D0065938

MARY E. WILKINS FREEMAN

Mary E. Wilkins Freeman

by Edward Foster

1956
New York

HENDRICKS HOUSE

Manufactured in the United States of America

Foreword

In the '80's, Mrs. Freeman—then Mary E. Wilkins—wrote a short story entitled "Old Lady Pingree" and set presumably in one of the villages of the West River Valley of Vermont. An aged spinster living in a decrepit family mansion, Miss Pingree did what she could to befriend her roomers—Jenny Stevens and her dying mother. Despite her own poverty, she twice attempted to make gifts to Jenny. They were refused. Then the mother died, and Miss Pingree knew that there was no money for the burial. Telling a "white lie" about her own resources, Miss Pingree gave the girl the savings which she had slowly collected lest she herself be buried by the town.

On the surface, this seems to be just another local color story centered in a strained, Victorian glorification of self-sacrifice. Yet for those who know and admire New England people of the small towns, it is a different thing—a rich and ambiguous representation of pride-within-poverty. For in many light touches of characterization, the writer suggests that Miss Pingree's "sacrifice" was at once noble and neurotic. In one aspect, it was compulsive giving, prompted by the need to maintain self-esteem. Lacking the Gothic touch of Faulkner's "A Rose for Emily," it is still a piece which he might have imagined; and, like all deeply conceived regional stories, it echoes in the mind.

In some of Mrs. Freeman's stories, poverty is lack of money for food and clothing; more often, it is poverty of environment. Economically and spiritually, her towns were too limited to provide growing space for the descendants of Puritan pioneers. The code said that they must be sturdily independent—and that they must conform. Somehow they did conform and retain independence, but their pride curdled in the process. Such, oversimplified, is the inner stuff of her most telling stories and novels. And it is never morbid, for

Mrs. Freeman always appreciated the thrust toward greatness which prevented her characters from accepting easy compromises.

More deeply than any writer of her time and perhaps of ours, Mrs. Freeman knew the meanness and the glory of pride-within-poverty.

She was born in Randolph, Massachusetts, in 1852 and died in Metuchen, New Jersey, in 1930. Two thirds of the years before her middle-aged marriage to Dr. Freeman and removal to New Jersey were lived in Randolph and one third in Brattleboro, Vermont. She was rooted in small town New England when the national life was surging in other directions. Stemming from good yet thin-blooded New England stock, she grew up in a family none too prosperous and dominated by the wife; somehow rose above family and village ways to record them with humorous, sympathetic, yet incisive vision; won for herself a comfortable living and an honored name among writers; and strove ceaselessly for a woman's happiness. "Louisa Ellis," the atrophied spinster of her story, "A New England Nun," is not a self-portrait; she hated those who made this identification.

Mrs. Freeman's elusive and winning spirit must be recaptured in small events or casual yet revealing words; she did not wear her heart on her sleeve. And no limited formula will do her justice. Yet the reader who surmises that the same twisted pride which works in her characters also shaped the author's personality may be within hailing distance of something roughly like truth.

My purpose is to analyze some of her best stories and novels and to present her life as writer, woman, and symbol of latter-day New England. Though she never wrote purely autobiographical fiction, her personality informs her stories more fully than has been assumed by earlier critics. Life and sensibility and fictional product should not be confused, but they can move along on the stream of time in such a way that themes will frequently cross.

A brief note on sources is needed. Books, articles, and town records are recognized in footnotes and bibliography, for they were very useful. My chief debt, however, is to Mrs. Freeman's friends and relatives, to the thirty elderly people who graciously helped me to know her and Randolph and Brattleboro. These are their names:

In the Randolph and Boston area: Mrs. Marian Boyd Allen, Mr. Willis Boyd Allen, Mr. and Mrs. Edmund K. Belcher, Mr. Joseph E. Belcher, Mr. J. Edgar Chamberlin, Mr. Herbert Clark, Mr. Herman W. French, Mr. William J. Good, Mrs. Harold Howard, Mrs. Arthur B. Mann, Mrs. Ellen T. Proctor, Mrs. George Sprague, Mrs. Nathan Irving Tolman.

In the Brattleboro area: Mr. Frederick Adams, Mrs. E. B. Barrows, Miss Helen Tyler Brown, Commander Pierce Brown, Mr. George H. Clapp, Reverend Edward Dahl, Mrs. Robert Dunklee, Mrs. Patrick Fenton, Miss Allie Morse, Mr. and Mrs. John E. Morse, Mr. Howard Rice, Mrs. Nellie Root, Mrs. Charles E. Severance, Dr. Allan D. Sutherland, Mrs. Edward Twitchell, Mrs. George W. Tyler, Mrs. John Steele Tyler, Mrs. P. K. White.

In the Metuchen and New York area: Mrs. Ada Murray Alden, Judge Thomas Brown, Mrs. Solomon S. Carvahlo, Mrs. Samuel Schenck.

Several crucial letters to Mrs. Freeman and many from her, all revealing of personality, were lent or given to me by Mrs. Allen, Mrs. Tolman, Mrs. Severance, Miss Todd, Mrs. John Steele Tyler, and Judge Brown.

It is saddening to know that my most effective expression of gratitude, a book about Mrs. Freeman which her friends and relatives could read, comes too late for most of them. They were fond of her. I also regret that it is impossible for me to say thank you again to Professor F. O. Matthiessen, who advised me at an earlier period.

E. F.

Georgia Institute of Technology

MARY E. WILKINS FREEMAN

CHAPTER

One

RANDOLPH, MASSACHUSETTS, is only fourteen miles south of Boston Common, but in the mid-nineteenth century it was not a suburb. It had its own sense of the past, its prominent families, its integrity as a considerably self-sustaining village. North Main Street was the road to Boston, and the trip by stagecoach required the entire morning.

The village honored many New England planning traditions. At the crossroads—there was no green—stood the Congregational Church, the town hall, and the tavern, all white and comely structures. North Main Street had many fine old homes. But for several decades, it had been moving toward the new era of business and industry; here, mingled with the homes, were the shops and small factories in which boots and shoes were made. Much of the work was still done by hand in the tiny sheds ("ten footers") which stood by the shoemakers' houses. Since Burrell and Maguire had recently opened the California and Australian markets for Randolph boots, everyone had work. The value of the 1852 product was over a million dollars.

South Main Street looked toward the past when every homestead was farm and home and shop for domestic crafts. Trim square houses, white with green blinds, stood behind their stone walls; back of them were barns, woodsheds, gardens, even farms of a hundred acres or more. Elms and catalpas shaded the houses; elms and walnuts arched the quiet dusty road.

Randolph's five thousand New Englanders of old stock respected themselves and the town. And their self-respect was supported partially by devotion to five gods—Work, Thrift,

Family, Gentility, and Jehovah of the Sacred Law. Yet in the first half of the nineteenth century the community founded upon these middle-class and Puritan ideals was not as solid as tradition would have it. Cash was always hard to get: the farms were meager, and domestic work on boots was poorly paid. Many of the energetic young men went off to the cities. When the Irish came in the late '40's, some families cut up their estates into building lots and sold to the newcomers. Cash was more plentiful. Yet the Irish were hated, for they were Catholics and competitors for jobs. The Know-Nothing Party—committed to opposition to foreigners, the papacy, and socialism—flourished in the town and elected nearly all state and local officers in Massachusetts in the '50's. The traditional order was clearly threatened.[1]

On October 31, 1852, a girl baby was born in one of the newer houses on South Main a few steps south of the town hall.[2] She was pretty but pindlin'; her parents feared that she, like their January baby, would die in infancy. But Warren E. Wilkins and his wife Eleanor vowed that this child would live if care and love could avail. They christened her Mary Ella though she would later call herself Mary Eleanor. A boy came to them three years later and died in his third year; seven years later, it was a girl named Anna. Though she lived, it was always "everything for Mary."[3]

The mother's family, the Lothrops and Holbrooks, were folks of consequence. The pioneer Thomas Holbrook was settled in Weymouth with Pastor Barnard's following by 1640;[4] in the 1850's his descendants were prominent landowners of East Randolph. When this village separated from Randolph in the '70's, it took the name Holbrook to honor its first family and to say thank you for a gift of fifty thousand dollars.[5] These were "fine genteel people of the old sort," these maternal ancestors of Eleanor Wilkins.[6]

Her father was a Lothrop—Barnabas who married Clara Holbrook and had seven children by her.[7] Founder Mark Lothrop, the second or third of the English line to come to

Massachusetts, was at Salem by 1643 and later settled at Bridgewater.[8] Various descendants distinguished themselves in the professions; Lothrop Stoddard, the popular lecturer and traveler of the '80's and '90's, was the grandson of Eleanor Lothrop Wilkins' Uncle Edward. Her father Barnabas, who died only a year before the birth of Mary Wilkins, had been a painter by trade and had accumulated considerable property. His well-designed, one-story house stood just north of the Wilkins place.[9]

In marrying Eleanor Lothrop, Warren Wilkins made a sensible choice. There were sweetness and strength in her rounded face with its dark eyes, small nose, and straight hair parted in the center, drawn back severely over the ears. Cheerful, practical, firm of will, she, if anyone, would be able to cope with his occasionally over-sensitive nature.[10] From her influence, the child might draw toughness of fibre and a great desire to make something of herself.

Randolph people did not know Warren Wilkins and his family as they knew the Holbrooks and Lothrops, but they believed that her talent came from him. Slim and tallish, he had blue eyes, fine features, a high forehead, light brown hair, and a full beard. There was nothing at all of the countrymen in him."[11] Trained by his father in the tradition of Samuel MacIntyre of Salem, he was a housewright and carpenter; at this time he and his brother George were building houses and shops in Randolph. He liked his trade and had a fine feeling for it.[12] Something of Calvinism survived in his extreme conscientiousness, his exaggerated sensibility, his occasional black moods. Usually, however, his eyes were bright with fun, and his wit was keen.[13]

Family tradition connected Warren with Bray Wilkins, a Welshman of Norman line, who settled in Salem in 1628 or 1630.[14] Warren's father, Amos S. Wilkins, seems to have been restless and ambitious. Born and reared in Beverly,[15] he settled for a time in Cambridge, married a Salem girl,[16] moved to Randolph where Warren was born,[17] returned to Beverly, fathered two more sons,[18] and died in his forty-first year.[19] His wife was lovely Mary W. Moulton of another Norman-Salem family.[20] The fourth Sir Thomas de Moulton will be remembered from Scott's *The Talisman* as a famous knight in the forces of Richard, Coeur de Lion.[21] A strain of literary talent ran in the family: C. W. Moulton edited *The Magazine of Poetry,* and Elizabeth Barrett Browning was a Moulton of the English line.[22] Some years after the death of her husband, Mary Moulton Wilkins married a Davis of Salem.[23]

Mary Wilkins was thus born into the traditions of the New England town. Perhaps she had some of the bodily and emotional sturdiness, the solid practicality of the Lothrop-Holbrook lines; perhaps she inclined toward the sensitivity of the Wilkins-Moulton strain. Certainly she would soon acquire the "New England conscience" and the conviction that she must be "beholden" to no one. She looked to be her father's child, or better, her Grandmother Davis's; for she was blue-eyed and unbelievably fine of features.[24]

For three years, Eleanor Wilkins gave nearly all of her thought and love to her delicate Mary, and there was always Mother Lothrop next door who would come in at critical moments. Then in '55, a sickly boy was born who lived for only three years. Though Mary retained her position as queen, she may have felt some of her mother's anxiety, her father's sense of helplessness. When the end came, she may have been puzzled and a little frightened by preparations for the funeral.[25]

But forgetting came soon, for there was much talk of Uncle George Wilkins and his engagement to Louisa Belcher. Soon he would be living in the Belcher house just north of Grandmother Lothrop's, and Grandmother Davis could come down from Beverly to live with him and his bride. Father and Uncle George told pleasant stories about their mother; they were looking forward to the time when they all could live almost in the same house. Mary, now seven, went to the wedding.[26]

Her favorite game was holly-gull, played with Father in

the kitchen while Mother was doing the dishes. He would draw up his chair opposite hers, would hold up his fist in which he held a number of kernels of corn. He would say, "Holly-gull, handfull, passel how many?" She was puzzled by the meaning of the magic formula, but she knew how to play the game. She would close her eyes in fierce concentration—"passel how many?"

"Twenty-three!" She had guessed right this time. She had won all of the kernels in Father's hand and a kiss too.[27]

Nearly every day brought some occasion for running over to Grandmother Lothrop's house next door at number 60. It was a low square house of a single story. Entering the doorway surmounted by its semicircular fanlight, one found the formal entry hall with the small parlor at the right, the best chamber at the left. Back of these rooms were the dining room, a great kitchen, and several tiny chambers at unexpected places. It was an odd arrangement of rooms; a child could be almost lost in it. Grandmother Lothrop told her how it happened to be built in that curious style—how her husband Barnabas, Mary's grandfather who had died a year before she was born, had been terrified by a wild wind storm which had demolished several Randolph houses; how he had decided to build a house low, spready, safe in any storm; how he had insisted upon having one windowless room into which he could retire until the storm subsided. She always concluded with a sharp fling at the folly of sleeping in little tucked-up bedrooms instead of good chambers just because folks had been scared of wind.[28]

Since Warren and Eleanor Wilkins were staunch Congregationalists, they took their daughter to meeting "as soon as she could go without crying for the bottle." The old Puritan observance of the Sabbath survived with little softening; it was still a day of almost uninterrupted preaching and prayer—morning service from ten-thirty till twelve, Sabbath School in the Vestry from twelve to one, a preaching service from two until three-thirty, young people's service at four, and prayer meeting from seven to eight in the evening. The day of warming pans was past.[29] The church had two stoves,[30] but it was much too chilly during the bitter mornings of January and February. Mary went to morning service with her mother and father and the Lothrop family. Sitting stiff and straight—except when she squirmed or looked out of the window, she listened to the sermons and prayers of a dignified man in long black coat, the Reverend Christopher M. Cordley. Later, in Sabbath School, she would at least have something to do. There were hymns, which she sang in a shrill thin voice; when all the children were seated in groups about their teachers, she supplied an occasional answer, learned from the *Quarterly,* to the questions. She might even be called upon to recite one of the Psalms, carefully memorized at home during the preceding week.[31]

The year 1859 was an exciting one for Mary. A baby sister, whom her parents named Anna Holbrook, was born; and she herself started going to school. Most children in Randolph started somewhat earlier—Mary was seven—but she had been considered too pindlin'.[32] School at old Number 1 kept from nine until twelve and from one to four-thirty with two recesses. Grades one to seven were taught by a single teacher, usually a young woman of education only slightly beyond the attainments of her older pupils. She was paid two dollars a week and sometimes her board and lodging.

The level of instruction was only a little better than that of precinct's second school, established in 1737, in which the subjects were "reading and spelling, repeating the Catechism, writing and arithmetic." For Mary when she entered, spelling, reading, and perhaps a little ciphering were the subjects. Her speller had much to say of vowels and consonants, diphthongs and triphthongs, monosyllables and polysyllables, and included many ponderous lists of words to be memorized. Occasionally, when the harassed teacher found time for it, the children took turns in standing before the class to read aloud from their progressive readers. It was no light matter, this reading for the class.[33] As one of the old readers phrased it, "To become a *good* reader is a valuable attainment. To ensure success, the first step is decision on the part of the scholar. The second is effort, and the third is perseverance. The purpose of mind must be as firmly fixed to break and abandon *bad* habits, as to establish and confirm *good* ones."[34]

Ciphering may have been better fun, if one can judge from Frederick Emerson's *The North American Arithmetic, Part First for Young Learners,* Philadelphia, 1859. Lesson Fifth offers, "Here are 5 little girls singing together, and 2 more are jumping together. How many are there in all?" By Lesson Third in Subtraction, the little ones have progressed to the arithmetic of inebriety: "There were 7 farmers, 3 of whom drank rum and whiskey, and became miserable; the rest drank water, and were healthy and happy. How many drank water?"

Such was the program. Usually the teacher could find little time for small children in the front benches. After endless periods of memorizing the speller, they gaped and squirmed and fidgeted. If a fly lit on the desk, it seemed a godsend.[35] Yet Mary liked her teacher and learned the dull lessons easily; obedient and well-mannered with adults, she had no difficulty with the formal aspects of her schooling.

Making her way with the other children was another matter. At home and in the neighborhood, she had had no playmates of her own age; Mrs. Wilkins had considered her too delicate to roam down South Main Street where other children lived. Knowing nothing of her small peers, she assumed that she would at once be accepted as the little queen she was at home. The first days at school were difficult. She was called "teacher's partial" and "little, dolly-pinky-rosy." Perhaps as much shy as proud, she was considered "stuck-up."[36] She was lucky to find one friend, little "Mary John" Wales. This one was Mary, daughter of John Wales, as distinguished from Mary, daughter of "Eph" Wales. Mary John's father farmed the old Atherton Wales place just across South Main Street from the school, a hundred acres stretching off to the west and south.

The girls went over to the farm when school closed. Though it was only a few steps south of the Wilkins' house, it was so much a part of the old rural way of life that Mary was really moving back in time to the '30's. Except in the coldest winter weather, they played much out of doors, and Mary came to know something of horses and cattle and the life of a farm. It was a big pleasant place. Flowers bordered the walk which led from gate to white house with green blinds; elms and catalpas and a single English walnut cast their shade over house and lawn and outbuildings. In the fall, the girls would gather walnuts to be stored for winter.[37]

A puzzling little house, a "ten-footer," stood near the road. Though it was used for storage now, Mary John said that her father and his brothers had used it for their work on boots before the factories had come to town.

Mrs. Wales—she had been Sarah Thompson of Braintree before she married John—sometimes let the Marys help in the huge kitchen in the back of the house. She did her cooking on a wood stove, but John's mother, Sally Wales, had cooked in the huge hearth that was at this time empty. John was usually in his fields; Mary saw him only when he brought in wood for the fire.

Mary heard much talk of the Wales family from time to time. Mrs. Wales said that it was Great-grandfather Atherton Wales who had built the house only twenty years after the Revolution. He had built for his son Jonathan with the understanding that he and his wife, elderly people at this time, should live in it with the children. After Jonathan and his wife died, the place came to the second Atherton, who married Sally Damon of Dedham. By her and by his second wife, Sarah Chessman French, Atherton had eleven children; and every room of the two story-and-a-half house was needed.

Mrs. Wales liked to talk about her "in-laws," John's brothers and sisters, for they were good people and had done well. Several of the brothers were doctors, living in their own houses near the homestead; Clara had married an Alden; Mary Ann, a French. In this way, nearly all of the old Randolph families had been intermarrying through the generations. Though John was the youngest son of Atherton Wales, he was the only one interested in farming; now the family place was his.

The Marys knew the kitchen well, and they could also go to the attic to play with a dusty old loom and a spinning wheel. For quiet games, they used the first floor sitting room, looking out on the road.[38] Mary Wilkins did not know that after much testing, she would return to this room and live in it for nearly twenty years; nor did she suspect that she was storing away in memory sharp images of farm and family life which would one day make the texture of her stories.

For the girl and her mother, the long snowy winter of Randolph was a serious matter; she was too "delicate" to be out very much. Once Father and Uncle George took her sleigh-riding on a cold and brilliant day. The trees held their white boughs against the blue of the sky. Mary laughed and her blue eyes shone. That, however, was just a single experience, because somehow she became afraid of horses. Skating and snow-balling, Mrs. Wilkins considered much too strenuous, so the child lived indoors through much of the winter.[39]

In the other seasons there were nice things for her to do. In April she made May baskets of strips of colored paper. Then came the fun of going to the woods in search of anemones, those bell-like flowers which were the favorites for May baskets. Almost every evening in May in the magic hour after sundown, Mary and Mary John and the others left their May baskets, great balls of flowers, swinging from the latchets of friendly doors. Then, laughing, they scampered away to watch from a tree or fence as the owner came to the door.[40]

Coming from school when the air was sweet and the meadows on either side of the road were brimful of grass and flowers, she loved to walk slowly, feeling the soft earth under her feet and the grass swishing about her ankles. She picked blackberries in July in the thicket behind Grandmother Lothrop's house, which also bordered on a shoe factory.

She was a quiet dreamy child, even a little lazy, yet there was something in her nature which now and then demanded the thrill of swift motion. She ran wildly to feel the sweep of wind against her forehead and the power and freedom of running. She ran until she gasped for breath and her cheeks glowed.

Mary liked the street hawkers and peddlers and wandering craftsmen, who were as much a part of village life as the meeting house.

"Mackerel, Mackerel!
Three for a quarter a dollar."

That was the mackerel man down from Boston with his wagon full of fresh silvery fish. The lobster man called,

"Buy lob!
Buy lob!"[41]

Some of these tradesmen, aware of the dearth of cash, did business by barter. The Soap-man offered a cake of soft soap in exchange for soap-grease saved by the housewife. Mrs. Jacobs, the China Woman, came once a month with a basket bulging with small images, busts, and perfume boxes, which she traded for castoff clothing. "But it had to be good." Every week brought "Little Moses," pack on back, to the Wilkins door. His line was dry goods, and he had been going from house to house as long as anyone could remember. They said he had a son who studied for the bar and became a great lawyer in New York. The Tin Peddler, who later appeared in Mary Wilkins' "A Humble Romance," might rap at the kitchen door at almost any time. "Good mornin', Marm," he said. "Hev you got any rags?" If rags were forthcoming, he weighed them in his spring-scales and offered in exchange new tinware from his cart, covered top and sides with gleaming pots and pans. There were others, too, the wandering tinkers and craftsmen—the clock-mender, the umbrella-man, the mender of chairs, the old man with his grindstone who sharpened knives and scissors. They were all "characters," going everywhere, knowing everyone, picking up bits of news and gossip, adding a touch of color to the prosaic pattern of village life. And they made a firm impression upon the girl's mind.[42]

Mary was not yet nine when news of Fort Sumter reached Randolph; at the time, it probably meant less to her than an item in *The Randolph Transcript* which folks were discussing on April 13; "A pleasant Sabbath in a Christian land is indeed a pleasant day; but much of the beauty and charm of the day is often lost by the harsh ungrateful sounds of rude boys or evil men who desecrate its Laws to games and hilarity. Query—I wonder if the magistrate and officers cannot put a stop to the ball playing and other rude sports which full grown men and boys habitually indulge in on the Sabbath day, in certain streets and locations in town. Let us see."

Father, Uncle George, and Uncle Edward Lothrop were, as family men, exempt from military service; Father's younger brother Eben responded to President Lincoln's call for volunteers.[43] Town meeting voted to borrow five thousand dollars that militia men called to active service might have six dollars a month for their families in addition to the government's small family allowance. There was a fine noisy send-off for the village's Company D. By the second year of the war, the town was paying one hundred dollars to each volunteer.[44]

Mary heard something of these events and perhaps shared a little of her father's anxiety as he tried to find news of Eben's regiment from the Boston and local papers. She surely knew that huge Army contracts for boots had come to the local factories, that McKay stitching machines were being installed rapidly,[45] that her father and Uncle George were working steadily on plant additions and alterations. Though Mother lamented rising prices, some money was going into a bank account.

Early in '62, Wilkinses and Lothrops were discussing Mr. Dwight, the pastor of their Congregational Church. Neither he nor his predecessor had been able to fill the boots of old Dr. Calvin Hitchcock, who for a full thirty years had preached the doctrines of Geneva in a form somewhat softened but still sufficiently austere.[46] If the faith of the founders was by this time clouded by generations of theological wrangling and by the rise of rationalism and Unitarianism, Dr. Hitchcock had had his way of making doctrine seem simple and inescapable to his flock. He ticked off the points on his fingers.

" 'One'—the little finger extended—'all men are depraved.'

'Two'—the next finger—'Christ died for all.'

'Three'—third finger—'the offer of salvation is freely made to all.'

'Four'—fourth finger—'all with one consent began to make excuse.'

'Five'—the thumb—'God chose some.' "[47]

Mr. Cordley, who succeeded Dr. Hitchcock, lasted for six years; Mr. Dwight was forced to go at the close of his third year.[48] Neither was especially liberal in theology or social thinking; but they had presumably been touched by newer tendencies.[49]

Mary's family discussed these matters, for religion was a vital interest. Uncle Ebenezer Moulton would soon head the Sabbath School, to be succeeded later by Uncle George Wilkins. If Mary at ten could not follow their discussions, she must at least have learned that theology in her family was bound up with deep personal feelings and that somehow faith and goodness were related to one's material success in the world. In her house, it was always assumed that the poverty of the poor was punishment for sin.[50]

Grandmother Lothrop died in December. Her son, Mary's Uncle Caleb, wrote in the calf-bound family Bible,[51] "She was taken suddenly ill and died in ten minutes without a struggle. Like her father her trust was in God her Savior." "God her Savior" and not Jesus—the phrase is revealing.

In these days Mary grew taller and thinner, and the roundness of her face lengthened into a fine oval. She was an appealing child—shy, wistful, loving of those she trusted; she was however a problem for her practical and energetic mother. Mary had the Lothrop will. Disliking her household duties, she avoided them, nor could she be moved by disciplinary tactics. She would lie awake for hours at night while the wildest fancies sped through her mind. Her small sister Nan was easier to understand; for she was a jolly child, always brimming with high spirits and forever playing with her cousin Harriet Lothrop next door.

Unless Mary were with her favorite Mary John, she was reading, reading, reading. She loved fairy tales, which to her seemed completely real.[52] One is inclined to agree with Professor Pattee's suggestion that there is an authentic flash of childhood reminiscence in her story "The Prism"[53] in which her heroine says, "Ever since I was a child, I have seen . . . or thought so, a beautiful little people . . . fairies and—such things . . . moving and dancing in the broken lights across the field."[54] Sometimes on winter evenings she sat silent before the hearth watching the tiny blue tongues of flame as they leapt and flickered around the logs. She dreamed of all the things she would do when she was a beautiful young lady and had everything she desired. Later in her own room, she placed the lamp on the chest of drawers and gazed long at her pretty face reflected in the mirror.[55]

In April of '65, General Lee surrendered to General Grant at Appomattox, and soon the Randolph veterans were returning to their homes and jobs. Warren Wilkins sold his house to N. I. Tolman,[56] since he was planning to enter the drygoods business with a friend, Orrin Slate, who was already established in Brattleboro, Vermont. Next year, in the name of his wife (or was it her money?), he purchased a superb residential site in a new section high above Brattleboro's business district.[57]

Did Warren and Eleanor Wilkins understand that the

Civil War and the vast economic changes which it dramatized had destroyed not only the agrarian culture of the South but also the precarious balance of farming and small industry on which the prosperity of Randolph rested? Were they intelligently alarmed by the decline in local population which occurred during the '60's[58] or by Burrell and Maguire's loss of the Australian trade in boots?[59]

In the absence of full statements by the relatives, such speculation is tempting; but the opinion of the cousin, Mr. Edmund Belcher, comes closer to the mark. Warren Wilkins, son of the restless Amos, was eager for a new venture at a time when venturing was in the air. His wife encouraged him because she, too, was ambitious for the family and especially for the daughters; in her estimate a merchant was a cut above a carpenter-builder. Mr. Slate had little difficulty in convincing them that Brattleboro was a more attractive town than Randolph. It had a reasonably solid base of varied small industry and a legend of daring merchandising. Everyone in New England knew of the Jim Fisks, father and son, and their gawdy and brilliantly successful peddling.

"Annual Spring Sale of Fisks Peddlers.
Friday afternoon, escorted by the Brattleborough [sic]
Cornet Band.
9 wagons 'handsome & convenient' (freight
wholly of dry goods valued at from
$25,000 to $30,000) drawn by
6 white horses, ribands in hands of
Tom Miner (the stage driver) followed by
2 coaches filled with solid business men;
then team with Fisk himself drawn by
4 bays—followed by
9 wagons of goods."[60]

And by this time, Jim Fisk, Junior, was known for other more mysterious and grandiose operations.

It was a Boston and Brattleboro man, Royall Tyler, who had written *The Contrast,* the first American comedy, and therein created the "stage Yankee." The Vermont town was also a famous spa: Dr. Robert Wesselhoeft's Water Cure had a national reputation in the '50's. (Mrs. Leverett Saltonstall, née Alice Wesselhoeft, is of the Boston branch of the family.) If the curative properties of spring water, a notion which the doctor brought from his native Germany, were overrated, none of his fashionable guests from Boston, New York, and Charleston could question the charm of the hotels, the exhilaration of walks into the hills, and the beauty of the music of Christian Schuster and his group of German musicians. Essentially, the cultivated Dr. Wesselhoeft had brought to bustling America a continental conception of leisurely living-out-of-doors which was new and pleasing. The Water Cure did not survive the Civil War, but some of the fine families which it drew to the town stayed on. And Christian Schuster would lead Brattleboro's musical life for another forty years.[61]

To all genteel and pious folks like the Wilkinses and Lothrops, Brattleboro also suggested Larkin G. Mead, Junior's, "Snow Angel." The story, which goes back to 1857, was first written by *The Brattleboro Phoenix:* "The denizens of 'Toad Hill' [the slight rise of ground north of the business district] were surprised, when coming down from breakfast New Year's morning to find a beautiful statue at the fork of the roads. . . . It was about eight feet in height and represented the Recording Angel that may be supposed to wait upon Time, making up her record at the close of the year. In her right hand was a style, while in her left she held the tablet on which the events were noted. It was modeled in snow the previous evening by Larkin G. Mead, and in a manner which was of itself sufficient evidence of his superior claims as an artist."[62] Reported nationally and internationally, the Snow Angel was more than a seven days' wonder. Replicas in marble were made; one, properly, found its place in the Hall of Statuary in the Capitol at Washington.[63]

Practically and sentimentally, much was to be said for moving to Brattleboro, and the die was cast in '65. But Mary was to have two more formative years in Randolph before the actual departure occurred.

In December, after months of talk in the family, John Codman Labaree was installed as pastor of the First Congregational Church.[64] From him, thirteen year old Mary learned the doctrines and the way of life that she never wholly abandoned.

Dr. Labaree was more than a country parson; the son of the president of Middlebury College, he was a man of good education and some spirituality.[65] He could not, one suspects, invoke Johnathan Edwards' vision of a God supremely powerful, majestic, mysterious, and lovable. By this time the great theology had been reduced to the flat orthodoxy of the Congregational "Bunker Hill Declaration of 1865": ". . . faith in God, the Father, the Son and the Holy Ghost, the only living and true God; in Jesus Christ the incarnate Word, who is exalted to be our Redeemer and King; and in the Holy Comforter, who is present in the church to regenerate and sanctify the soul. With the whole Church we confess the common sinfulness and ruin of our race, and acknowledge that it is only through the work accomplished by the life and expiating death of Jesus Christ that believers in him are justified before God, receive the remission of sins, and through the presence and grace of the Holy Comforter are delivered from the power of sin and perfected in holiness. We believe also in the organized and visible church, in the ministry of the Word, in the sacraments of Baptism and the Lord's Supper, in the resurrection of the body and in the final judgment, the issues of which are eternal life and everlasting punishment."[66]

To those who respond to any well-worded statement of Protestant Orthodoxy, these words will seem impressive. But Haroutunian has sufficiently shown that the inner stuff of the system was no longer felt. It was not understood that "the good which God seeks and accomplished is the display of infinite being, a good which transcends the good of all finite existence. If the misery of the sinner is conducive to such a display, which it must be because sinners are in fact miserable, then it is just and good that sinners should be punished with misery. . . . The test of piety [within a true Calvinism] was the worship and the service of God in spite of, nay because of, the disagreeable facts of human life."[67] Dr. Labaree told his congregation that he was preaching the faith of the fathers,[68] but this statement, however pardonable as a necessary simplification, was not quite accurate.

Thinking of Mary Wilkins' later religious growth, one surmises that she could have thrived on a clearly tough religion, an authentic Calvinism conforming with the facts of life and spirit; or on a clearly soft faith, a modern liberalism or humanism. She could not, one suspects, thrive on the faith of Dr. Labaree which was at once soft and tough. All through life she attempted—without the necessary framework of either psychology or mature religious doctrine—to bring together apparently irreconcilable propositions: God is good and all-powerful; God has given us his sacred law; men follow the law and still suffer pain and frustration.

Dr. Labaree was middling in size and appearance; his voice, however, was full and beautiful, his manner impressive. Sermons, he kept relatively short, though he prayed for "everything from the Sandwich Islands to darkest Africa." He was loved and respected, yet what lingers in the minds of those who remember him is chiefly his emphasis upon the sacred duty of coming to meeting every Sabbath; his condemnation of cards, dancing, and drink; his insistence upon the centrality of the Ten Commandments in the Christian way of life.[69] Mary never forgot the terrible Tables of the Law; she had got religion—of a sort—and did what she could to live with it. She had also learned much of the Bible—its poetry and prose and memorable stories, and the Bible would serve her well.

School was more interesting in these days, for she was sitting in the last row of Number One. Having successfully performed the mental gymnastics of *Colburn's Intellectual Arith-*

metic, having survived the dreariness of the earlier years of reading, she had now reached the higher levels of the readers. She learned to stand on her feet before the class at the Friday afternoon rhetorical exercises and to read such brave effusions as Campbell on "The Sacking of Prague" or "Cato's Speech over His Dead Son," using the gestures and inflections of the old school of elocution. She may even have performed on exhibition days before the gentlemen in black, the "Superintending School Committee," though one suspects that she would have been too timid to do credit to either herself or her teacher. She wrote excellent themes, one may be sure, on Industry, Thrift, and Temperance.[70]

School was more interesting, yet its influence hardly equalled that of day-to-day life in her home, at Uncle Edward Lothrop's, at Uncle George's, at the Wales homestead. In so far as preaching and schooling carried over to living, they were blended with the cultural ideal of these homes.

Work, Thrift, Family, Gentility, the righteousness of the Ten Commandments—her men and women folks agreed in worshiping at these altars. Mary learned quickly that her people were determined to "be something."[71] That determination involved working and saving, if possible with zest and a grand sense of achievement; if impossible, working and saving anyway, grimly, with a tight-lipped sense of consecration. Of course they were working for the family, and there was some division of labor. The Wilkins and Lothrop men were the providers, not brilliantly successful, and the heads of families, half conscious of being ruled by their wives. The women raised the children, kept house, secretly longed for more successful and dominating husbands, and made what they could of the men they had. They also performed most of the rites of gentility (Augusta Belcher organized the Ladies Library Association in 1852) and administered, with some pastoral aid, commandments three, five, and seven of the Law of Moses. Number eight, "Thou shalt not steal," was rather more the province of the men; for them it had come to mean business integrity and the holiness of property rights.

Mary learned this code from her elders and much more almost as sacred. She learned that in the woman's world, some of the facets of human nature ignored by the code could still find expression. Craving beauty and distinction, her mother could have a flower garden and a speckless house. New England women could even boast of their neatness, ironically: "Come right in, if you can—for the dirt."[72]

Mother, Aunt Louisa, and the grandmothers could gossip too. There were so many things to say of Abby —— who had bought a new bonnet for May's first Sunday when everyone knew she had had one the year before, about the cake Mrs. —— had contributed to the church social, about Hatty —— and what she was doing for her backache, about the disgusting way that chit Sarah —— was chasing the boys (you would think she had no pride at all), about the rumor that old Lucius —— had finally popped the question after calling on Martha —— for nearly twenty years. There was always a funeral to be discussed with proper relish for the details of the appearance of the corpse and the conduct of the mourners.

One suspects that the girl sensed that these women, even in their cattiness, were holding on to life, that she recognized that this endless chatter about seeming trifles was important. She could not understand—nor could they—that the code was no longer adapted to the human needs of Randolph people.

If the men were to retain the dominance in the family which the code demanded, they needed more pay and better jobs than Randolph could provide. The girls needed beaux and the wives needed husbands who could love because they were confident. As it was, according to William J. Good, the men postponed marriage interminably, and the women were obliged to get themselves husbands from other towns—or remain single. The code glorified independence—and conformity to tradition, but Randolph did not provide a setting in which these conflicting ideals could be reconciled. It was a breeding place for nervous tensions—tensions which Mary did not understand but must have felt within her own home. One of the family stories seems to have left a disturbing impression, for it would appear nearly thirty years later in the grim novel *Pembroke.*

It was Mother's story of the house in which they were living. It had been built in the '30's by Grandfather Barnabas Lothrop for his son Barnabas Junior, Eleanor Wilkins' brother. Barney was engaged to Mary Thayer, one of Randolph's belles. Her wedding dress was ready; the house was finished too except for painting.

Sitting one evening in the kitchen with Mary and her family, Barney became involved in a bitter argument on politics. Mr. Thayer was a Democrat; Barney, a Whig. In a fit of rage old Thayer drove Barney out of the house, telling him never to enter again. Assuming the patriarch's right to rule his family, he said that no daughter of his would ever marry Barney Lothrop.

Mary accepted her father's decision yet hoped for a reconciliation. It did not occur. There was no yielding in either of these men, and the issue was deeper than politics. Barney had loved and still loved Mary with the steadfastness of a strong spirit. After the break he always seemed a different person, "as if something inside had snapped"; but he could not bring himself to sue for pardon. Old Thayer had never yielded, and he never would. After a time Barney left Randolph, and the incident might have been forgotten but for the unfinished house. There it stood on Main Street, its unpainted clapboards weathering to a drab gray. Barney Lothrop's house stood tenantless for ten years.

If one sided with Barney against old Thayer, Mrs. Wilkins said that it was "just Mr. Thayer's way." It was also "just Barney's way" if he were held to be in the wrong. Then she explained that when she and Warren Wilkins were engaged,

Barnabas Lothrop Senior decided that they should have the unfinished house.[73]

Early in '67, Warren Wilkins was planning to leave Randolph: he would go to Brattleboro, join Mr. Slate, and obtain a house. Then the family would follow. Before his departure, he stopped at the Lothrop house for a minute, dug a small piece of paper from his vest pocket, and after halting preliminaries, read from it. It was a poem by Mary. It seemed pretty to him, and he was proud of his daughter. The Lothrops were not impressed. Uncle Edward Everett summed up their feeling by remarking, "Lot of good that will do—letting that child write poetry!"[74]

CHAPTER

Two

BRATTLEBORO, VERMONT, lies in the Connecticut Valley about ten miles above the Massachusetts line and ninety by rail from Boston. The power of swift Whetstone Brook where it flows into the river had attracted the first settlers in the middle of the eighteenth century. Along or near the brook were the village industries and many of the workers' homes. Main Street crossed the Whetstone and ran north-to-south parallel with the river; from the back of the shops on the east side, there is a view, a little breath-taking, of the Connecticut, the island and bridge, and Mount Wantastiquet on the New Hampshire side. Well to the north is the comely but rather irrelevant Common. The finer homes were on Toad Hill near the Common and on Elliot, Green, and High Streets which moved out of Main Street, rising sharply on terraces.

Walking along Main Street from Brook to Common, Warren Wilkins in '67 must have felt himself part of a thriving and impressive town. Had he taken the long view from Prospect Hill on the south, he might have seen Brattleboro as a toy town—white, pretty, almost fragile—in its setting of river valley and rugged dark hills rising to the west and north.

He and his partner Orrin Slate had their dry goods shop on the river side of Main Street at the foot of High at the exact point where business yielded to mansions, churches, and the town hall. Next to him was the book store of the greatly respected Joseph Steen. It was an excellent location for attracting Brattleboro's ladies.[1]

Unable to build immediately on his Oak Street lot, Mr. Wilkins found a small cottage for his family, 3 Chase Street, west of the Common.[2] There he brought his wife, his mother, his two daughters. If the house was outrageously cramped, it would at least serve for a short time.

Mary, now fourteen, was ready for the excellent high school headed by Mr. B. F. Bingham, a teacher of uncommon force and ability. In the stately porticoed building on its terrace above Linden Street, Mary studied Latin, natural philosophy, algebra, arithmetic, geometry, and rhetoric. As in Randolph, she recited at the Wednesday afternoon rhetorical exercises and wrote one or two dramatic sketches for production at evening entertainments.[3] She was a good scholar—serious and keen in learning.[4]

It was pleasant for her to walk down to Father's shop after school closed and to drop in next door at Mr. Steen's to look at books and magazines. Quite as much as her teachers, he could stimulate her interest in literature. If the nation were headed fast into materialism, the new spirit was not strongly felt in Brattleboro and not at all in Mr. Steen's.[5]

Occasionally, at 3 Chase, she would be drawn to the front door by an odd visitor, an old lady who asked for something to eat and mumbled in a disturbing way. The Marsh Building of the Vermont Insane Asylum was only forty yards north of the Wilkins house, and many of the patients wandered freely around the neighborhood. Back to the northwest equally distant was the Asylum's burial ground, a small square plot walled by dark pines and hemlocks. Once in a great while, there was a quiet burial ceremony, followed later by the placing of a stone memorial. On one of the old ones, appears this inscription: "To the memory of / Abram N. / Son of / J. S. Horton / of Grand Rapids, Mich. / who died in Brattleboro / Jan. 7, 1855 / Age 32 years 1 month / He sleeps far from home & in a / strange land."

Though Miss Wilkins in later life spoke frequently of the

various other houses in which the family lived, she never mentioned 3 Chase Street.[6] Perhaps she was embarrassed by its extremely small size; conceivably it was associated with her first glimpses of psychic terror.

Mr. and Mrs. Wilkins quickly joined the Centre Congregational Church on Main Street.[7] Though painted brown, it still retained its simple beauty of line. The Wilkinses heard a few of the last sermons of the Reverend George Palmer Tyler, a son of Royall Tyler and the only one of the four "preaching Tylers" to serve in his own town. He had studied at Yale and the Union Theological Seminary and taught the same Hopkinsian divinity which Mary had learned in Randolph; he was also tender, witty, genial, something of a poet, and the favorite cousin of Mrs. Nathaniel Hawthorne.[8] Sitting under him and gradually meeting his friends and relatives, the Wilkinses would begin to understand the special role of the Tylers in the village. Somewhat later, with pardonable rhetoric, Henry Burnham described it in this way: "It was not the mission of this old and distinguished family to set in motion the wheels of industry. . . . So large a family of almost purely intellectual proclivities, furnishing six collegiates, four of them ministers of the gospel, is, we believe, rarely, if ever, found in the past or present history of any town in New England. As there is no end to the good arising from the highest department of our nature, the beneficial influence of such a family, upon a community almost wholly utilitarian, it is impossible to fully estimate. Their first coming to that high hill overlooking the whole town seems to us as the morning dawn of intellectual life in this region, or, the beginning of an Elizabethan age in Brattleboro."[9]

In one way or another, the Wilkinses learned of Brattleboro's other fine families—Bradleys, Cabots, Chapins, Eatons, Esteys, Fullers, Goodhues, Higginsons, Hunts, Meads, Scotts. A few of the ladies called on Mrs. Wilkins to ask how she liked the town, where the family came from, how old her daughters were; but she was obviously embarrassed by the Chase Street house and none too happy in welcoming guests. Mr. Wilkins, now better dressed than ever before, served many of the ladies in his shop and brought home to noon dinner his budget of small news. Mary met some of the sons and daughters at school. Though there was little snobbery in the town, it was still a nut that had to be cracked; valuing the kernel inside, the Wilkinses were determined to crack it—at least for their daughters. And why not? Wasn't a Lothrop and a Holbrook as good as a Mead or Bradley? Mrs. Wilkins also knew that her Mary was just as pretty and smart as any of the daughters of old families and that she was certainly getting along well in school.[10]

Mrs. Wilkins and her husband took their daughters to the Lyceum Series in Town Hall.[11] The 1868-1869 series included the humorist D. R. Locke (Petroleum V. Nasby) and Colonel Thomas Wentworth Higginson,[12] and Mary was impressed by this first experience of celebrities. She might have been drawn toward the Colonel's sister, "Miss Anna," whose Asylum Street cottage, near the Wilkins' house, was Brattleboro's salon. "It was," according to G. L. Walker, "one of the very choicest privileges . . . to be admitted to the fellowship of that pleasant home where she lived amid the associations of books and family treasures, and of friends of culture and refinement. A most modest and retiring soul, but how potent an influence for all things good and lovely! As kind-hearted a woman as one may ever hope to see, but how her indignation flashed at every obtruded display of snobbishness or wrong. Hers was a home where the old-fashioned art of rational conversation preserved its traditions undecayed. One could be sure in going there of an alert and responsive interest in every topic of literature or of public concern."[13]

Pretty and bookish Mary Wilkins would, one suspects, have been welcomed by Miss Anna Higginson; in her circle, she might have grown rapidly in poise and spirit. But her best friend of the period, Mrs. C. E. Severance, said that Mary was too proud to make any tiny gesture which would lead to an invitation. In some indirect way, however, the influence of Miss Anna and especially her enthusiasm for the Transcendentalists would reach her.

The fall of '69 brought three disasters to Brattleboro. Black Friday, September 24, saw the price of gold, cornered by Gould and by the now hated Jim Fisk of Brattleboro, at a point which ruined many business men including some of the shakier local concerns. In the preceding year, Mr. Wilkins had purchased, along with Joseph Steen, the two stores with their apartments above, which were called a "block."[14] Though he considered himself prospering, he actually knew little about buying and was timid about collecting accounts. Orrin Slate, the partner, was shrewd enough to move out of the business in panicky '69;[15] hence Mr. Wilkins was left with a charming manner and little skill in business.[16] It may be assumed that his wife, at least, was worrying.

From Saturday, October 2 through the following Monday, everyone in the village was frightened. The rain began on Saturday night and came down in torrents for thirty-six hours. Whetstone Brook, around which the factories were built, rose until by noon Monday it reached the highest point in its turbulent history. It carried everything before it—bridges, factories, houses, lumber. Its current was so powerful "that it swept across the Connecticut River, striking the eastern bank near the further abutment of the bridge to the island. . . . Soon after two in the afternoon the east end of the bridge began falling, and with a mighty crash it tumbled over and went down the river." Two persons were killed, and the loss of property was estimated at three hundred thousand dollars.[17]

Since the Steen-Wilkins block stood a furlong north of Whetstone Brook, it was in no danger; yet the family could not have escaped the general sense of panic and disorganization caused by the flood. Mary would later use the incident for a climactic moment in the novel *Jerome.*

Fire followed hard upon flood. "About 2.30 o'clock on Sunday morning, October 31, Night Watchman 'Vet' Burlingame discovered fire in the kitchen of the saloon of A. E. Eayrs in Central block . . . and ran to the lower Main street shop of Estey & Company to have the whistle blown, which was delayed for some minutes, and after more delay two bells were rung. The fires . . . soon worked both north and south, and within three hours all of the buildings on the west side of Main street between High and Elliot streets were consumed by the devouring element. The large building on the corner of High and Main street . . . , the great market occupied by W. F. Richardson, the grocery and flour store . . . , the building used by E. A. Eayrs as an eating saloon, and by B. N. Chamberlain as a hat store, with lodging apartments above—all were destroyed. The raging mass of flames then swept across an alleyway to the south, and in an incredibly short time the three-story Brattleboro House . . . was completely enveloped. Superhuman efforts were made to save property, but very little was saved."[18]

There can be no doubt that Warren Wilkins was haled out of his bed by the alarm. His store was directly opposite the northerly end of the burning block; buildings on his side were several times on fire. But they were saved.

Mary graduated from Brattleboro High School in 1870. Her record in studies had been excellent; socially she was still an uncertain quantity. Despite her fine features, blue eyes, and reddish gold hair—despite her sweetness and depth of spirit, she did not attract the town's likelier sons. Mother and Father decided that she must have further advantages. Despairing of building their own home, they sold the Oak Street lot[19] and rented 8 Putney Road next to one of the Tyler houses.[20] Somehow they found enough money to send Mary to Mount Holyoke in the fall.

The Seminary had been conceived in heroic terms: "We will pray," said the founder, Miss Mary Lyon, "but let us also do, and do now."[21] Its purpose was to offer "a thorough intellectual training combined with careful religious culture" which often led to service in foreign missions.[22] Though Miss Lyon died in 1849, the "spirit of the institution" was still living when Mary enrolled in 1870.[23] Courses were full and rigorous, student schedules heavy according to our standards. Much Latin, algebra, physiology, Bible, and composition—these were the courses of the first year.[24]

Mary was also expected to "do now" her share in the domestic work of the "family." "Each girl," according to one of her contemporaries, "was enrolled in a 'circle' with a Senior as leader. Work was changed from time to time, so as to avoid monotony. Most of the periods were of an hour, with a half hour extra on Wednesday, recreation day. . . . Two matrons superintended the housekeeping in domestic hall where food was prepared and dishes washed. Great sheet-iron bake ovens were ranged along the wall in which bread was baked, a barrel full of flour being used each day. Then there were the huge iron pots in which the food was cooked. Cornelius, the friendly oldish man of all work, tended the furnace, carried wood for cooking, handled trunks, and so on. But all the rest of the work, even hard cleaning, was apportioned to the girls themselves.

"Rules were serious matters in those days, and not lightly to be broken. 'First class exceptions' . . . included absence from church, from recitations or from meals, as well as tardiness. 'Second class exceptions' comprised minor offenses, such as breaking study hours, walking over wet floors (on Wednesdays), having room or wardrobe out of order. Once a day each girl was required to report any infractions of rules to her designated teacher. Either she was excused or told to 'report to the front seat.' This ordeal was faced on Saturday mornings when the entire Seminary gathered in Seminary Hall. . . ."[25]

Mary at eighteen was getting the discipline which she had lacked at ten.

There was "an interesting revival near the close of the winter term. It was preceded by weeks of earnest prayer. Mr. Durant and Rev. H. M. Parsons . . . conducted the public services and conversed privately with inquirers. 'Everyone knew that the Holy Spirit was here. When one after another tremblingly or joyfully told of her new found love, we blessed the Master who had so abundantly fulfilled his promise. . . .' Among our two hundred and sixty pupils, only ten manifest no interest."[26]

Mount Holyoke was too much for Mary Wilkins. Many years later she put down her memories of the college in a letter to a classmate. "I was very young . . . and went home at the end of the year a nervous wreck, so I fancy I may be somewhat confused about the whole. What I am sure of is that I ate so much beef in different forms and so many baked apples that I have never wanted much since. I have often wondered why they looked out so beautifully for our young morals, and did not vary our menu more. As I remember, I did not behave at all well at Mt. Holyoke, and I am inclined to attribute it to monotony of diet and too strenuous goadings of conscience."[27]

In the following year, she had a few courses at Mrs. Hosford's Glenwood Seminary, a school for girls in West Brattleboro. One of her classmates, the late Mrs. P. K. White, recalled the morning drives in the mail coach and the return in the late afternoon and remembered Mary as an uncommonly talented student.

Such was her formal education, completed in the nineteenth year, chiefly literary, and unusually full in these days when higher education for the female was still widely questioned. It did not supply the poise and easy friendliness which Mrs. Wilkins probably desired for her daughter, nor did it kill her interest in literature.

Meanwhile Brattleboro was rebuilding much of its business and industrial section. Edward Crosby, formerly of little Marlborough in the country back of Brattleboro, had built a sizable grain business as eastern agent for one of the western mills. Chiefly on his reputation, he borrowed heavily, bought out the owners of the burned Main Street properties, and proceeded to erect an entire long block of three-story brick business buildings. When his bank began pinching, Crosby sold half his block and finished the other half with his gains. Loyal George Brooks returned to Brattleboro, after having made a fortune elsewhere, and built the handsome Brooks House at the northern end of Crosby Block. The Block and the hotel represented one of the boldest village ventures of this period.[28]

One day Warren Wilkins was discussing his daughters with a friend. "Nan," he said, "is a good musician and will be able to take care of herself. But Mary—she has no talent, and I don't know what she will do to make a living."[29] Mrs. Wilkins might have added that Nan would also marry early and well. Though still little more than a child, she was gay and sweet and pretty in a dark way. She was already going to many little parties and bringing her friends to the house. Mary, attractive also but withdrawn, was always curled up in a big chair with a book or gazing out of the window. And both Warren and Eleanor Wilkins knew that in view of the family finances, she should soon be marrying.

It was not that Miss Wilkins disliked young men in general; she thought and dreamed in a normally romantic way. It was that she could not imagine herself falling in love with any of the boys who came her way in Brattleboro; they seemed to her dull, clumsy, self-conscious, and appallingly young. It was fun for her to sit demurely and let them babble while she peered beneath the youthful swagger; she could not take them seriously. Since she wished to be like other girls and to please her mother, it was a disturbing situation and also humiliating. Always, deep in her imagination, was a princely person—something of all her fictional heroes, something of her gallant and feckless father—who would one day claim her hand. He would take her away from these people who loved her but without understanding her real nature.

Then Mary met Evelyn Sawyer, one with whom she could talk. They discovered a common bond at once: they both despised the same people. The daughter of a Newfane merchant who was by this time doing well in Brattleboro, Evelyn was invited everywhere. Though she could be completely charming when she wished, she demanded lightness of touch in conversation. For her some of the Brattleboro teas were interminable agonies. What could she, a lovely blonde in the early twenties, say to an elderly gentleman slightly deaf, his wife who talked only of crocheting and operations, three indignant spinsters, and the callow youth of seventeen invited, as an afterthought, for her? There was one compensation. Mary Wilkins would drop in that evening after supper; they could pop corn at the fireplace and say deliciously catty things.

When they went calling together, Evelyn was forced to make the conversation. Mary sat with an expression of angelic sweetness, put in a shy word occasionally. Afterward at the Sawyer's she reenacted the scene—every gesture, mannerism, every revealing flash of character.

Mary knew that most people in Brattleboro preferred Nan to herself; she also knew that the incomparable and worshiped Evie Sawyer found her much more interesting.[30] Avid readers both, they talked about their discoveries as they read Auerbach, Dickens, Emerson, Greek mythology and philosophy, Hawthorne, Sarah Jewett, Poe, Mrs. Stowe, Thackeray, Taylor's translation of *Faust,* Thoreau, a "lot of poetry."[31] The listing is casual because this was casual reading, yet it was surely lifting them out of the rigidities of the village code.

On warm still nights in the summer they strolled down Walnut Street to a bench, hidden from the street by trees and bushes, from which they could see the river. There it lay before them, silver-gray in the moonlight, and down below, a dark uncertain bulk, the island, and nearer shore, the dancing reflection of the village lights. Across the river rose the dark mass of Mount Wantastiquet, reflecting its curving crest in the water. There they talked quietly of great vague questions raised by their masters. Though still orthodox in her bones if not in her mind, Mary found the romantics intensely stimulating; Goethe's deity or Emerson's was crowding out the Jehovah of Dr. Labaree. Even at this moment of night and lapping water and hushed woods, she was feeling herself part of a great breathing oneness.

From Emerson she did not need to learn self-reliance; for something of ambition and inner confidence was already alive in her spirit. Yet it was heartening to know that this reaching up and out was to be counted a good and vital thing. "Society everywhere is in conspiracy against the manhood of everyone of its members. . . . Whoso would be a man must be a nonconformist." Encouraged by the rising tide of feminism, Mary knew that she was right in reading "man or woman" for the single word of the text. Then she and Evelyn would be talking of dresses and people and their beaus. Mary might tell of her afternoon's drive with an awkward youth snared for her by her mother. Poor boy, he had tried so hard to be pleasant, and she had helped him so little, saying nothing at all but intentional banalities. Anyway, she would not have to be bothered with him again.[32]

In the summer of '73 came one who seemed worthy of all her wit and beauty, real or fancied. He was tallish, solid of build, handsome in a mustached and clear-featured way. A recent graduate of the Naval Academy, he wore his ensign's uniform admirably.[33] He was also a Tyler, a grandson of Chief Justice Royall, a second son of the Reverend Thomas Pickman.

Hanson Tyler was on leave after a stay in Havana, living

just across the lawn with his father, step-mother, and Aunt Amelia Tyler of the school.[34] Inevitably, he and Mary met, walked to the Post Office and back in the bright morning, drove in the long afternoons to Spofford Lake or the old Royall Tyler place at Guilford, smiled in Prospect Hill Cemetery at the four marble nymphs who leaned against the obelisk hewn by Larkin Mead to honor murdered Jim Fisk.[35]

Hanson Tyler was enough of a man for any woman: later he was known in the Navy for courage, humor, hard drinking, and bad health. They called him "Horse" Tyler. He substituted twenty-two guns for twenty-one for His Majesty and later explained that twenty-one were to honor the King, one for good old Joe Gish.[36] He also had the sweetness of spirit characteristic of his family. Perhaps he knew girls unusually well; he seems to have been close to several of his young cousins. This is part of his letter to Cousin Edie written when he was fifteen:

"Allow me to delicately hint that having nothing better to do I will answer your note—allow me also to tenderly insinuate that I am very much obliged to you for it & that it was a *most good* one considering that you had *nothing to say.* [Both Hanson and Edie are in Brattleboro, living in the same neighborhood.] Fan just passed, under way for your house; I sent word by her that I was trying to answer your note. Allow me to remark that Vishnu the Fakir, and originator of Gift Exhibitions, proposes to give everybody a present who attends his first entertainment, which will be Wednesday evening, Sept. 12, 1866. I have only got thirteen more days to stay in town, so I am going to enjoy them as much as possible, for I shall not have another chance to cronie with such a most best crowd in a long time. . . .

"I've just filled my pipe & am having a smoke. While I was filling the pipe George laid [sic] on the sofa & cracked jokes—but they were of no account, so I won't spin them to you. I'm awful hard up for something to say. I will here remark that

Vishnu, the Fakir gives an entertainment at the Town Hall on Wednesday evening, Sept. 12, 1866.

"John C. Tyler is just passing the window & looks like a wet hen on a cold morning.

"You can give my love to Sister Kittie & Lina & Sally & Fannie and kiss me for them all. George is trying to think of something to write in your album. Why don't he put
'The girl who feign would choose a mate
Who'd ne'er in goodness fail her & c.'

"Well this is a *most poor* note, but please answer it soon, & believe me to be forever

Y'r aff.ate Cousin,
H. R. Tyler U. S. N.

P. S. Remember that *Vishnu,* the *Fakir* gives an entertainment at the Town Hall—Wednesday—Sept. 12th."[37]

By the summer of '73, Hanson Tyler would be talking of his brother John Steele—mortally wounded in the Battle of the Wilderness and idealized by the whole family; of the endless doings and sayings of grandfather, grandmother, and their four preaching sons; of the cousins and their beaus and parties; of his own days at Annapolis and his recent cruises; but the lightness, the humor, the lovable quality of the boy would remain. Pressed by Mother and Nan and Evie Sawyer, Mary confessed that she was very much in love with her ensign.

Did he love her? Saying goodbye as he departed for a cruise, he gave Mary a photograph and promised to write. A sweet bit of verse brightened her album. He loved her quite as much as Cousin Edie or the other girls of the "most best crowd"; he also loved all the Tylers, the Navy, and his career. Though Mrs. Wilkins was virtually certain that Mary would eventually marry her glittering ensign, her daughter merely hoped and dreamed.

She tried teaching in the fall at Miss Sawyer's school for girls on North Street; the principal was a relative of her friend Evelyn. Lacking incisiveness and caring little for her pupils, Miss Wilkins was a poor teacher and resigned at the close of the spring session. It was a disappointing experience chiefly because the family needed her earnings. Economic conditions in the country were bad; and Mr. Wilkins' lack of business ability was glaringly apparent.[38] With the September failure of Jay Cook came the crash which was followed by seven lean years.[39] Wilkins sold his stock, retained his interest in the Steen-Wilkins Block, and returned—with dim prospects —to his trade as carpenter and builder. Since little building was under way, he sometimes worked in the shops of the Estey Organ Company.

Though the Wilkinses had come to Brattleboro with high hopes, they were now reduced to proud and shabby gentility. For their pretty and talented daughters, they continued living on respectable Toad Hill as long as possible; but they were in straits almost desperate. Sensing real need, one of the neighbors, in a considerately tactful way, brought in an occasional supper dish, always a delicacy. Mrs. Wilkins accepted with stiff courtesy. Later she insisted upon reciprocating by offering a good soup in her most costly tureen. Though still witty on occasion and fully presentable in black suit on a Sunday morning, Warren Wilkins began to slip into the background. The neighbors thought of him as a "putterer" and as one who was always doing little services for others, partly perhaps to maintain his own dignity.[40]

Even in a panic year, Brattleboro had a diverting literary sensation. Charles Dickens, it will be remembered, had died in 1870. Shortly afterward, one T. P. James, who called himself a master printer, came to town with his "alleged wife." He worked for a time in one of the print shops, then announced that he was retiring into the deepest seclusion. As Dickens' medium, he would complete *The Mystery of Edwin Drood,* left unfinished by the novelist. So great was the excitement caused by this announcement at a time of general interest in spiritualism that metropolitan papers sent reporters to interview James. They went away puzzled. On October 31, 1873, the completed *Mystery* was issued. It sold widely in the United States and in England and was "commented upon favorably by many Dickens critics."[41]

In '75, Mr. Wilkins hit upon a scheme for increasing the family income, a plan roughly like this so far as it can be understood from the records of the Town Clerk. His interest in the Steen-Wilkins Block yielded each year a tidy sum in rentals; he could mortgage his share in the Block to obtain cash and still retain the rentals; with the cash, he could have some interest in a small frame apartment building which he would erect for a friend. The Wilkins family would live in one of the apartments. The site was newly opened Grove Street which rises sharply from Main. At number 17, Wilkins built a curious adaptation in frame of the old houses of Washington Square, which he could have seen in the course of his buying expeditions to New York. Soon the family was living in the second floor apartment on the western side.[42]

Though only sixteen, charming Nan Wilkins was engaged to another of Christian Schuster's musicians, the young organist Arthur Barrett. Mary was still the favored sister in the family, but it was Nan who was known and loved in the town.[43] In May, Evelyn Sawyer married a brilliantly schooled physician, Dr. Charles E. Severance.[44] Though Mary had several other friends, the doctor's decision to move to Shelburne Falls, Massachusetts, was a severe blow.[45] There was no one to take the place of the adored Evie.

Mrs. Royall Tyler, Hanson's Aunt Laura, received from him in November a long and amusing letter written aboard the U. S. Str. Monongahela. Two sentences fit into this story: "I hardly know whom to write to; I have not heard from anybody for ages and don't think I owe anybody any letters. As 'leaf by leaf the roses fall,' so one by one the girls have fallen off whom I used to be friendly with when last at home."[46] Had Mary Wilkins ignored his letters to her? Or was it rather that he did not write? Certainly she still remembered him vividly.[47]

A few weeks earlier, Miss Wilkins had had a birthday—her twenty-third. Since the family purse was about as lean as usual, it was clear that she should be doing something. Perhaps she was "waiting" for Hanson Tyler; if not for him, at least for a young man more interesting than the beaus who had come her way. Careers for women were not totally unheard of in this day, but what? Much later she told Mr. Henry W. Lanier that she had wished to be an artist.[48]

Though the town was not an art center, something of a tradition did exist. John Larkin Mead, Junior, was by this time a famous name in sculpture. Influenced by their artist mother and the Italian painter Gambadella, whom she had brought to Brattleboro in the late '30's, the Hunt boys had turned toward art. Richard was a fashionable architect in New York, the designer of the Tribune Building, of Newport and Fifth Avenue residences in the style of the French Renaissance. William had studied painting under Couture, become a disciple of Millet, and returned to introduce the Barbizon painters to Boston. In this year, he was doing two superb murals for the Capitol at Albany.[49]

Mead and the Hunts were of course "emigrants," especially notable figures in that vast movement away from New England or from village to city which had been under way since the '30's and '40's. Brattleboro could not use their talents, yet their careers were in some sense part of the local tradition. They were discussed at home; to a degree they inspired all of the young people like Mary Wilkins who were attracted to the arts.

Quickly she made two discouraging discoveries. Oil paints in tubes cost money. Moreover it is not enough to mix them well; they must be applied skillfully to canvas. Hence she turned to writing.

"I started with poems, religious. I took myself quite seriously then, also my work. I showed these efforts to a Vermont clergyman, and he told me that I was a genius, or to that effect. I thought he knew. Fortunately, I never offered these poems for publication, and they are non-existent."[50] (Warren Wilkins boasted of Mary's poetic flights when Hattie Lothrop came from Randolph for a visit.)[51] "Then I wrote children's verse for a little Fall River magazine. It did not pay, but the editor was extremely kind. She wrote me encouraging letters which really meant more than dollars though the family purse was very lean."[52]

In the next year—May 27, 1876—Nan Wilkins died suddenly of a "disease of the mesenteric."[53] She had been unwell for some time; yet she was so intensely alive, so gay and bright that her death at seventeen must have seemed shocking. She was taken to Randolph for burial in the family lot. Having nothing suitable to wear, Mary borrowed black from a neighbor.[54]

CHAPTER Three

Two of the Wilkins children, Edward and Mary Clara, were buried in the family plot at Randolph. Nan was placed beside them. Naturally there was some visiting of relatives and friends; then Warren, Eleanor, and Mary returned to Brattleboro.

Through the long summer, the Grove Street apartment seemed quiet to Mary. Though sharp grief and rebellion subsided quickly, the thought of Nan was always there when Mary went into her sister's room. Yet her mother and father, however much or little they understood her vague aspirations, could be counted on for the affection which she deeply needed.[1]

Fall and winter brought small events. The Lyceum season included the Boston Lyceum Opera Company, Bayard Taylor, whose translation of *Faust* Mary knew well, a certain Mrs. Mary Asherwood who had something to say about "Superfluous Women,"[2] a subject sufficiently significant in a region which had been losing too many of its young men to the West or to the cities. Though only slightly interested in politics, Miss Wilkins could hardly have ignored the Hayes-Tilden campaign and the disputed election; for Rutherford B. Hayes, born in Ohio, was the grandson of Rutherford, of the old Hayes Tavern in West Brattleboro and was also related to the Elinor G. Mead of Brattleboro who had married William Dean Howells.[3] Vermont, it seems, was a good state for one's father to have come from.

The rhythm of her life was gentle and slow with much time for reading. Sometimes she put down her book to gaze idly out of the window. There was nothing very interesting to see—just a pleasant row of frame houses on the other side of Grove Street, the green of the maples, and an occasional passer-by. Yet she would sit at the window hour after hour—looking and dreaming until the neighbors began to think it odd that this undoubtedly clever young woman should use her time in such a way. Why wasn't she doing something?[4]

The infrequent callers, usually for her mother or father, held little interest for Mary. "You are fond of people, and I never have been," she wrote in an undated letter to Evelyn Severance. These are curious words to have come from one who would later win distinction as an analyst of New England character, yet they should not be rejected. Miss Wilkins was fascinated by the interplay of motives, by the underlying web of emotion and tradition, by the incident of dramatic potential; but for the people themselves she cared little at this stage of her growth. One must except the few close friends who could meet her on her own level; to them she offered lasting devotion.[5]

And she adored bright children. Now and then, small Florence Pratt would look in, and Mary would read fairy stories for her in a high and rather sweet voice, enjoying both the tale and the child's delight.[6] She craved a bit of deviltry and found it hard to come by: one night she dressed in man's clothes, gazed at her image in the mirror, later told one of her friends that it was a "thrilling experience."[7]

In 1877 the leanness of the family purse necessitated another move. The Reverend Thomas Pickman Tyler and his wife invited the Wilkinses to live with them at 9 Tyler Street: Mrs. Wilkins would keep house for the family.[8] Knowing the independent spirit of father, mother, and daughter, one wonders how they were able to accept this situation. It smacks too much of shabby gentility.

Yet it must have been pleasant, in some ways, for them to

live with the Tylers. Pickman, a semi-invalid in his early sixties, was still a winning and handsome person. He was the eighth son of the old Chief Justice and his wife Mary and the youngest of the four "preaching Tylers"; after Trinity College, Hartford, and the General Episcopal Seminary, he had married a Brattleboro girl and headed the local academy for a time. Then for nearly thirty years, he had served Episcopal congregations in Ohio and New York State. Precarious health held him to smaller churches and at length forced him into Brattleboro retirement in his middle fifties. Yet Pickman Tyler was a man of intellectual distinction and great personal charm.[9]

One of the three sons of his first marriage was Hanson Tyler, whom Mary Wilkins had not at all forgotten. After the death of his first wife, Dr. Tyler married in Batavia, New York, Diana O. Brown, the widow of one of his wealthy parishioners. It was with Brown money, they said in Brattleboro, that he built the 9 Tyler Street house.[10]

If the Wilkinses lived there in a menial status, they at least lived well. They were in the neighborhood that they knew best but closer to the Connecticut River than ever before. On a summer afternoon, Mary could enter through the Tyler Street gate, cross the east lawn shaded by its horse chestnut and linden, and go on to the sward at the back which stretched down almost to the river. Seated under a pine, she could see the smooth water through an opening between trees and bushes and then look up to Mount Wantastiquet on the eastern shore. For the musing and reading which she loved, it was a matchless setting.

The house was large, roomy, and pleasant: the Wilkinses surely lived without crowding, for there were five bedrooms on the second floor. Pickman Tyler and his lady may well have appreciated Eleanor Wilkins' efficient housekeeping and have done what they could to make mother, father, and daughter feel at home.

Now a Master, Hanson Tyler was off on cruises, still the

wary Yankee not easily led into marriage. His leaves of August and October, 1877,[11] may have been spent in his father's house; but no knowledge of this matter nor of Pickman Tyler's attitude toward the friendship with Miss Wilkins is available. Did he read to her these teasing words of Hanson's letter of November 19, 1877?—"Doesn't it seem kind of curious that people with wives get so much sympathy when away from home while we poor lads who haven't the good luck to have a family are supposed to be perfectly happy everywhere? . . . I have some pretty pictures hung about my room and standing on my bureau. The latter are of young ladies with whom I have had flirtations at various times of my life. The one I like best has the prettiest frame and of course occupies the position of honor in the centre of the bureau."[12]

Mary Wilkins living in the same house with Hanson Tyler when he returned on leave—if he did so return, talking daily with his father who was receiving periodical letters from him, meeting casually and often other Tylers who knew of the friendship—it is a piquant situation which might have left memories in the minds of friends and relatives. But almost nothing remains.

She must have learned much of all Tylers living and dead, for Pickman was the tireless and enthusiastic family historian. For many years he had been collecting letters, mulling over them, corresponding with the huge connection, above all cherishing and making plans for editing Grandmother Tyler's Book. Long outliving her husband the Chief Justice (she had died as recently as 1866), Grandmother Mary was still a beloved presence in the family.[13] Her journal caught up its history from the Boston and Braintree days of 1738 down to the Vermont establishment, closing in 1810. Eventually it would be edited by Frederick Tupper and Helen Tyler Brown and published by G. P. Putnam.

In the '70's, it was a manuscript to ponder sentimentally. In it Revolutionary times lived in the vivid memories of

Palmers and Hancocks: Mary Tyler had been a Palmer, and the family connection was impressive. Yet she writes frankly of the family's most impoverished days and of her parents' struggle to rear and educate their children. Slowly her own sturdy character emerges from the pages, and we are ready to accept the father's judgment of her: "Those of us who know you feel that you are good, amiable, and, what is of infinite more importance, have fixed and firm principles of action."[14]

Equally fine for Miss Wilkins, if she was searching for anchorage in the New England past, was Royall Tyler's description of his West Brattleboro farm in 1801. "The farm we have purchased is in a retired spot upon the brow of a large hill, about one mile . . . from [West] Brattleboro meeting house. . . . The farm consists of about 150 acres, the greatest part of which . . . is well fenced and under good improvement. We have wheat and rye now in the ground, springing up as the snow leaves it, and promising a sufficiency of those grains for our bread and pies. We have two large orchards, and two smaller ones coming on, and expect to make some fifty or sixty barrells of cider. . . . We have plenty of good pasturing and expect to cut enough hay to winter thirty head of cattle. Our neighbor, Mr. Peck, takes the farm, at present, at halves. . . .

"Mrs. Peck is an excellent dairy woman and he is a regular farmer. . . . With the farm, we purchased farming tools, young cattle, hogs, poultry, and twenty-three sheep, who have increased the flock by eight lambs; and it would amuse you to see Sophia and the children surrounded with sheep, lambs, geese, turkeys, and hens, feeding them from their hands. The house is entirely secluded from a view of any neighbors; though on the crown of a hill, it is yet in a hollow, but the necessary buildings around it give it the air of being a little neighborhood; a large barn and a shed, corn-barn, chaise-house, smoke-house, ash-house, etc."

Mary Tyler continues. "All this time my dairy and spinning

wheels were busily attended . . . by myself, with the assistance of one and at times two girls. Our sheep furnished wool and we raised flax. I spun all the thread I used for years, whitening some, and coloring some, and some keeping flax color. . . . For twelve or fifteen years we made the children's clothes summer and winter for common wear. . . . The farmers' wives gave me credit for making excellent cheese and butter, but we did not have enough cows to shine in that way."[15]

Another Tyler, Aunt Bessie Tyler Billings, took Mary on long drives to Putney, Guilford, and the West River Valley villages, drives which supplied thought-provoking contrasts. Aunt Bessie was niece to Pickman and to his sister Miss Amelia, who had a school for younger children. After her husband Captain Cornelius Billings had been killed at the Battle of the Wilderness, Aunt Bessie had returned to Brattleboro, living with Miss Amelia and teaching under her. Her son had followed Hanson and the other Tylers to study at the Naval Academy.

Like so many of her family, Aunt Bessie was sensitive, intelligent, and sweet of spirit. Mary Wilkins liked her, felt safe with her. And she enjoyed the drives into the Valley towns to visit with Bessie's friends and relatives.[16] When she wrote later of the "beauty of Brattleboro" and its lasting effect on her life,[17] she may have been thinking as much of the Valley and its villages as of the big town on the Connecticut. For in the reticent way of hilly country cut by swift streams, it is incomparably lovely.

These rides may have supplied some of the experiences and insights which would later speak in her stories. In the late '70's, this was a beautiful and anemic country. To the south was Guilford, the village to which Royall Tyler brought his bride—population 1379 in 1850,[18] 1096 in 1880.[19] Following the river north, they came to Putney—1423 in 1850,[20] 1124 in 1880;[21] or they could drive northwest, following the West

River to Newfane—1304 in 1850,[22] 1031 in 1880,[23] and then Townshend—1351 in 1850[24] and 1099 thirty years later.[25]

Summer for this country, writes Harold F. Wilson, was the period 1790 to 1830—the opening of new farms, the development of small industries;[26] 1830 to 1870 brought autumn—a thriving sheep industry and the stimulus of railroad building but also the competition of the West and the cities.[27] By 1877, when Miss Wilkins saw the Valley and its villages, it was winter.[28]

"What shall the New England farmer do? He cannot compete in cereals with the West; in fruit and vegetables with Delaware and New Jersey; in cattle with men whose herds run summer and winter on the free ranches of the government; in wool with the unhoused flocks of Texas and California, of New Zealand and Australia; in butter with Nebraska and Iowa; in dressed beef with Armour's syndicate; in the labor market with the local manufacturers."[29]

Miss Wilkins may have been especially interested in Newfane, for it was in this village that the worshiped Evelyn Severance had grown up. A shire town bordering on the West River, settled in 1776, Newfane had been a thriving and important center in the '20's and '30's. A superb inn was built in 1793 along the north side of the common; in the days of John Quincy Adams came the fine Greek Revival Courthouse, the Union Hall, the Congregationalist Church—all grouped symmetrically within the common. Nicely placed were the business and residential areas; off to the north was Newfane Hill, the original settlement.

But when Mary Wilkins and Aunt Bessie Tyler Billings came to this village in the '70's, they must have noticed that the Newfane Hill settlement had disappeared and that Newfane, however lovely, was moribund.[30] They may have remembered that Evelyn Severance's father had disposed of his Newfane business and had come to industrial Brattleboro to prosper. "Had come from"—it was always that phrase, for the more ambitious or energetic or artistic ones could be fond of villages like Newfane, but they could not stay. The good farms were in the West; the careers in business or industry or the arts were in the great cities.[31] Newfane, like the other Valley villages, was hanging on grimly and without rational hope.

Miss Wilkins and Mrs. Billings were not economic historians; presumably they did not consult census statistics nor inquire into the health of local agriculture and industry. They would hardly discuss emigration from the Valley or from Randolph, Massachusetts; for they were of course a girl and a widow out for a pleasant drive and a few calls.

Neither, however, was a fool. They certainly must have noted deserted farms and seen mills sagging into ruins; talking with the women folk, they must have noticed that the word *mortgage* was spoken too frequently, that old people seemed to predominate in these communities, that mothers said much of their sons who had gone away, that young women spoke grimly of their marriage prospects. Here, in the Valley towns, Miss Wilkins had come upon a subject though she was hardly prepared to recognize it at the moment. It would be a rich subject too, a subject of tragic overtones; for the stay-at-homes whom she met were not weak and indolent people. They still retained many of the strongest qualities of New England character.

Though Aunt Bessie Tyler Billings died in 1878,[32] it is fully possible that Pickman Tyler and other friends occasionally invited Mary to drive with them into the Valley, that her knowledge of the towns and their people may have continued to grow. Moreover, her eyes would now be open for similar situations which could be encountered in Brattleboro, West Brattleboro, and the immediately neighboring country. She was still experimenting with verse and tales for children, but the "copy" and the sensibility for her characteristic adult stories were developing rapidly.

The telephone came to Brattleboro in 1878. Major F. J.

Childs and others associated with American Bell had a contract for installations in Vermont, western New Hampshire, eastern New York, and northern Massachusetts. The first Brattleboro line ran from Town Hall to the Brooks House, carrying music for the entertainment of the hotel's guests.[33] Though eventually the Valley towns would have their telephones and would be less isolated from Brattleboro and the nation, the immediate effect was presumably a sharpening of the contrast between the phoneless village and the larger town which moves with the times.

Brattleboro moved with the times—the corrupt times—in another way: on July 16, 1880, *The Weekly Reformer* ran the banner headline "A Big Crack in the Upper Crust." "The most startling crime which ever broke upon this country, and possibly as it may turn upon all New England, is revealed in the collapse of the First National Bank of Brattleboro, which is ruined by the defalcation of its president and former cashier, Silas M. Waite. The extent of the crime is not determined yet, but it is not likely to turn out to be less than $100,000 and is likely to go much higher—possibly to three or four or five times that amount. No one certainly knows the whereabouts of Waite himself, who left town Thursday and is supposed to have skipped the country.

"For some days there have been signs of approaching explosion. Men who have known the workings beneath the surface of local finances have expected it for several years, and some of Colonel Waite's enemies have tried to bring it on by petitions to the comptroller of the currency at Washington for an investigation, but Waite's great ability and shrewd management has checkmated them every time, until within a week.

"Last Thursday Col. Waite left town. Since then, the bank has kept its doors open and apparently done business as usual, though it is said that it has been careful about paying out any very large sums of money. Yesterday, in the afternoon the rumor got upon the street that it had refused payment, as was the fact, on two or three large checks, against really good parties. As the bank had always been famous for its accommodating disposition in letting its customers overdraw their accounts *ad libitum,* this immediately aroused suspicion. The news spread in whispers from mouth to mouth, until along in the evening, when enough facts got bruited about the street, so that it was generally understood that the 'First National had gone up.' "[34]

Did Waite's defalcation signify a big crack in the integrity of Vermont finance? Hardly, for the later record has been excellent. But in 1880, the incident had a shattering effect in Brattleboro. Is it permissible to surmise that Waite's crime may have strengthened Miss Wilkins' tendency to look toward the past and toward the village as symbols of old moral strength?

Then the winter of 1880 and a crushing blow: Mrs. Wilkins died on December 9th.[35] She was only fifty-three, a vigorous, capable woman who could be ill spared by either husband or daughter. For a time, Mary's self-consciousness and the feeling that she was needed by her father helped her to endure the loss. However, she was essentially a clinging and affectionate girl, still much dependent upon her mother; and there were times when grief was overwhelming. Only after many years would the keen sense of loss disappear.[36]

Now father and daughter must leave the Tylers; they moved to a house on North Street, where Mary kept house and experimented with verse and possibly stories.[37] People in Brattleboro thought "she was always rummaging through old books and copying their style": much of her writing was weak enough and would merely collect dust in the "box full of things" which she humorously mentioned in later years.[38] But now, more and more frequently, she was seeking publication. Little Helen Brown, of the Tyler connection, was puzzled by the process. Why was pretty Miss Mary always going to the post office with a large envelope, then carrying away the same envelope three or four weeks later?

At last came a bit of recognition. A ballad, "The Beggar King," was accepted by D. Lothrop's *Wide Awake,* one of the better magazines for children, and appeared in the issue for March, 1881. For it Miss Wilkins received ten dollars.[39]

"The Beggar King" is a fanciful expansion in some fifty galloping stanzas of the old nursery rhyme:

> Hark! hark! hark! The dogs do bark!
> The beggars have come to town,
> Some in rags and some in tags,
> And some in velvet gowns.

It tells how a great host of beggars beleaguered the King's city, how the Beggar King demanded that the King of the city marry the Beggar Princess, how the King looked upon this shy and comely maid and "loved her at a sight," how she was splendidly arrayed in "a crocus-bordered petticoat, robes stiff with threads of gold, satin shoon, and lace in spices rolled," how the King was delighted with his bride, and the Beggar King, her father, sadly rode away.[40] Miss Wilkins is completely at home in this metier: she smoothly manages the ballad stanza and its internal rhymes; the story swings along with gusto; the images flash with bright and romantic beauty.

In the same year *Wide Awake* printed four other poems by Miss Wilkins, and one of the local papers recognized her small success. "Miss M. E. Wilkins of this village is evidently becoming a favorite contributor with the young folks' magazine publishers. The April St. Nicholas has a poem from her pen, "Cross Patch," each of the 24 stanzas of which has a vignette illustration. The April Wide Awake has a three-page "Story of Miss Muffett," also by Miss Wilkins, with full page illustrations, and Good Times (Boston) has a short Sunday school exercise written by her for six girls."[41]

In January, 1882, her first adult story, "A Shadow Family,"

won a fifty dollar prize offered by *The Boston Sunday Budget*.[42] It is not difficult to sense the importance of the fifty dollar prize: surely it was a fine thing for Mary to show the check to her father, to know that she was beginning to be somebody in a town which respected the arts.

By this time, the tradition rested not merely on the old names—Royall Tyler, Christian Schuster, Larkin G. Mead, Junior, Miss Anna Higginson, the Hunts—Richard and William—but also upon some younger people. The artist Robert G. Hardie was beginning his career; Mary and Lucien Howe and Harriet Brasor were giving promise of the distinction they later achieved in music; and Samuel M. Crothers, of the Unitarian Church on Main Street, was turning toward the essay in which he was to become a master.[43] Brattleboro was not Boston, but perhaps it was almost as good a town for the artist or writer in the early stage of a career.

Before the leaves were fully green, the Brattleboro paper told Miss Wilkins of the passing of Mr. Longfellow and Mr. Emerson. She had known neither of them personally, nor had she visited Cambridge or Concord. Yet Emerson, at least, had been one of her spiritual fathers; she was loyal to the Randolph pastors and the Village Code but perhaps more deeply committed to the teaching of "Nature," "The American Scholar," and "Self-Reliance." A quarter century later it would be the latter doctrine that she would pass on to young writers.[44]

The summer was quiet—much reading, keeping house for father, a few visits with her friends, occasional concentration on poems, tales for children, or more ambitious short stories for adults. Always devoted to her father, she was now disturbed because he was losing his youth so rapidly. His hair was entirely gray; though he still laughed, it was laughter that no longer came easily. He talked now and then of moving to a warmer climate.[45]

Century for September ran a Wilkins poem, "Sweet Phyllis," a graceful trifle in the manner of Robert Herrick. Since Gilder's was one of the nation's three distinguished periodicals, the ladies of Brattleboro were impressed: one of them, who had never spoken to Miss Wilkins before, greeted her warmly when they met on Main Street. After they separated, Mary said to her companion Miss Allie Morse, "Did you notice that? That's because *Century* printed one of my poems." Her eyes were gleaming with amusement.[46] *Wide Awake* was as usual printing her poems and children's stories steadily—fifteen poems and the fairy story "The Pumpkin Giant."

Early in the autumn, Mr. Wilkins left for Gainesville, Florida. There he could work on a construction job in a climate which would help him to regain his strength. Mary was not quite alone, for she had Augustus, her cherished tiger and white striped cat.[47]

Her thirtieth birthday came on October 31. Was she thinking about Nan and mother and father, about Hanson Tyler and Evelyn Severance, about her "work," which seemed to be all that remained to her? Could she write the stories for adults on which a career as writer could be based?

"The simplest road to success," she noted later, "is the best. There is really little to do except to provide one's self with good pens, good ink, and paper, a liberal supply of patience, sharpen one's eyes and ears to see everything in the whole creation likely to be of the slightest assistance, and set to work. . . .

"A young writer should follow the safe course of writing only about those subjects she knows thoroughly, and concerning which she trusts her own convictions. Above all, she must write in her own way, with no dependence upon the work of another for aid and suggestion. She should make her own patterns and found her own school. . . . The keynote of the whole is, as in every undertaking in this world, faithful, hopeful and independent work."[48]

Soon Miss Wilkins was working on a subject which she knew thoroughly, one of those tales which the women were always telling in Randolph or Brattleboro. The setting is the shoe town, Leyden, smaller than Randolph and, if anything, slower and more stolid. David Emmons, a shoe worker, began courting Maria Brewster when both were in their thirties. He had his own little cottage and garden patch; Maria lived with her father and mother. She was cheerful, ruddy-cheeked, good of heart. Though David was "slow," he was also sweet-tempered and solidly reliable. Nothing stood in the way of the marriage.

One Saturday evening David almost popped the question, and hopeful Maria was soon buying pearl-colored silk for her wedding dress. That was when they were about forty, but David did not move on to a real proposal. Ten years later, Maria had the silk made into a dress, for again it seemed that David had made up his mind. But again he retreated. The father died, leaving Maria—now sixty—with a very old mother. Leyden folks were then sure that David and Maria would be married, that he would rent his house and come to the Brewsters'.

Through all of these years, David never failed to make his weekly call. And there was a friendly arrangement whereby he brought vegetables from his garden for Maria and she did his baking and tidied his house on Saturdays.

When David was seventy and she was sixty-eight, Maria gave the pearl-colored silk dress to a cousin's daughter: it became her bridal gown.

One Sunday night, David stayed a little longer than usual. He said, " 'I'm gettin to be an old man, you know, and I've always been slow-goin'; I just couldn't seem to help it. . . . You don't lay up anything agin' me, Maria?'

" 'Yes, I know, David, all about it; you couldn't help it. I wouldn't worry a bit about it if I were you.' "

Next morning Maria was called to David's cottage. He was

dying. She leaned over him to hear his faint words. " 'Maria'—a thin, husky voice that was more like a wind through dry corn-stalks, said—'Maria, I'm—dyin', an'—I allers meant to—have asked you—to marry me.' "[49]

Miss Wilkins titled this story "Two Old Lovers," sent it first to *Lippincott's,* got it back after a few weeks with criticism she could not understand; then she tried *Century, The Atlantic,* and, at length, *Harper's Bazar.** There Miss Booth looked at the manuscript and laid it aside, judging from the childish script that a school girl was the writer. Later she read it and wrote off a quick acceptance.[50] Miss Wilkins never forgot the arrival of that note with its enclosed check for twenty-five dollars. Over forty years later when she was acknowledging the Howells Medal presented to her by Hamlin Garland, she compared the occasion to that other great day in Brattleboro: ". . . when I had taken the letter of acceptance and the check from my post-office box . . . , I did not walk home. It was before the days of the airplane . . . but I flew. I felt my wings spring from my shoulders capable of flight and I flew home.

"Twenty-five dollars! I may not be telling the exact truth when I say that I had visions of endowing a great public charity. I concluded to wait until I received ten dollars more for a story, and contented myself with buying small gifts. . . ."[51]

It is easy to understand the joy brought by this first major acceptance; but the purchase of "small gifts" at a time when the money was surely needed for the barest necessities—it seems puzzling. Then one remembers the stiff pride of Mrs. Wilkins who gave a gift of soup in her finest tureen when she was beholden to her neighbor. Miss Wilkins was, one suspects, returning past favors, regaining the right to hold her head high in Brattleboro.

Early in April came a telegram from Gainesville, Florida:

* This spelling of *bazar,* which is still recognized by lexicographers, was employed by the editors of the magazine.

Warren Wilkins was at the point of death. Mary went at once to Randolph, presumably expecting to join Uncle George and proceed to Florida. When she arrived, he had already departed. Soon came another message, saying that her father had died on April 10, only a few hours after the coming of his brother.[52] Working on a building operation, he had suffered a chill which quickly developed into deadly fever.[53] The body was brought to Randolph; for the third time within seven years, Mary Wilkins in mourning rode to the cemetery just east of town.

Now she was alone.

Perhaps, like her heroine in *By the Light of the Soul,* a novel which one of the cousins[54] deems considerably autobiographical, she fell into a mood of bitter doubt and questioning. "It had not occurred to her that whereas she had lost her mother, she could also lose her father. It seemed too heavy a hammer stroke of Providence to believe in and keep her reason. She had thought that her father was losing his youth, that his hair turning gray had much to do with his altered looks. She had never thought of death. It seemed to her monstrous. A rage against Providence, like nothing which she had known before, was over her. Why should she lose everything? What had she done? She reviewed her past life, and defended herself like Job, with her summary of self-righteousness. She had always done right so far as she knew. Her sins had been so petty as hardly to deserve the names of sins. She remembered how she had once enjoyed seeing her face in the looking-glass, how she liked pretty new dresses, and she could not make them seem very culpable."[55]

After the funeral Miss Wilkins returned to Brattleboro, staying with the Wheeler family of the Grove Street house built by her father.[56] With the sharp spur of writing for her living, she turned quickly to her work. Luckily—it had come just in time—Miss Booth of *Harper's Bazar* was deeply impressed by the stories: "The Bar Light House" appeared in the issue for April 28, 1883, "A Symphony in Lavender" on August 25, "A Tardy Thanksgiving" on December 15. The inferior "Little Mary Witlow" was accepted for the May *Lippincott's,* and there were the usual contributions to *Wide Awake*. D. Lothrop issued some of the verse in a little volume called *Decorative Plaques.*

Though the Wheelers were always kindly, Miss Wilkins wished to be in Randolph for the Christmas season. Packing her bags, taking Augustus as usual, she journeyed again to the town which might be called home; she would stay with Mary John Wales and visit Hattie Lothrop, Uncle George and his wife, and the other relatives. The one recorded event of the visit appears as an advertisement in the *Norfolk County Register* for December 8, 1883; "Lost on South Main Street, a large striped tiger and white cat. Had on, when lost, a leather collar marked 'M. E. Wilkins.' A suitable reward will be paid for his return to John Wales on South Main Street."

Providence was this time merciful; later references to the pet indicate that it was returned. It is also interesting to note that the incident, considerably transformed, appeared in "An Object of Love," one of the stories of *A Humble Romance.*

Early in '84, Miss Wilkins stayed for several months in the home of Dr. and Mrs. Charles E. Severance, at Shelburne Falls, a town of northwestern Massachusetts not far from the Vermont line and Brattleboro. Evie Severance was still her dearest friend, perhaps the only one who understood her deeply. In the spring, the friends could sit on the lawn at the rear of the house, talking gently as they looked at the placid Deerfield River and the hill rising sharply from its banks. For Mary and Evie, this must have been virtually a return to the setting of their Brattleboro confidences and a precious experience.

They also drove down to Deerfield. Miss Wilkins, as might be expected, fell in love with the old town and eventually used several of its houses and traditions in her stories. And there were calls at the Shelburne Falls home of Miss Katherine Mayhew, who would later introduce Miss Wilkins in New York and Brooklyn. Meanwhile at the Harper's office the idea that an M. E. Wilkins story was something rather distinguished had been gradually growing, and Miss Booth of the *Bazar* convinced Mr. Alden of *Harper's New Monthly* that "A Humble Romance" should be accepted for his June number.[57]

Short of an acceptance by *The Atlantic,* nothing could have been more satisfying for this young woman who was striving for recognition. *Harper's* was the most popular literary magazine of this period.[58] Of course there were the usual concessions to the genteelism of the times: its pages contained nothing which could not be read aloud before the entire family.[59] Yet Mr. Alden was selecting good fiction for his readers. In addition to "A Humble Romance," the June, 1884 issue included a striking story by John Esten Cooke, "Grace Sherwood, the One Virginia Witch"; in subsequent issues during the next three years would appear stories by W. D. Howells, Frank R. Stockton, Rose Terry Cooke, Sarah Orne Jewett, Harriet Prescot Spofford, Edward Everett Hale, George W. Cable, Brander Matthews, Helen Hunt Jackson, Elizabeth Stuart Phelps, Thomas Nelson Page, and "Charles Egbert Craddock." With the exception of Bret Harte, each of the important regional and realistic writers of the period would be represented by at least one story.

"A Humble Romance" glances back to Miss Wilkins' childhood in Randolph and her memories of the tin-peddler and his jiggling, rattling cart. In the story, he is Jake Russell, middle-aged, awkward, very kindly; and he is courting Sally, Mrs. King's plain little kitchen drudge. He proposes abruptly and is accepted after Sally understands that he means marriage. " 'I wouldn't go with the King, if it wan't to—go—honest—' " Jake and Sally wed that same day are granted three months of happiness in idyllic tin-peddling. Then an ugly complication—Jake's wife, whom he had thought to be dead, reappears.

A separation must occur, but Sally and Jake are reunited when the first wife obligingly dies.[60]

In bald summary, "A Humble Romance" seems inferior to "Two Old Lovers" and other pieces which had appeared in the *Bazar;* certainly the second incident is trite and trashy.[61] But by this time, Mr. Alden seems to have known that the M. E. Wilkins blending of humor, sentiment, and close analysis of New England village character was pleasing his readers. For her, the *Harper's* acceptance was superb recognition: continuing to write for the *Bazar,* she would reach the women readers; in *Harper's New Monthly,* she would be writing for the entire American "literary" public of her time.

On May 31, 1884, the estate of Warren E. Wilkins was settled. Mary, his only heir, received $969 in cash and a half-interest in the "Steen-Wilkins block," the small business property purchased originally in 1866.[62] The next question—where to live?—was not easy to decide. Miss Wilkins had no very close friends in Brattleboro; in Randolph, there were Uncle George Wilkins, the cousin Hattie Lothrop, and her old schoolmate Mary Wales. The kindly Wales family had invited her to stay with them. Since a maiden lady without close kin could hardly expect anything more attractive than a home with devoted friends, she decided to live with Mary John and her family. She packed her belongings, put the beloved tiger and white cat in his basket, and boarded the old Vermont and Massachusetts for Boston—and Randolph.

John Wales and Mary John met her at the station. If John Wales talked gloomily of the decline of the shoe factories and hard times on the farm, his daughter was as usual buzzing with news of the doings of the women folks. There was talk of the *Harper's* acceptance and the settlement of the estate.[63] Mary had come back to Randolph as something of a personage; she had a little money, a small steady income from the Brattleboro property, and at least the foundation of a career. She could, if she wished, hold her head high.

They drove past the three houses on South Main which she

knew best—Uncle George's, Uncle Edward's where Cousin Hattie was still living as she waited for one or another of the slow Randolph swains, and then her own house now occupied by the Tolmans. Farther down, they came to the Wales place which would be home for—well, for a time. It was good to see Mrs. Wales again—the kindly dark eyes, the rounding face, the white hair parted in the center and drawn back over the ears.[64] Receiving her greeting, Miss Wilkins remembered Mary John's way of saying, "Mother is the sort of woman who takes in every stray kitten."[65]

Since Frederic Wales, the elder son, had died in the '70's, there were now only the mother, father, Mary John, and a son John in the big house. They had marked good rooms for Mary Wilkins, really the whole north side of the house. She was to have the small parlor on the right as one enters, behind it a study with a curious old fireplace—a room which had been the kitchen, and one or two chambers on the second floor. Gradually, they would be decorated in her own taste.

If Mary John was a "come-outer," her mother and father honored the Randolph gods—Work, Thrift, Family, Gentility, and Jehovah of the Sacred Law. They rose early, worked hard, and went to bed betimes; and they never missed church. Mary was expected to conform only partly with their ways, for she was after all a writer. Her schedule was up at seven for breakfast with the family, an hour of "setting things to rights," a walk to the post office in the center of town, a chat with Cousin Hattie or other relatives on the way back, then dinner with the Waleses at noon. In the afternoon, she read or wrote in the small study. A neighbor might call after tea; more frequently, Miss Wilkins returned to her study. With the tiger and white cat, she would curl up in an arm chair to read or to muse. Later, old Augustus was succeeded by a pair of kittens, Punch and Judy; but there would be no other change in the those evenings in the study.

She enjoyed running up to Boston with Mary John for shopping, for she followed fashion closely. Since Randolph, with its late marriages, drew the line at thirty-five, she did not consider herself a maiden lady. She would be thirty-two in October, and her mirror showed a mouth which drooped a little at the corners. Yet she was always "Dolly" Wilkins, still pretty in a fragile, exquisite way. She knew that her blue eyes and red-gold hair were lovely, and she was fiercely determined to remain attractive. With Mary John, she bought Parisian hats; soft dull silks in brown or rose; and guimps of fine lace to soften the sharp line of her profile.[66] Later she would write, "A man may write something that will live for the sake of something ignoble, and a woman may write something for money with which to buy a French hat."[67]

And Mary John—how did she fit into the pattern of Dolly Wilkins' life? Miss Wales liked men and never married. Of an age with Mary Wilkins, she was less personable: her dark eyes were bright with fun and intelligence, but her features were rather heavy and her figure, frumpish. Though she never rebelled openly against the village code and indeed exemplified some of its virtues, she did her own thinking.[68] A Randolph attorney and shrewd student of local ways considers her typical of the antinomians, who were always held in check by the pastors but never fully converted to orthodoxy. She may well have believed that the true Christian has no need for Jehovah's law, and such heresy could have been appealing to the "come-outer" in Mary Wilkins.[69]

Certainly Mary John was a managing woman in a household in which the men folks were unimportant. Her father, a quietly good man, was struggling doggedly to keep the farm going at a time when farming did not pay. Miss Wilkins would later represent him as a "kitchen colonel" in a story by that name, a husband who does woman's work and is dominated by his wife. The son John had a rebellious nature and yearned toward city life; lacking education, he stayed on the farm. When Miss Wilkins came to live with his family, the women folks decided that John could no longer have his meals with the family: he would eat with Herbert Clark, the hired man.[70]

Mary John was strong, practical, partly emancipated from the code; and these were qualities which Dolly Wilkins valued. She could rely on Miss Wales for managing many aspects of her life and could always call upon her intense devotion and admiration.

Mary John was not especially possessive: she urged her friend to accept a place in Randolph's social life and also to travel. Though Mary rejected the first idea, she did screw up her courage for a trip to New York and Brooklyn in the winter of 1884-1885.[71] Miss Katherine Mayhew, whom she had met at Evelyn Severance's, suggested to Kate Upson Clarke that it would be interesting to know this young woman who was writing such sensitive stories about village New Englanders. Miss Wilkins visited Miss Clarke at her Brooklyn home and met many of those who liked her writing. One of the guests was Miss Booth of *Harper's Bazar,* then near the end of her career and of course delighted to meet her "discovery." Miss Wilkins performed tolerably. She surprised the ladies by having almost none of the country cousin manner; meeting her, they could not understand her kinship with the village characters of her fiction, but they could value her sweetness and her quiet sense of humor.[72]

Mary Wilkins was coming a little out of her shell as she began to feel more certain of her position as a writer and to sense the easy security of life in Randolph with the Wales'. But her work was still the real center of her existence: she wrote easily, she liked to write, and she was writing proudly for her living. She continued sensibly with juveniles—poems and stories for *Wide Awake* and the others. In '86, D. Lothrop collected the *Wide Awake* stories and issued them as a book, *The Adventures of Ann.* Her best ideas and highest skill went into short stories for *Harper's Bazar* and *Harper's New*

Monthly; in each year the *Bazar,* a weekly, would use five or six pieces and the *Monthly,* one or two.

In the spring of 1887, Miss Wilkins was talking with Mary John and Hattie Lothrop about reading the galleys of her first book for adult readers.[73] It was a collection of twenty-eight stories which had appeared in *Harper's* or *The Bazar.* The Harpers were the publisher, and the title *A Humble Romance and Other Stories* had been suggested.

CHAPTER

Four

WHEN *A Humble Romance* appeared in 1887, it produced no sensation among American critics. In a perfunctory notice, *The Critic* reviewer remarked: "They are tales of New England life, told with a good deal of originality and cleverness."[1] *The Literary World* of Boston relegated the volume to "minor fiction," admitting however that the "simplicity, purity, and quaintness of her stories set them apart from the outpouring of current fiction in a niche of distinction where they have no rivals."[2] The warmest commendation came from the most distinguished critic—Mr. Howells writing in "The Editor's Study" of *Harper's Monthly*. After caviling at occasional suggestions of sentimentality, he concluded, "They are good through and through, and whoever loves the common face of humanity will find pleasure in them. They are peculiarly American, and they are peculiarly 'narrow' in a certain way, and yet they are like the best modern work everywhere in their directness and simplicity."[3] The reading public apparently agreed with Howells, for *A Humble Romance* gained almost immediate popularity.[4] And it remains today one of Miss Wilkins' two or three best volumes of stories.

Though the story is the thing, something is to be gained by glancing at several aspects of its origin. What, first, was the writer using for copy? For characters and situations, Miss Wilkins went directly to her own experience and that of her family and friends. She and her own people were at the center: her own experience of life and death, her "disappointment," her phantasies often projected into middle-aged and elderly women, her mother and father, Grandfather Lothrop and his wife, and the aunts and uncles of Randolph—especially the pattern of weak husband and strong wife. In herself and in her immediate family, she knew the life, the cultural ideal, the character traits of the middle-class New England villager. She wrote of what she knew best. Only a little of the evidence for this statement will appear in the present chapter; more will accumulate as we turn to later volumes.

Though she tended to see her family in nearly all other families, many of the germs of stories came from gossip and from neighborhood tradition. From the talk of her parents and their friends in both Randolph and Brattleboro, from the lore of the Wales family and connections, from talk with Bessie Tyler Billings' friends of the West River Valley, from other similarly immediate sources, she picked up the revealing incident or the hint of strongly marked character which was enough to spur her imagination. Not far from 9 Tyler Street in Brattleboro were two old spinsters living in an ancient home owned by the Bradleys. Though they were pitifully poor and could pay no rent, no one could have turned them out; for they were ladies of good family. Since they had only one black silk dress between them and would go to meeting in nothing less elegant, they went by turns. That situation, related to me by Miss Helen Tyler Brown, was a source of indulgent amusement for Toad Hill people in the '80's; Miss Wilkins used it as the starting point for "A Gala Dress." It is hardly necessary to add she saw these sisters as "copy" because she and her family knew much of pride-in-poverty.

The casting of the stories of *A Humble Romance* suggests the same blending of fact, experience, and sensibility. The emigration of many young men from Randolph and Brattleboro during Miss Wilkins' formative years was a fact: census reports show men over twenty slightly less numerous than women of the same brackets. In the stories, the preponderance of female characters is exaggerated—over fifty women and only twenty-three men. Many young girls, somewhat fewer young men are used; only occasionally are these young people full-bodied and closely studied characters. The tart figures are the middle-aged or elderly spinsters and widows and, at a lower level of intensity, the middle-aged bachelors and widowers. Admitting exceptions, one remembers the men as a poor lot. In "Gentian," Miss Wilkins made much of an old couple. All of these characters are of the middle class, though some have "seen better days"; many are pitifully poor. In selecting her characters, Miss Wilkins was at once highlighting social and economic facts—the emigration of the young men, the preponderance of older people, the poverty of the villages—and reflecting her own experience and sensibility. Certainly, she was not guided by a rigorous devotion to the typical and the representative.

Her form is the local color story. That blunt statement is made with misgivings because the term has been applied to so much fiction that is merely dialect or atmosphere or the "quaint" customs of the "natives." It has been used to characterize Harte, Woolson, Cable, and Jewett at their very good best and also Harte's tired stories of his later period in London and hundreds of ephemeral pieces which littered the magazines from 1870 to 1900. But *local color* need not be a pejorative label; it can be understood to denote not merely surface aspects of a story but also an impulse, a sensibility, an attitude toward a particular moment in the development of a traditional culture. So understood by Alexander Cowie, the term serves well as a quick clue to the medium which Miss Wilkins employed.

Cowie writes, "The colors in a local-color story are likely to be sombre, but they serve to emphasize the seriousness of the form. Decline and decay are often a central theme: a generation is passing away. The setting is an isolated one: a pocket in the hills, a village remote from railway or main highway, a seaport town beyond its prime, a river hamlet, a Great Lakes outpost, a settlement begun in hope but finally by-passed by 'progress.' The community may have had an illustrious past, but it has no future. . . . Economic enterprise is slack: people do the old things in the old ways. Opportunity for individual improvement is scant; escape from personal problems, difficult. . . .

"Yet the author, who has probably lived in such a milieu, has a special affection for it. . . . The scene is often beautiful, and the characters, though outwardly 'unsuccessful,' are, as groups, at least, strongly individualized. Living close to God and nature . . . they exhibit a quiet stoicism, and they hold high the simple virtues of loyalty and response to duty. . . . Unmodified by contact with the outer world, they develop personal traits to the point of eccentricity.

"[The writers] are better in motivation than in episode. They make much of origins and aftermaths, and they excel in 'atmosphere.' Some of them overload their stories with descriptions of the physical setting, but many of them achieve a finely poetic quality in their descriptions. Hardly less significant is the emphasis laid upon speech peculiarities. . . . The form developed best in a sequestered region amid people bound together by tradition and generally acquiescent to the social order in which they find themselves."[5]

Though this is a roomy definition, it must be further expanded by noting that the local color story may be either romantic or realistic in tone. In 1887, Howells was praising "fidelity to physical and social conditions" and "absolute and unswerving realism" but also "sublimity," "a passion for nature," "brief romances," "pensiveness lit with humor."[6] It is only the simplification of a literary history concerned necessarily with major trends which leads us to subject Miss Wilkins' stories to standards appropriate to a clearly realistic intention. Her form, then, was the local color story, and it was a form within which she could express many facets of her complicated spirit.

She learned it, presumably, by reading Auerbach, Hawthorne—a local-colorist in his devotion to a declining tradition, and at least Mrs. Stowe and Miss Jewett among her immediate predecessors and contemporaries in New England.[7] She lived and felt her way into it by being the daughter of Warren and Eleanor Wilkins and by growing up in Randolph and Brattleboro in the '50's, '60's, and '70's.

More significantly, she wrote her own signature on the local color story. Partly, her originality was a matter of technical skill. It will be remembered that she had given nearly a decade to apprenticeship in poems for children and adults and stories for children before Miss Booth accepted "Two Old Lovers." Her models in verse were the English ballads, Herrick, and the English romantic poets;[8] craft for juvenile stories, she presumably learned from her contemporaries of the periodicals for children.

She also read Dickens,[9] Tolstoy, and possibly de Maupassant. From Dickens, she may have learned something of her skill in managing the mood of tragicomedy and much of the value of homely detail. Tolstoy's tale, "Three Deaths," affected her deeply, as she would later tell Miss Jewett;[10] and it is probable that she read some of his other stories. Mrs. Severance did not list de Maupassant among Miss Wilkins' enthusiasms; and the first English translation of his stories, *The Odd Number,* was issued in 1889. However, the friend did not pretend to be familiar with all of Miss Wilkins' reading, and she had quite enough command of the language for knowing the French realist in his own tongue.

Though there is no need for insisting on a Tolstoy or de Maupassant influence, this possibility should not be ruled out. Technically, the most striking characteristic of the Wilkins story is its pace and directness—the short and wiry sentence; the short paragraph; concision in narrative, expository, and descriptive elements; boldness in moving fast to the scene developed in dialogue. These aspects of form lend themselves easily to statistical comparisons. At each of these points, the Wilkins story of *A Humble Romance* and later volumes closely resembles Tolstoy of "Three Deaths" and other tales and a representative sampling of de Maupassant stories, whereas, at the same points, it differs sharply from the practice of Mrs. Stowe, Bret Harte, and Miss Jewett. To say this much is not to compare Miss Wilkins with Tolstoy or de Maupassant for either stature or sensibility.

Without seeking to define her formal adaptation of the local color story in terms more precise, one may say that she learned from her experience with verse and juveniles, from her English and American predecessors and contemporaries, and possibly from Tolstoy and de Maupassant. Certainly, the result was an admirable quickness, simplicity, and directness.

Her unique gift to the local color story was of course her own sensibility. Aspects of this sensibility have been mentioned briefly; others will emerge as the study continues. A short note may be useful here.

One is thinking of her need for affection and for recognized achievement, twisted but unsubdued by the frustrations of her early life; of that aspect of the code which glorified independence and nonconformity; of the prophets, Emerson and Goethe, who helped her to know and trust her own aspirations. Miss Wilkins was at once a woman and an artist, and she demanded all that she could get and much besides. Spiritually, she was obliged to live in at least three ages—the Puritan village of the late eighteenth century which still survived to a degree in Randolph; the vigorous idealism of Concord in the 1840's in books and, faintly, in the spirit of Brattleboro and in the minds of her editors; and the relative rigidity and decadence of her immediate environment in Randolph. She was at once within and outside the spirit of the culture from which she drew her themes and characters; she loved—and almost hated the people of whom she wrote. Out of this partially neurotic ambivalence comes much of her intensity and her deepest insight into her characters. Luckily, for her sanity and our pleasure, she had the Yankee's coolness and his ability to manage a smile from time to time. And if this sensibility seems much like that described in Cowie's analysis of the local color tendency, the circumstance should not be surprising. Miss Wilkins was unique only in her intensity, in her strong grip on whatever of past and present seemed alive.

Looking more closely at the stories of *A Humble Romance,* one must admit at once that they are uneven in quality, that some show the weakness of local color at its lower levels—sentimentality and over-dependence on atmosphere. Even its title is enough to make the modern reader suspicious of "A Symphony in Lavender."[11]

Caroline Munson is gradually revealed as a sweet and emotionally undeveloped spinster of nearly fifty, a woman whose personality has been assimilated to the lilac bushes of her comely home in Ware. She tells the narrator of a dream she had in her early twenties—a dream of a young artist whose face was at once beautiful and repulsive. Later she met the young man of whom she had dreamed, and they became friendly. When he proposed, she was again conscious of his dual nature, but the evil and ugliness seemed to predominate. Caroline Munson rejected him. The narrator, who knew the man, remarked that Miss Munson had chosen wisely.

This subject is an initiation, the protagonist's first discovery of evil in the world; and it is one of the richest available for the artist. Hawthorne would have intensified the invocation of evil, as in "Young Goodman Brown"; however shadowy and allegorical the resulting tale, it would have been morally impressive. James would have given us evil within a complex web of symbol, psychological analysis, and realistic detail. Miss Wilkins refused to cope with more than the safe surface of her subject.

For angle of narration, she used the first person confidante—a woman a little like herself visiting in a town reminiscent of

Shelburne Falls, Massachusetts. The device is useful for creating the lilac atmosphere and slowly revealing Miss Munson's secret. It is also unfortunate. The narrator is entirely too much the summer visitor; she is more knowing than Miss Munson but still too obviously reticent and genteel. The effect of "A Symphony in Lavender" is not symphonic; it is merely a wistful little air by MacDowell. Though one should not demand that Miss Wilkins use Freudian insights for probing the emotions of Miss Munson, it is fair to remember that she knew enough of women to avoid confusing them with lilac bushes.

The effect is much more impressive when, as in "Gentian,"[12] the mood is tragicomical and the approach to character and situation more direct. This story is built on the situation which initiated Ibsen's, "A Doll's House" though there is no record of Miss Wilkins' acquaintance with the play. Loving her old husband "Alferd" deeply, Lucy Tollett must sit quietly watching him die; for he refuses doctors or medicine and will accept no advice. Alferd is the typical stiffnecked male of Wilkinston. Lucy used the suggestion of her sister and put the tonic gentian in her husband's tea. His health improved. But Lucy Tollett was obliged to deal with her own conscience and the village code; she was tormented as she remembered that she had disobeyed and deceived her husband. When she confessed her sin, Alferd said little but acted drastically. He prepared his own victuals. There was a separation, very difficult for both Lucy and Alferd, and eventually a reunion. Alferd "came to see" that his pride must bend before Lucy's devotion.

Like most of the pieces of *A Humble Romance,* this story was written for *Harper's Bazar,* a woman's magazine; a woman was writing for women. Yet it can be enjoyed by women and men, by almost any woman and by the men who are aware of the absurdities of the male animal. Alferd Tollet is always there—willful, whimsical, set in a patriarchal determination to rule his own household. He is permitted to "tower like a grand giant" in the eyes of his adoring wife, but for the reader he must remain a comic and pathetic shadow.

For this is Lucy Tollet's story as is deftly suggested by the angle of narration. As in nearly all of her stories, Miss Wilkins is—in a narrowly technical sense of the term—the third person omniscient author: she presents at will the subjectivity of all her characters. Most stories of the '80's were told in this way. But the thought of the sister is revealed only once and that of Alferd twice whereas we are taken again and again into the mind of Lucy. Thus Miss Wilkins moved far toward one of the shrewdest devices of the modern writer—restriction of subjectivity to the chief actor. "Gentian" is the story of one woman; it is finely concentrated.

Viewed outwardly, Lucy and her sister are struggling first to save Alferd's life and later to regain for Lucy her proper status as a loved and respected wife. But the sister serves chiefly to supply bold ideas which Lucy must take or leave with full acceptance of responsibility. The real conflict (and this is characteristic of the Wilkins story) is within and involves basic aspects of the spirit and of the village code. Lucy is torn between love of her husband and the code's demand that she remain an honest and obedient wife, the code clearly functioning as an aspect of her conscience.

It is a meaningful conflict, and its emotional values are heightened by other aspects of Lucy's nature. Even at seventy, she is apparently timid and girlish; she has been so long subordinated to her domineering husband that one would consider her incapable of unconventional action. Put to the test, she found great courage within herself.

It may be difficult for the modern reader, who is unaware of the strength of the village code even today, to feel the full daring of Mrs. Tollet's decision. Judge John E. Morse and his wife, of South Newfane, Vermont, are an old couple not unlike the Tollets. This is what happened when they heard Miss

Wilkins' story. The judge merely chuckled at appropriate moments; his wife whispered at several points to mine. When she understood the initial situation, she said, "Why, this is just like the Judge and me. He's so feeble and he needs something. He can't get up in the morning. But I can't do anything with him." When Mrs. Morse heard of Lucy's decision to put a tonic in her husband's tea, she whispered, "O, I'd never dare do that! I've never disobeyed him, and I've never deceived him. I wouldn't dare." That incident occurred in one of the West River Valley towns which Miss Wilkins knew and nearly seventy years after the writing of "Gentian."

The conflict is a serious matter, but it is imagined in the mood of tragicomedy. Sly touches of humor here and there notify the reader that no very drastic conclusion is to be expected. Hence we can enjoy the contrast between Lucy's meekness and her moment of daring. Especially, we can chuckle at Alferd's terrible silences when the male ego is threatened.

"Old Lady Pingree"[13] has its flaws—overmuch reliance on providential developments and a rather mechanical building of intensity by repeating the initial situation of conflict. Nevertheless it is a moving story and a suggestive comment on the need for self-esteem, which is the strongest mark of the people of Wilkinston. The setting is lightly suggested but highly important as a phase of theme and characterization. We seem to be in one of the Valley towns which has long been losing good sons and daughters to the West and the cities. Aged Miss Pingree is living in the old mansion of her family; she and the big house, which assumes symbolic value, are all that remain of a solid and highly respected family.

She might be merely the most pathetic of the old ladies of the volume; for she is a spinster of eighty, abjectly poor, and alone save for impoverished roomers. But pathos is not the intended effect. The inner conflict is centered in the demands of two phases of Miss Pingree's pride. She must be generous;

she also must be buried like her folks, not by the town. Objectifying this conflict, Miss Wilkins created a situation in which her heroine must choose between giving or keeping her burial money.

The writer skillfully foreshadows the major conflict by a slight episode in the exposition. Miss Pingree has two eggs fresh from her hens—one for her tea, one for her breakfast. But she remembers that her invalid roomer Mrs. Stevens must also need something hearty because her daughter Jenny has had no work through the week and has been unable to buy food. The decision made, "she climbed stiffly up the stairs, which were fine old winding ones. Then she knocked at a door on the landing.

"A thin, pretty-faced young woman opened it. Nancy proffered the egg. She had a stately manner of extending her lean arm.

" 'Here's a new-laid egg I thought your mother might relish for supper, Jenny,' said she.

"The young woman's sharp, pretty face grew red. 'Oh, thank you, Miss Pingree; but I—don't think mother needs it. I am afraid you will rob yourself.'

"Nancy held her wide mouth stiff, only opening it a crack when she spoke. 'I've got plenty for myself, plenty. I shouldn't use this one before it spiled, mebbe, 'ef I kep it. I thought p'rhaps it would do good for your mother's supper; but you can do just as you like about takin' it.'

"The young woman accepted the egg with reserved thanks, then, and Nancy went stiffly back down-stairs.

" 'I guess ef Jenny Stevens hadn't took that egg, it would have been the last thing I'd ever offered her,' said she, when she was in her sitting room. 'I don't see how she ever got the idea she seems to have that I'm so awfully poor.' "[14]

The details of setting and physical appearance are slight—only fine old stairs; Nancy's "stately manner of extending her lean arm"; the reddening of the young woman's "sharp, pretty face." Yet they do much to define the personalities which are revealed more boldly in speech and action. And it is characteristic of Miss Wilkins' best method that Jenny and Miss Pingree are essentially the same person, a person who must maintain self-esteem in an impossibly difficult situation. Giving is obligatory; receiving involves an intolerable loss of face. One may suspect that the idea of the sinfulness of poverty is hovering over the scene. Obligated to her mother, Jenny yields on this occasion; yet Miss Wilkins has sufficiently suggested the bitterness of her inner struggle.

The story develops in intensifications of this situation. Jenny attempts to pay her rent; Nancy refuses to accept the money, for the plight of the girl and her mother is desperate; Jenny leaves the money behind. When the mother dies, there is no money for her burial, no relatives who can help; she will have to be buried by the town. Though it was horror of burial by the town which had spurred Miss Pingree to save a small sum of money, she insisted that Jenny accept that money. "Here, child, there ain't any need of your going on the town. . . . This ain't all; I've got some more."[15] That was the white lie without which Jenny could not have accepted.

There is no need for recounting the disappointingly sentimental solution in which both Jenny and Miss Pingree are provided for in very kindly if somewhat implausible manner. It is enough to notice that Miss Wilkins found one of her richest subjects in "Old Lady Pingree," developed it with a sympathy and understanding which brings to mind the pride-in-poverty which was part of her family heritage; that the result is tragicomedy leaning a little toward one aspect of high tragedy. Obviously, this aspect is not the fall of the protagonist, for that is averted. It is rather the conception of the character as a noble nature flawed by a pride which is to be admired even while it is distrusted.

Just how "big" is the Wilkins story? On the one hand, the local color impulse, with its commitment to the commemoration of types and ways that were passing and to actions off the main line of national development, seems pointed toward the essentially limited. The very shortness of the short story is another limitation. Remembering the slightness of "A Symphony in Lavender," thinking of the situations around which the stories are constructed, noticing the absence of issues or personalities worthy of even an inner page story in the '80's and '90's, one concludes that Miss Wilkins easily conformed with the limitations of a minor art form.

But is the matter so simple? It has been suggested that she at once accepted and rejected the limitations of the declining culture of the Yankee village. Frequently, her central characters are demanding not the small satisfactions which can be salvaged after defeat in the main action is admitted but rather victory in the main action. They demand and struggle toward love and honor and a sense of achievement. And as the intensity of this demand increases, one feels that the writer is rebelling against the limitations which form imposed.

"A Conflict Ended"[16] nicely illustrates the ambiguity of this situation. At one level, it is just another love story for women readers of the late '80's. Young George and Margie are engaged; they quarrel when George insists that Margie must make a home for his difficult mother; they are reconciled when Margie yields. George says that another arrangement for the mother has been worked out. The important matter, as he sees it, is that his fiancée has accepted the womanly role of submission. On the realistic level, the woman wins: she will not have his mother in her house. On the level of principle and conformity with the code's prescriptions for man and woman, the man retains the honors. With this insight, much older Esther Barney, the chief figure of the story, is able to effect a reconciliation with stiffnecked Marcus Woodman; they can marry after an estrangement of twenty years' duration.

Here, again, are the little people of the local color story, yet the motives are strong. For all of the characters, men and women, the need for love is intense, and each demands a love which does not compromise an equally imperative need for recognition and status in the village. It is a love and honor conflict—a subject grand enough for Virgil's Fourth Book of *The Aneid* and Shakespeare's *Antony and Cleopatra.*

Structurally, "A Conflict Ended" is awkward, for the subject is too big. The story is told within the feminine subjectivity of Esther Barney. Thinking of the estrangement of George and Margie (Esther is a milliner and Margie, her assistant), Esther tells the girl of the cause of her own break with Marcus Woodman. The result is a lengthy cutback. " 'That makes it the hardest of anything, according to my mind—when you know that everybody's laughing, and you can hardly help laughing yourself, though you feel 'most ready to die.'

" 'Ain't that Mr. Woodman crazy?'

" 'No, he ain't crazy; he's got too much will for his common-sense, that's all, and the will teeters the sense too far in the air. . . .'

" 'You turned him off because he went to sitting on the church steps?'

" 'Course I did. Do you suppose I was going to marry a man who made a laughing-stock of himself that way? . . . You see, he got up an' spoke in that church meeting when they had such a row about Mr. Morton's being settled here. . . . He said Mr. Morton wa'n't doctrinal; that was what they all said; but I don't believe half of 'em knew what doctrinal was. . . . Well, Marcus spoke in that church meeting, an' he kept getting more and more set every word he said. He always had a way of saying things over and over, as if he was making steps out of 'em, an' raising of himself up on 'em, till there was no moving him at all. . . . Finally when he was up real high, he said, as for him, if Mr. Morton was settled over that church, he'd never go inside the door himself as long as he lived.

Somebody spoke out then . . . an' says, "You'll have to set on the steps, then, Brother Woodman." '

" 'Everybody laughed at that but Marcus. He didn't see nothing to laugh at. He spoke out awful set, kinder grittin' his teeth, "I will set on the steps fifty years before I'll go inside this house if that man's settled here.' "[17]

All that, Esther said, had happened twenty years earlier, and Marcus had been sitting on the church steps every Sunday morning through all of those years. And they had never been married: Marcus could not yield, she could not marry a man who had made himself ridiculous in the town.

Esther's recital is quoted because it says so much of her and of Marcus and because it is a flawless bit of semi-humorous writing. But however fine in itself, it destroys the movement and the balancing of characters and motives in the story. Coming about midway in the development, it is a moment of conflict much richer than any which follows; the remainder of the tale is anticlimactic. And for this reader, it shifts too much of sympathy and interest from Esther Barney to Marcus Woodman.

For Marcus, religion seemed to be important; for Esther it was a minor matter to be humorously dismissed. For Marcus when forced to choose between the ridicule which will follow yielding and the ridicule involved in backing his oath, the second seemed the less objectionable alternative; for Esther, who is also proud, there seemed to be no understanding that the man was obliged to choose between difficult alternatives. For both, the choice was honor—without love—for a twenty year period. Moreover, it is a situation in which the code, the congregation, and the entire community are implicated. One aspect of the code pushed Marcus to his strongly individualistic stand while another forced conformity upon him—an inconsistency which has been causing trouble from Winthrop's day right down to our own. And the fact that the congregation fell off in numbers after the installation of Mr.

Morton—mentioned by Miss Wilkins at the opening of the story—indicates that Marcus may have had reason for his stand.

Sympathizing as one must with Miss Wilkins' feeling that somehow there must be a commonsensible solution in a coil of this sort, one concludes that her own is too facile. For once, her sympathy with the feminine as against the male point-of-view seems not misplaced but arguable. The truth is, of course, that her little people of "A Conflict Ended" are really big people in the fullness and intensity of their demands and that the subject, with its involvement of individuals within a complex social order, requires the scope of the novel. Technically, "A Conflict Ended" partially fails, but it also leads one to suspect that Miss Wilkins might one day successfully widen her range.

For the purpose of subordinating Marcus Woodman and highlighting Esther Barney, Miss Wilkins slurred a religious issue. That is not to say that religion was a minor matter in her own thinking. She had, to be sure, partially put aside the orthodoxy of Dr. Labaree, yet she would remain sincerely a seeker through all the rest of her life. And it is the most overtly religious of all of the stories of *A Humble Romance* which seems to me freshest and the most satisfying. In "A Tardy Thanksgiving"[18] a great spiritual issue is fully objectified within the bounds of the local color story.

The title is discouraging. One assumes at once that Miss Wilkins was commissioned to do a Thanksgiving story for *Harper's Bazar,* remembers the hypocrisy so common on the occasion, and expects the worst. Yet even the opening pages bring the conviction that the writer had gritted her teeth and resolved to tell an honest story.

Mrs. Muzzy told old Mrs. Field that she was going to neither her sister's nor her brother's for Thanksgiving dinner. She would stay home and do her pig-work. Mrs. Muzzy was a squarely built woman, and her thinking was clear and straight. She had lost her husband in a recent accident, and her daughter had died of consumption. She told Mrs. Field that she had nothing to be thankful for; she would simply go about her pig-work, whatever the neighbors might think. (One suspects that Miss Wilkins is adapting the Book of Job to a New England village setting, that the justice of God is brought to bar.)

When her niece Lizzy came to talk about the loss of her beau to the Hammond girl, Mrs. Muzzy advised independence and a show of spirit. The girl caught some of her intensity of feeling and said that she too would put aside Thanksgiving and help with the pig-work. (Now two women are drawn together in protest against Jehovah's will.)

Through a gray holiday morning, the women worked together in the kitchen. At ten, Lizzie answered the doorbell. She returned to say that her George Allen was taking her to his house for dinner. Mrs. Muzzy accused her of shamelessness in playing second fiddle to the Hammond girl. " 'I would for *him,*' cried Lizzie."[19] As she went off happily with her boy, Mrs. Muzzy went on with the pig-work. (One woman has capitulated to arbitrary but lovable male majesty.)

Soon Mrs. Muzzy dropped a kettle of boiling lard on the floor and her own right foot. She lifted the kettle to the stone hearth, cut off her shoe and stocking, and powdered the shockingly burned foot with flour. Then she quietly waited for someone to come. (Outraged Jehovah has spoken from his whirlwind, but the woman does not cringe.)

At length, Lizzie's mother was at the door, a large plate in each hand. Seeing Mrs. Muzzy's condition, she said that this was not the moment for Thanksgiving dinner. Mrs. Muzzy: " 'I want to eat some turkey an' plum puddin' before I'm an hour older, an' keep Thanksgivin'. I said I wouldn't, but the Lord got ahead of me, an' I'm glad he has.' "[20]

So Miss Wilkins has written her Thanksgiving story and Jane Muzzy has eaten turkey and plum pudding in a properly grateful spirit. But grateful for what?

Both she and Lizzie had contested with the arbitrary but not unlovable male: Lizzie called him George Allen, for Mrs. Muzzy his name was Jehovah. For surely one is intended to accept this interweaving of the sub- and main plots and its humorous and feminomorphic vision of the relation between Jehovah and his subjects. Ultimate capitulation is expected; for Job did, according to Scripture, bow before the greatness of God; and the husband did, according to the code, rule the wife in the Yankee home.

But within the humanistic religion of the story, it is greatly important that woman (or humanity in general) should not grovel, that the need for status and recognition should not be violated. Lizzie yielded rather too easily; Mrs. Muzzy yielded only when her strength had been tested and proved adequate. She can sit down to dinner with Him, not at his right hand, but certainly above the salt. Richly and rightly self-confident, she is now ready in spirit to play second fiddle for Him. And we must credit Miss Wilkins in having anticipated the modern psychologist's theory that self-love and self-confidence must precede humility and the love of others.

CHAPTER

Five

IN the spring of '87, some of the Randolph ladies were reading Miss Wilkins' story "A New England Nun" of Louisa Ellis who broke her engagement with Joe Daggett because she preferred "serenity and placid narrowness" to her birthright of marriage. Since the writer was nearly thirty-five, the ladies were tempted to identify her with Louisa Ellis: one of them, writing anonymously for the *Register* made the identification reasonably clear in these "sweet" and surely well-intended stanzas:

> "A plain and simple house of other days,
> With clustering honeysuckle at the door,—
> (Where all have open hearts and kindly ways,
> And kindly deeds are done forever more,)
> Shelters a village maiden, with the gift divine,
> To make of earthly common things, life's sparkling wine.
>
> "Artless she is as a Quaker maid of old,
> She tells her perfect story, straight and true,
> And all her homely tales of life unfold
> At heart, unfailing sweetness through and through.
> No faintest taint of modern freedom mars her page—
> Healthful and pure throughout, alike for youth and age.
>
> "Happy the quiet little country town,
> Where arching elms adorn the one long street,
> That keeps within its confines *as its own,*
> A writer now so famous, still so sweet.
> Heaven bless her! As she slips the westering way along,
> Add fadeless glory to her story and song."[1]

One suspects that Miss Wilkins was bitter when she read these lines. She did not wish to be identified with the spinsters of her stories; she was not "artless" nor did she find much serenity in "stepping the westerly way along." In a certain way she needed Mary John, Cousin Hattie, Uncle George, Uncle Edward, and Randolph; she was fond of them too. Yet she needed increasingly to get away:[2] that summer she went to Martha's Vineyard with Miss Wales, and later she made extended visits to Chicago, New York, and Old Point Comfort in Virginia.[3] She needed friends who understood writing, whose range of vision transcended Randolph limits. Perhaps she was even ready for a little of the "taint of modern freedom," whatever that might be.

She enjoyed going to the J. Edgar Chamberlins' in Boston. Mr. Chamberlin was a short man with brown hair and close clipped mustache, low spoken, thoughtful and gentle. Reading widely in the advanced writing of the period and knowing many authors, he wrote a column, "The Listener," for the *Boston Evening Transcript*. Sensitive and intelligent Mrs. Chamberlin had her ways for making "Dolly" Wilkins feel at home. She could talk with them easily about books—her own and other ventures into realism. Occasionally, they would laugh together over her yarns of Randolph or Brattleboro eccentricities, stories too trivial or absurd to be written for *Harper's Magazine*. They discussed their impression that every New England village hides a mysterious secret or a hidden crime, a notion which would return to Miss Wilkins in later years and lead to such stories as "The Long Arm," *Madelon*, and *The Alabaster Box*.[4]

Hamlin Garland, "intense and very serious in a plaid Windsor tie and frock coat," was another of the Chamberlins' guests; and he described their evenings in *Roadside Meetings*: "Chamberlin and his wife were ideal hosts and had the one open fire known to me, and I recall that as we all sat about the hearth fire on this night, Mary Wilkins told ghost stories in the light of it, and my admiration of her grew with acquaintance. She was a fair, small, blue-eyed girl at this time . . . quiet, almost shy in the presence of strangers, but in Chamberlin's home she was ready, in her low-voiced way, to do her share of the entertainment. . . . Miss Wilkins was a charming talker, humorous in her laconic way, but her succinct low-voiced comment was often lost in the joyous clamor of less important voices."

Garland called on Miss Wilkins in Randolph and remembered that "her home might have been used as a typical illustration for her characters. Its cakes and pies, its hot biscuits and jam were exactly right. I felt large and rude like that man in one of her tales 'The New England Nun' [Garland joins the ladies of Randolph], who came into the well-ordered sitting room of his sweet-heart with such clumsy haste that he overturned her workbasket and sat down on the cat. That she was taking my measure at the same time I was taking hers was certain. Her keen glance was almost as intimidating as that of Howells."[5]

There were other out of town visitors—Mrs. Margaret Sangster,[6] who would soon be editing *Harper's Bazar,* and the young Scot, James Barrie who had written *Auld Licht Idylls* and *A Window in Thrums.*[7]

Family affairs were centered in death and marriage. Little, exquisite Grandmother Davis, who had been living in the home of Uncle George Wilkins, died in 1887.[8] She had been loved by the whole family. But in these days the women were talking mostly—and with proper pride and reticence—of the marriage prospects of Uncle George's Carrie and Uncle Edward Lothrop's Hattie. They were both clever and pretty—Carrie a little taller than Mary Wilkins but like her in the sharpness of her features and blueness of her eyes; Hattie, dark-eyed and tiny of face and figure. Though all too many of the likely young men were going west or moving off to Boston, it was assumed that these girls must marry well. The swains who stayed in town took their own good time in choosing wives: they called and called but did not propose marriage. Cousin

Dolly heard much talk of beaux when she stopped of a morning at Uncle George's or Uncle Edward's: often it was laughing and spirited chatter, but she sensed and understood its undertóne of bitterness.

Carrie Wilkins charmed a young man of another town—Arthur B. Mann, of Central Falls, Rhode Island. The wedding was in September of '88. Mothers and young matrons were of course not unmindful that Miss Dolly and Miss Hattie were also in need of husbands. "You'll be next, dear," was the proper reassuring phrase.[9]

While the snows of March, 1890 were still lingering, Miss Wilkins gathered up her luggage and set off for Old Point Comfort, Virginia. She would live in this modish resort at the mouth of the Chesapeake and see something of nearby Williamsburg and Jamestown. Cousin Hattie Lothrop and Mary Wales accompanied her as guests;[10] it was Mary John who managed all traveling arrangements.[11]

By May 20 they had returned to Randolph to find that Uncle George Wilkins, the head of the family, was critically ill.[12] Since the death of her own mother and father, Miss Wilkins had come to depend upon Uncle George in various ways; and she loved him for his sweetness of temper and utter integrity. In certain moods she would always need the support of the village code: he was this code at its best. She stayed with Aunt Louisa, his wife, and with the neighboring Lothrops through the days of his illness. It was a trying time. George Wilkins was not a wealthy man; but as a pillar of the First Congregational Church and an officer in various Randolph organizations, he had made many friends.[13] And they must call to learn of his condition. Mindful of them, he gave them a message: "Tell them I send my love and to meet me up there." He died on the afternoon of May 30.[14] Mr. Huxford, of the *Randolph Register* called him "an upright and just man" and reported his quietly fine career with unusual fulness.[15]

It was a New Englander of the same essential integrity—and

much richer mind—who was by this time Miss Wilkins' chief editor. Henry M. Alden of *Harper's New Monthly* was a man of fifty-four—tall, rugged, angular. His hair and beard were always unruly. To understand him one had to notice his expressive, deep-set dark eyes and his speech—deliberate, low-voiced, always kindly.[16] There was a little of the genteelism of the period in Alden's thought but more of the transcendentalism of the preceding generation. "He believed in the innate goodness of human nature and in the innate depravity of dogmas. . . . Despite their dates [*God in His Word* appeared in 1890], his writings express the spirit of New England in 1840, its vague but deep religiosity, its moral idealism, its innocence of evil."[17]

If he demanded of Miss Wilkins her own best writing, he was not the man to hold her within rigid conceptions of either subject or form in fiction.[18] He recognized, it seems, the inchoate nature of the local color story and its susceptibility to an accent either romantic or realistic. Less ardent than Howells as a champion of realism, he saw Miss Wilkins' sensibility more truly than did any other critic of the period. With fine insight, he wrote in 1900, "Anyone supposing that Miss Wilkins derives her stories from studies of New England life and character is grossly mistaken: she is, first of all, an impressionist, with a dominant subjective motive, her fiction taking an outward shape from an inward prompting, having only such connection with life as there is in the texture of a dream."[19] The statement is deceptive in that it includes no word as to the cultural factors which shaped the "subjective motive," otherwise quite sound.

It appears then that Miss Wilkins was encouraged to go her own way. After she and Mr. Alden had become friendly in correspondence, he invited her to visit in his home at Metuchen, New Jersey. She grew fond not only of her editor but of the first Mrs. Alden and her daughters Annie, Harriet, and Carolyn, all of about her own age, talented to a degree, and unmarried. The Aldens were good hosts, and she visited them frequently. Her friends of the cities were in effect pulling her away from the village. But she always returned to Randolph because she believed that she could not write elsewhere.[20]

She was very comfortable at the Wales'. Hers was the north side of the house, both the first and second floors. Her sizable parlor was cluttered like most rooms of the period. Touched by the "aesthetic style," it was bright with color in the draperies and in the hanging of many-hued Chinese reeds which screened a closet on the left where books were shelved; an Italian primitive triptych, a blending of sombre color and old gold, hung above the table. A piano, a Boston rocker, some nondescript lesser pieces were there as reminders of her home in Brattleboro. Grass matting quietly covered the floor, yielding suddenly in one corner to a tiger skin. A framed photograph of Hanson Tyler in uniform rested on one of the tables.

Back of the parlor was her study, once the kitchen of the Wales house, where she read and received her friends. For writing she needed the seclusion of a room on the second floor. She could look out of its windows to the elms of Main Street and beyond to the coastal hills. In this room at a low table and amid the plainest things, Miss Wilkins wrote her stories. Occasionally her eyes would grow bright with fun; more often they were dark and impenetrable as light lines of concentration creased her forehead.[21]

Later she would define her feeling for her work: "I may say, never write unless you are sure you have something worth while for a subject. I may say, never write unless you feel that you must. But I really wonder if those rules do apply so generally that the world might not lose much good work if they were strictly observed.

"Without the slightest doubt, many a writer sits down to her task without the faintest idea concerning its ultimate outcome, and does, nevertheless, very good work. She is the writer who observes the law of sequence in writing, and there are many like her. Once started she progresses and reaches good results simply because her mind is of the sequential order—possibly I might even term it the creative order. . . .

"The feeling that one 'must write' is an even more doubtful proposition. It is, I conclude, supposed to argue such inspiration, such seething of the central fire of genius, that expression or disaster must ensue. In reality a man may write something that will live for the sake of something rather ignoble, and a woman may write something for money with which to buy a French hat. . . . It is never the kind of spur which signifies, but the speed which results from the prick."

Here she is stating, perhaps over-stating the concept of the artist as a "professional"; but her conclusion moves off in a different direction: ". . . if a woman be at liberty to write, let her write as if she were running a race in the sight of the world. . . . She must write above all things the truth as far as she can see the truth."[22]

Her writing of these years was always centered in the traits of the New England villagers—her own people; and as in the Brattleboro years, she used all of the possibilities of this subject. Juvenile poems and stories were still going to *Wide Awake,* stories to *St. Nicholas; Giles Corey,* a tragedy for the stage, was under way. Of the stories for adults on which her chief reputation rested, the majority appeared in the weekly *Harper's Bazar;* Mr. Alden would usually accept two each year for the *Monthly.* For truth and fame and French hats and a living, Miss Wilkins was playing the field.

It may be assumed that she found keen pleasure in knowing that her stories were admired. She received friendly letters of commendation from Lowell and Holmes.[23] From Miss Jewett came an enthusiastic appreciation of *A Humble Romance* to which Miss Wilkins replied, "You are very lovely to write to me so about my stories, but I never wrote a story equal to your 'The White Heron.' I don't think I ever read a short story, unless I except Tolstoy's 'Two [sic] Deaths,' that so appealed to me."[24] She met Mr. Howells and may have been strengthened by his recognition that they were hewing somewhat the same line. "He was eager to disclaim credit for her growing reputation. 'Miss Wilkins' work makes its own way,' he said."[25]

M. E. Wilkins stories were read in England and on the continent. From France came a request for permission to translate; *A Humble Romance* was issued by David Douglas of Edinburgh and by Heineman and Balestier of London and Leipzig. The English accepted the stories quickly: " 'There is something like a craze in England over Mary E. Wilkins,' noted an observer in *The Critic* in 1890."[26] Her English publisher wrote on August 27, 1891:

"Dear Madam:

I do not know why I should not tell you what I am sure you will be interested to hear; that Mr. Henry James who is a dear friend of mine, has lately been taken with an enormous enthusiasm for your stories. He has been reading them all one after another—both volumes—and has the greatest opinion of them. . . ."[27]

"Both volumes"—evidently Mr. James read *A Humble Romance* and *A New England Nun:* the first collection had been out for four years; the second was issued in April, 1891. And it is this second collection of twenty-four pieces which is usually and rightly deemed the strongest of Miss Wilkins' many volumes of short stories.

To be sure, the Wilkins story—a good one—remains the Wilkins story; it is hard to discover any real technical growth as one moves from the first to the second collection. Like so many of the local colorists, Miss Wilkins had hit pay dirt fast and would never greatly surpass her first effort. But the number of fresh and striking pieces in the second slightly exceeds that of the first.

Though *A New England Nun and Other Stories* will be presented here by analyses of five stories, this is the moment to pause for consideration of terminology. In the introduction to the study of *A Humble Romance,* Miss Wilkins was classified as a local colorist, understanding the term in the inclusive sense preferred by Professor Cowie. If she had not also been labeled at one time or another *idealist, romantic, impressionist, realist,* and, by this writer, *naturalist,* one would gladly let the matter rest. For consideration of this slippery terminology does not greatly increase the enjoyment and understanding of the stories.

A beginning may be made in this way. If all fiction is illusion and compact of the arts of illusion, all of the modes must be viewed as points on a scale leading away from unpatterned life. And every writer of fiction—even Zola when he bemuses himself with the language of science—is giving us "life" filtered through a sensibility. A "rich" naturalism, such as Joyce's, which makes room for all human behavior from the crudely animalistic to the moment of worship, marks the point on the scale least removed from "life." The order as one moves further from life might then be realism, impressionism, and romanticism touched with idealism. And it seems that the local-colorist may write within any of these modes or any blending of them.

Confronted with this terminology of the literary critic and historian, Miss Wilkins, like most artists, made little attempt to understand and less to force her writing within any category other than local color. Called upon to write a short preface, she used the language of the realist and the social historian.[28] Such was the fashion of the moment. And certainly she was devoted to some sort of truth; she was, in some sense of the term, a realist. But despite the prefaces, she also told friends that until she was labeled by reviewers, she had no consciousness of writing within this mode.[29] Mr. Alden wrote tellingly of her impressionism, "with a dominant subjective motive"; Charles Miner Thompson would later use the phrase "an idealist in masquerade."[30] All of these elements are in her writing and in addition much that is frankly romantic within the spirit of Emerson, more than a touch of the symbolism in which the image of moral or social significance is sustained throughout the story, and even some understanding of a naturalism rooted in cultural determinism.

Considering characteristic stories of *A Humble Romance* and *A New England Nun,* the critic is forced into a grotesque litter of terms something like this. Miss Wilkins wrote local color stories of an inner feeling at once romantic, naturalistic, and symbolic and of a surface texture realistic and impressionistic. And such, in so far as these terms are meaningful, was her way of voicing her truth, her own intensely personal interpretation of life and character in the New England village.

The need for such distinctions becomes obvious as we move to "The Revolt of Mother,"[31] the most popular story of *A New England Nun,* and to Miss Wilkins' later attitude toward it.

The tale is so well known that a very short summary will bring it back to mind. When Mother—Mrs. Sarah Penn—discovered that Father was planning a new barn on the site reserved for a much needed and long promised new house, she reminded him of his duty to his family and especially his daughter. She showed him what a poor thing the old house was. Father said nothing, a favorite tactic of the Wilkins' male, and proceeded with his barn. As the barn was nearing completion, he went away on business for a few days. Jesting ironically, the daughter suggested that they move into the barn; Mother took up the suggestion. When Father returned, he found his women-folks comfortably established in the new barn, which made an excellent home. After recovering from the shock, Father said that he had had no idea that Mother was so set on having a good house.

Though this intrigo is by no means Miss Wilkins' most distinguished story, it well deserves its extremely wide popularity. In her later life when her work was hard to place with editors, the writer came to hate it. She wrote in 1917, "In the first place all fiction ought to be true and 'The Revolt of Mother' is not true. . . . There never was in New England a woman like Mother. If there had been she certainly would not have moved into the palatial barn. . . . She simply would have lacked the nerve. She would also have lacked the imagination. New England women of the period coincided with their husbands in thinking that the sources of wealth should be better housed than the consumers. . . . I sacrified truth when I wrote that story, and at this day I do not know exactly what my price was. I am inclined to think coin of the realm."[32]

Reading this comment, one is reminded of the gulf between creation and criticism. It is a broad gulf now and was broader during Miss Wilkins' years of writing. Here by narrowing the broad concept *truth* to conformity with average Yankee character traits, the writer was unfair to several truths and values which "The Revolt of Mother" clearly achieves.

It is quite possible (one dares not dispute the point with Miss Wilkins) that Mother would not have moved into the barn. But in a local color story, even in a realistic local color story, we demand nothing more than a compelling illusion. Mother *seems* real, for sure knowledge of Yankee traits and much canny thinking went into her creation. At every point but one, she is the approved wife and mother of her time—thrifty, genteel, industrious, solicitous to serve her husband, mindful of his patriarchal dignity. Her revolt was limited to a single issue; the idea was her daughter's; Mother took it up considerably because it seemed to her wrong that the girl should be forced to bring her beau to such a miserable place as the old house. At every point her management of the situation—once the die is cast—conforms strictly with the customs of her type. Having won her limited engagement with Father, she returns at once to her conventional role. The single departure—if it is a departure—from the truth of character has been deftly covered; the illusion has been preserved.

Though this comment must be written to meet the author on her own ground, it is rather pointless for understanding the story itself. "The Revolt of Mother" is really satisfying because it has the quality of a comic folk tale, rooted not so much in specifically Yankee traits as in attitudes common to much of the western world. We all share Mother's feeling that a family should be decently sheltered; we are amused by the battle of the sexes—anywhere; and we cheer when any worm turns.

The comic quality is just beneath the serious surface of the story. It is partly in the contrast between the farcical action —barn becomes house—and the deadly intensity of mother and father. In a wilder way, Faulkner achieved a similar effect with Henry and his "missus" in "Spotted Horses." And Father, a type already familiar, is a fine humorous character. Saying almost nothing in the entire story, he bears himself like a Norse god who has no need for words. Through forty years his ego has gorged on the rich food of deference and respect. Then at the first real challenge the inflated ego collapses.

Writing with shrewd insight and high spirits in 1890, Miss Wilkins was at her comic best in "The Revolt of Mother"; her later condemnation of this story suggests only that she had lost her appreciation of this mood.

An overly rigid regard for "truth" as conformity with average traits or with incidents of common occurrence would lead to criticism of one aspect of the next story, "A Gala Dress."[33] Based upon Brattleboro lore already mentioned—the two old sisters who went to meeting on alternate Sundays because they had only one black silk dress, it nevertheless involves improbable incidents.

It had been decided that Miss Emily Babcock should go to the Fourth of July picnic and wear the dress. Prying Matilda Jennings, who had never had anything better than black alpaca, suspects that the Babcocks have only the single black silk and resents their air of slight superiority. They had seen better days; Matilda came of the plainest stock and had always been poor. It was she who went to the picnic with Miss Babcock. While Emily enjoyed the festivities, Matilda maneuvered miserably to keep the darns and patches of her alpaca out of sight. They returned in the evening by a path through the woods. Matilda suddenly stepped aside. Emily walked on, stepped into a nest of firecrackers, and scorched the flounce of the black silk.

That was catastrophe. Previously, each sister had had her own trimming for the dress so that it had seemed to be Emily's when she wore it and Elizabeth's when her turn came. But now trimming could not cover the evidence of the burned flounce even if it were mended, and Matilda would have the proof she had been seeking.

Conveniently a western aunt died. Elizabeth made a crape flounce for the black silk and went to meeting the following Sunday in mourning. Though Matilda questioned keenly, Elizabeth had an adequate reply ready. Then came a trunk of the aunt's things including two black silks. Miss Emily and Miss Elizabeth went to meeting together for the first time in many years. When Matilda called to pry, she said that folks were pleased to see the sisters going out again together. There had been some talk of trouble between them.

Elizabeth stood up. " 'If you want to know the reason why we haven't been out together, I'll tell you. We had just one decent dress between us, an' Emily an' me took turns in wearin' it. Emily an' me never had a word in our lives, an' it's a wicked lie for folks to say we have.' "[34] She also explained the gift of the two dresses.

Matilda said she would tell no one; maybe she had had to know because she had never had a black silk. Elizabeth offered her the nicely mended original dress. There were tears in Matilda's eyes as she took it. She went toward her own house but returned quickly. " 'Look here,' said she, with a fine light struggling out of her coarse old face, 'I want to tell you—I see them firecrackers a-sizzlin' before Emily stepped in 'em.' "[35]

And that is the droll and pungent piece that Miss Wilkins made of a bit of Toad Hill lore. Without the presumably invented Matilda, there is no conflict; without the firecrackers —no major complication; without the death of the aunt of the two black silks—no solution. The two incidents smack of improbability. But in understanding Miss Wilkins' art, this comment again seems relatively unimportant. It is better to ask, Of what stuff is the illusion created?

At the center, one must as usual insist, is the writer herself —her own experience of pride-in-poverty, her awareness of the intense conflict between the New England conscience and the need for keeping up appearances, her sensitivity to minute distinctions of breeding and position as they were felt in Brattleboro. Slight as it is, "A Gala Dress" was felt deeply and honestly.

This feeling was objectified by the techniques of impressionism rather than strict realism. In a completely "truthful treatment of material," the speech should be that of Brattleboro rather than Randolph. To be sure, both towns are within the same sub-region of New England speech, according to the formulations of Hans Kurath;[36] yet minor differences must have existed, differences that could have been rendered by a meticulous realist. Yet comparison of the dialect of "A Gala Dress," rather obviously set in Brattleboro, with that of other stories set in Randolph, reveals no significant differences. All of the characters speak a language of the rather generalized village which might be called Wilkinston. Moreover, the distinction between the social levels of the faintly aristocratic Babcocks and the lower middle class Matilda Jennings might have dictated some distinction between their ways of speaking. But no—the same dialectal expressions are given to all three. Only at the close, when Miss Wilkins desires to mark strongly Matilda's honesty *and* low breeding, does she bring out an especially resounding solecism: " 'I want to tell you—I *see them* firecrackers. . . .' "[37]

Generally—and this statement applies to nearly all of the Wilkins stories—the dialectal flavor is not strong. There are some clipped forms—*goin', tootin', an'* for *and, 'twas, s'pose;*

but they are hardly more common in a New England village than in any other region. A few words are spelled to indicate dialectal pronunciations—*perticklar, ruther, obleeged, heerd, jest*—for *just*. More of the flavor of local speech is conveyed by such locutions as "peekin' an' pryin' and tellin' things" . . . "be beholden" . . . "I'd jest as soon show it as not" . . . "You're gettin' of it all fagged out" . . . "Mind you don't cut it rippin' of it off."[38] So collected, these dialectal forms may seem an important element in a story; read in context, they are not especially striking. For Miss Wilkins chose to give us only a light suggestion of village speech, a suggestion which would fuse easily with the general texture of her prose.

Turning to her own voice in prose—the passages of narrative, exposition, and description, one senses the danger of all extreme comments. She has been praised as a skillful impressionist, damned as one who never mastered presentable prose; she has been considered completely the conscious artist, totally the primitive. And there happens to be some rightness in all of these opinions.

Until 1895 or thereabouts, Miss Wilkins seems to have been content to write the sentence which came easily to her pen. The median length in "A Gala Dress" is thirteen words—a short sentence not greatly different from that needed for juvenile stories for older children. Occasionally, and with powerful effect, she rapped out a very short period—"It was too true."[39] Occasionally, for descriptive purposes, details are gathered together in an extended sentence—"The sisters cast a dismayed and indignant look at each other; they both arose; but the door flew open, and their little square tea table, with its green-and-white china pot of weak tea, its plate of bread and little glass dish of butter, its two china cups, and thin silver teaspoons, was displayed to view."[40] That one comes off because the details are poignant, not because they are arranged within the sentence with any very striking skill.

Though one might guess that nearly all sentences are of the grammatically simple type, there is actually some variety.

Of the first fifty in "A Gala Dress," 44% are simple, 36% compound, and 20% complex. In their effect on the reader, the first two types—curt, direct, emphatic—are relatively similar; 80%, then, lend themselves to the sharp and intense presentation of flashes of action and of sensuous experience. Only twenty permit the subordination and the more quiet and studied effect of the complex type. In a single story, this is pungent prose, admirably adapted to impressionism in details of description. Passing to a second or third, one begins to be conscious of shrillness and monotony.

Occasionally, the illusion is broken by a fault in wording or grammar in the descriptive or narrative passages. "In the midst of her grief and disappointment she *devolved* a plan for keeping up the family honor."[41] "Her daughter, who was after her own kind, was *all the one* to whom she could look for sympathy and understanding."[42] "There *was* some kindly women in the village."[43] "No one but Nature tended these old graves now, and she seemed to be *lapsing them* gently back to her own lines, at her own will."[44] But for *lapsing them,* one might argue that the solecism results in a poetic quaintness. In estimating the effect of these trivial flaws, it should be remembered that they were found not in one story but here and there at wide intervals in *A New England Nun* and a volume of juveniles written at about the same time. Mr. Alden's comment should probably be accepted: "Anyone who writes stories like Miss Wilkins' can do what she likes with the English language."[45]

Her best work for illusion is of course done with words for symbol, for setting, for describing persons. Here one comes closer to the center of her talent and sensibility.

The symbol of "A Gala Dress" is naturally the dress itself. It is described first in flatly realistic terms: "The dress was black silk, and had been in its day very soft and heavy; even now there was considerable wear left in it. The waist and overskirt were trimmed with black velvet ribbon."[46] Writing with no more eloquence than the village seamstress could command, Miss Wilkins has convinced us that we are concerned with a real dress. But we live with the black silk throughout the story, come to know and feel it as the Babcocks do, sense its involvement with their need for recognition. And we become ready for a metaphoric and psychological exaltation of the black silk. "To their notions of etiquette, black silk was as sacred a necessity as *feathers at the English court*. They could not go abroad, and feel any self-respect in those flimsy muslins and rusty woollens, which were very flimsy and rusty. The dainty care with which they made [the black silk] endure so long was wonderful. They held up their skirts primly when they walked; they kept their pointed elbows clear of chairs and tables. . . ."[47] If the dress is the major symbol, it is developed with the luminous detail—especially in the last sentence—which is typical of impressionism.

The characterization of the Misses Babcock posed a pretty problem: they must fuse almost into a single figure, yet they must be nicely and swiftly discriminated. Here details are working to represent them as one: "There was about these old women and their belongings a certain gentle and deprecatory reticence. One felt it immediately upon entering their house, or indeed upon coming in sight of it. There were never any heads at the windows; the blinds were usually closed. Once in a while a passer-by might see an old woman, well shielded by shawl and scooping sun-bonnet, start up like a timid spirit in the yard, and softly disappear through a crack in the front door."[48] Then, after a finely wrought description of the interior of the house—"Never a door in the house stood open, every bureau drawer was squarely shut. A whole family of skeletons might have stood well hidden in these guarded recesses; but skeletons there were none, except, perhaps, *a little innocent bone or two of old-womanly pride and sensitiveness*."[49] If the moral sensitivity is not unlike Hawthorne's, the sly and gentle humor of the conceit might have pleased Katherine Mansfield.

But Elizabeth and Emily must also be distinguished and contrasted. At first, it seems that the distinction is very simple: Elizabeth is strong, Emily is weak. "Elizabeth uplifted her long, delicate nose with its transparent nostrils, and sniffed. Apparently, her sister's perverseness had an unacceptable odor to her. . . . She carried herself with so much decision that she seemed to keep every inch of her stature *firm and taut,* old woman that she was. . . . She wiped her spectacles, set them *firmly,* and began examining the hem of her dress."[50] And Emily: "She arose, showing a height which would have approached the majestic had it not been so *wavering.* . . . Emily *oscillated* wearily over her sister and the dress."[51] Yet Miss Wilkins was not content with a simple contrasting of the relative strength of Elizabeth with the relative weakness of Emily; the characterization must be given another twist as the tale develops. So it transpires at the climactic moment that Emily has a little vein of daring and imagination; she proposes, and firm Elizabeth backs her up.

The same art is employed in the creation of Matilda Jennings; but only one detail, the most imaginative, need be cited. Miss Wilkins is moving rapidly to build the mood for the denouement, and we must feel a brightening of Matilda's spirit even though we remain conscious of her crudeness. It is done by invoking the qualities of garden flowers. "The peppery sweetness of the nasturtiums came up in her face; it was quite early in the day, and the portulacas were still out in a splendid field of crimson and yellow. Matilda turned about, *her broad foot just cleared a yellow portulaca which had straggled into her path,* but she did not notice it."[52] This is the moment when Matilda had decided to tell the truth. After a calculation at once moral, aesthetic, and totally feminine, Miss Wilkins had decided that the broad foot might miss the yellow portulacas.

"A Village Lear"[53] is a piece which would be heavily stressed if one sought to make a case for Miss Wilkins as "realist." Though the term is used in this work to denote nothing more than one of the points on the scale from unpatterned "life" to exoticism and frank subjectivity of the romantic mood, it has frequently been employed to connote a temperamental bias toward the grim and sordid, as in de Maupassant, and "unflinching honesty" in setting down the record of mean lives. Within this concept, "A Village Lear" seems thoroughly realistic.

The story opens with a scene of skillful characterizing action. Old Barney Swann, the Lear of the story, is asking for the love of his daughter's boy. " 'Jest look a-here, Willy!, said he; 'jest look a-here! See what gran'pa's got: a whole stick of candy! He bought it down to the store on purpose for Willy, an' he can have it if he'll jest come here an' give gran'pa a kiss. . . .'

"But the child drew back, and shook his head violently, while his frown deepened. . . .

"The old man stepped back and began again. It was as if he were enticing a bird. 'Now, Willy,' said he, 'jest look a-here! Don't Willy like candy?'

"The child did not nod, but his blue, solemn eyes were riveted on the candy.

" 'Well,' the grandfather went on, 'here's a whole stick of candy come from the store, real nice pep-mint candy, an' Willy shall have it if he'll jest come here an' give gran'pa a kiss.'

"The child reached out a desperate hand. 'Gimme!' he cried, imperatively.

" 'Yes, Willy shall have it as soon as he gives gran'pa a kiss.' The old man waved the stick of candy; his sunken mouth was curved in a sly smile.

"The child began to take almost imperceptible steps forward, his eyes still fixed on the candy. His grandfather stood motionless, while his smile deepened. Once he rolled his eyes delightedly around at Sarah. The child advanced with frequent halts.

"Suddenly the old man made a spring forward. 'Now I've

got ye! he cried. He threw his arms about the boy and hugged him tight.

"The child struggled. 'Lemme go!—lemme go!' he half sobbed.

" 'Yes, Willy shall go jest as soon as he gives gran'pa the kiss,' said the old man. . . .

"The child put up his pretty rosy face and pursed his lips sulkily. The grandfather bent down and gave him an ecstatic kiss. . . . The child snatched the candy and fled across the yard.

"The old man laughed, and his laugh was a shrill, rapturous cackle, like the high notes of an old parrot. He turned to the young woman. 'I knowed I could toll him in,' he said; 'I knowed I could. The little feller likes candy, I tell ye.' "[54]

The scene is surely skillful, and it has precisely that quality of tough-minded objectivity in the presence of the painful which marks much highly praised realistic or naturalistic fiction. It should also be marked as the first and nearly the last example of this especial quality which will be found in Miss Wilkins' writing. Its uniqueness is not in the motive—the old man's hunger for the affection of something young and fresh; Miss Wilkins never hesitated to build stories around the basic needs of persons of any age or type or social class. That awareness is part of her strength. Barney Swann is unique among her characters not in his motive but in his action. He is abject. He is buying affection and, if proud like so many others, he is proud only of a pitifully contemptible skill. " 'I knowed I could toll him in.' "[55] No matter how far down they are driven, her other spinsters and widows and bachelors and widowers always retain certain traits of human dignity as they grasp for what they must have.

Barney Swann is in a situation roughly like King Lear's. For sixty years he has had status of some sort by sticking to his cobbler's bench and acquiring a bit of money and property. Recently he has been induced to turn everything over to his daughters Ellen and Malvina. He was to stay with the elder,

Malvina, and to visit Ellen occasionally. Though neither was entirely vicious, the arrangement worked badly. After the first revealing incident, we are given a second of the same nature: Barney sold his watch-chain to buy a gift for Annie, Malvina's daughter, who is soon to be a bride. When the wedding came, Barney had a cold and was excluded from the ceremony. Frantically he tried to give his gift as bride and groom left the house to ride away. That expedient failed. Barney's spirit was broken; contracting a cough, he soon died. To a neighbor, Sarah Arnold, Miss Wilkins gave the role of the kindly Cordelia, and it was she who cared for the old man at the end.

One suspects that there may have been an old man like Barney Swann in Randolph. The flash of description with its suggestion of limited intelligence is utterly convincing: "Barney Swann was a small, frail old man; he stooped weakly, and did not look much larger than a child, sitting there on his bench. His face too, was like a child's; his sunken mouth had an innocent infantile expression."[56] Equally plausible is the daughter Malvina; she is not wicked; she simply lacks all understanding of her father. All that is solid and "realistic" characterization.

But it must be said again that these are not the realities of New England character which are characteristic of Miss Wilkins' fiction. For better or worse, she was rarely interested in the meanly pathetic. And because the subject is meanly pathetic and nothing else, the evocation of Shakespearian tragedy in the title seems unfortunate. If the paralleling of the action of *King Lear* is too obvious for comment, the shrieking differences in inner feeling also need no remark. The title, "A Village Lear," could be defended by interpreting it as an ironic comment on the gulf between village mediocrity and Elizabethan grandeur of spirit. That would be to say that Miss Wilkins anticipated Mr. Eliot's use of this device by a good thirty years. It is an attractive speculation, but there is nothing in the tone of the story to lend it plausibility.

Read lightly, "A Solitary"[57] might seem to be another piece in the same manner; indeed one of its two characters is an old man at least superficially in a plight like Barney Swann's. Yet if due weight be given to decision of the denouement, this story must be regarded as quite outside the bounds of realism, as an expression fully personal and even more cogent than "A Tardy Thanksgiving." Its subject is the loneliness of two men.

Though it was snowing hard, Nicholas Gunn sat on his doorstep and let the flakes fall upon him. He seemed calmly passive. He did not look up as an old man struggled up the road from the southward, coughing in a deep and rattling way. When the old one asked for shelter, Nicholas said no; but he yielded when the coughing grew worse. The old man stayed for twenty minutes, then went on. No words came from Nicholas Gunn.

Later in the afternoon, Nicholas had his dinner of cold hasty pudding—an act of asceticism, for he would have preferred to heat his porridge. Then he tramped the road to the north for a long way and at length returned to the store at the village center. All heads turned toward him as he entered. "There was hardly a man there as tall as he. He went across the room with a kind of muscular shamble; his head, with its wild light beard, had a lofty lift to it."[58] He bought Indian meal and matches and went out. The men of the store laughed at this Nicholas Gunn who was living alone on meal and water even while he was worth a tidy fortune.

Next morning the old man passed Nicholas' place again and was invited to come in to rest. Thus it happened every morning; but beyond a bare good morning, nothing was said. Then a night of heavy snow in January, and Nicholas again heard the old man's voice. He put the fellow in his cot, rubbed his feet, covered him well; he made a fire and cooked porridge. Warmed and strengthened, the old man could tell his story.

He had been staying with his half-sister who kept boarders—doing chores for her, going every morning to the store for meat. Now the boarders were so annoyed by his cough that his half-sister had decided that he must go to the poor house.

To escape that indignity, he was on his way to the town from which his family had originally come. He had a little money and was determined to pay for his lodging.

When light came, he was eager to be off. Nicholas said, " 'You're goin' to stay just where you are. I've fought against your coming just as long as I could, and now you've come, an' I've turned the corner, you're goin' to stay. When I've been walkin' in the teeth of my own will on one road, an' havin' all I could do to breast it, I ain't a goin' to do it on another. I've give up, an' I'm goin' to stay give up.' "[59] He went to the store for victuals, talked with the half-sister about his plan for the old man, returned and made breakfast for him.

He said, " 'I don't know but you've heard stories about me that I wa'n't quite right. I've had lots of trouble, an' it come mainly through folks I set by; an' I figured out a way to get the better of it. If I didn't care anything for anybody, I shouldn't have no trouble from 'em; an' if I didn't care for myself, I shouldn't have any from myself. Well, I was all wrong. I've got to go through with the whole of it like other folks, an' I guess I've got grit enough. I've made up my mind that men's tracks cover the whole world, an' there ain't standin' room outside them. I've got to go with the rest. Now we'll have breakfast.' "[60] And it was understood that the old man would live with Nicholas Gunn.

We now speak of the alienation of man from the universe, from other men, and from himself, and usually in existential terms. But this sense of the "human predicament" is not a new thing. Mary Wilkins knew it though not as deeply as Kafka. Arthur Machen was perhaps the first to feel it as a poignant aspect of her sensibility: "You may feel pretty certain that real literature has always been produced by . . . a certain loneliness of soul. . . . And this is my plea for Miss Wilkins. . . . She has painted a society in which each man stands apart, responsible only for himself and to himself, conscious only of his soul and his God."[61] The comment fits many of her characters but none more perfectly than Nicholas

Gunn. His withdrawal with its overtones of masochistic ascet-icism is almost complete, and it involves a rebellion against religious and social orthodoxy more drastic than that of Mrs. Muzzy in "A Tardy Thanksgiving." This is alienation and loneliness with a vengeance.

Though Miss Wilkins could deeply sympathize with the intense individualism and the stubborn integrity which were one aspect of this withdrawal, she also saw it as a destruction of personality. Gunn must be brought back—plausibly and with no sentimentality—not to the Congregational Church but to an acceptance of his involvement with other men. As pure theology, her solution is less interesting than that of "A Tardy Thanksgiving," for there we learned something of the nature of God and of his way with man. "A Solitary" does not advance this inquiry, but it strikes hard at the vicious concept of "freedom from" as distinguished from "freedom for." Here, touched lightly, is the humanistic religion toward which Miss Wilkins was groping.

Louisa Ellis of "A New England Nun"[62] gained negative freedom—freedom from—and thought she had something of value. Such is the ironical thrust of this story of a capacity for love perhaps originally weak and then long unused. It has been considered Miss Wilkins' definitive study of the New England spinster.

Miss Louisa is revealed first at her exquisitely prepared tea—alone and contented. When Joe Dagget called, there was a bit of decorous chat, but Louisa could not overcome her feeling that a man is a clumsy creature unsuitable for a parlor in which each object must remain in its appointed place. In a month, she and Joe would be married. They had become engaged in their early twenties; then Joe had emigrated to make his fortune, an enterprise which had consumed fifteen years. During that time, Louisa's mother and father had died, and she had become accustomed to living alone in the inherited house.

Since she had given her word, there could be no question of

turning aside from marriage, yet she thought sombrely of all the changes in her ways which married life would bring.

One night Louisa strolled down the road a little way. Sitting on a low stone wall, she overheard the talk of a couple near her—Joe Dagget and Lily Dyer. She was a blooming and womanly person who helped Joe's mother. Louisa gathered that they were in love yet firmly agreed that Joe was in honor bound to herself. When he called next evening, she artfully sounded his inclinations and explained her own. They reached an understanding and parted tenderly. The threat of marriage was removed; Louisa got what she wanted—gentle and unexacting life in her own house.

Firm, direct, objective to a degree, yet hauntingly suggestive, this story was chosen as title piece for the 1891 volume and has remained one of Miss Wilkins' most respected shorter things. The slight but fully plausible plot moves naturally to its climax—Miss Ellis' striking yet easy decision to free her man for marriage with Miss Dyer. The denouement is equally quiet. It is precisely the absence of desire and striving which is the story's grimly ironic point.

The quality of conviction in the closing moments depends of course upon the earlier presentation of Louisa's neatly sterile design for living—a blend of atmosphere, poignant detail, and low-keyed incident in which Miss Wilkins excels. There is even a touch of sly humor in the rendering of Joe's call, and it becomes broader as the writer comments upon the aftermath.

"When Joe Dagget was outside he drew in the sweet evening air with a sigh, and felt much as an innocent and perfectly well-intentioned bear might after his exit from a china shop.

"Louisa, on her part, felt much as the kind-hearted, long-suffering owner might have done after the exit of the bear.

"She tied on the pink, then the green apron, picked up all the scattered treasures and replaced them in her work-basket, and straightened the rug. Then she set the lamp on the floor, and began sharply examining the carpet. She even rubbed her fingers over it, and looked at them.

" 'He's tracked in a good deal of dust,' she murmured. 'I thought he must have.'

"Louisa got a dust-pan and brush, and swept Joe Dagget's track carefully."[63]

Rightly, we are nearly always within the subjectivity of the spinster and can share her discovery that a man—even gentle Joe Dagget—is rather masculine. Tone is deftly maintained. Despite much evidence that Miss Wilkins understands her Louisa Ellis, the touches of humor and satire seem to say that the writer is outside of the story. If tone breaks at any point, it is only at the close where the condemnation of the spinster's choice is expressed too stridently. "If Louisa Ellis had sold her birthright, she did not know it, the taste of the pottage was so delicious and had been her sole satisfaction for so long. Serenity and placid narrowness had become to her as the birthright itself."[64]

Considered technically, "A New England Nun" is a superb story, and no doubt it seemed to have a certain realistic toughness in its day. Less brilliant and sinister and tragic than Mr. James' Olive Chancellor of *The Bostonians,* Louisa Ellis may well have seemed the typical New England old maid. By linking the emigration of the young men, a village fact, with the emotional atrophy of the young women who stayed behind, Miss Wilkins seemed to say that—but what exactly did she say?

She did not here or elsewhere write as a feminist; she did not speak of the village code as Puritanism in its last gasp. She did satirize and flatly condemn her spinster heroine, but so many of the questions whose answers would have yielded real understanding are never raised. What of the whole relationship—general and sexual—between Louisa's mother and father? Of what sort of "love," if any, was she capable when she and Joe were engaged in their twenties? Miss Wilkins tells us something of that love but not enough. "Fifteen years ago she had been in love with him—at least she had considered herself to be. Just at that time, gently acquiescing with the gentle drift of girlhood, she had seen marriage ahead as a reasonable feature and probable desirability of life. Her mother was remarkable for her cool sense and sweet, even temperament. She talked wisely to her daughter when Joe Dagget presented himself, and Louisa accepted him with no hesitation. He was the first lover she had ever had."[65] But what "wisdom" did the mother impart, and why was Joe the first and only beau?

It is easy to dismiss these questions by noting that Miss Wilkins was contriving a short story and not a novel. Then one remembers that only one of them—the general relationship between wife and husband, especially the struggle for prestige and dominance—is raised in the novels. It seems that "A New England Nun" is a triumph not only of art but of reticence.

To this point, interpretation has remained largely within the story. Now it is necessary to consider its autobiographical values.

It is one thing to join Mr. Alden in his recognition of a strongly subjective element in Miss Wilkins' writings; it is quite another to assume that each spinster in one of her stories is a simple projection of herself. Each story must be considered separately and with suitable caution. The point is made here because Hamlin Garland and Willis Boyd Allen, who knew the writer, have at least inferentially suggested the identification of Miss Wilkins and her Louisa Ellis.[66] Knowing that her parents had died while she was relatively young and perhaps guessing at the Tyler episode, they found the speculation difficult to resist. In my opinion, they were mostly mistaken.

They ignored telling considerations. Miss Wilkins roundly condemned the spinster of the story. She had a career, Mary John, other men and women friends, and a fairly rich social life; Louisa Ellis seems to have had only her house and the time-killing activities within it. As for the return of the emigrant lover, the volume *A New England Nun* contains two other pieces in which he comes back and finds his sweetheart eager for marriage. These stories are "The Scent of Roses" and "A Discovered Pearl." Assuming, as one fairly may, that all three had their origin in day dreams of the return of Lieutenant Tyler (Miss Wilkins would be remembering him vividly even in the last years of her life), all one can say is that twice she projected something of herself into the womanly role and that once, in "A New England Nun," she exorcised an image of atrophy which may have been deeply disturbing. No one of the stories seems to take us very far into her complex inner life.

CHAPTER Six

Towns, like people, age, and their economic arteries harden. Newer regions, seeking a place in industry, profit from their freedom to manufacture unfettered by old traditions. The "shoe town" Randolph was aging in the '80's and '90's. Though the factories, now owned by the Irish, were still making a profit, they found it increasingly difficult to meet the challenge of newer plants in Brockton. Between 1880 and 1900, Randolph population declined from 4027 to 3933; Brockton rose from 13,608 to 40,063. In the '50's, Randolph had been the larger town.[1]

Yet some attempt was made to maintain the older and more vital spirit. It was not, unfortunately, a bold gesture toward dealing with fundamental issues—the relative decline of the shoe industry and the need for new plants and a balanced economy. It was an effort by the Randolph Business and Improvement Society to better public services and provide an "entertainment course."

A few items from *The Randolph Register* will reveal the uncertainty of these impulses. The editor insisted in 1887, without too much conviction, that "the town is not dead, not sleeping, but alive."[2] The entertainment course brought a variety of fourth-rate programs to Stetson Hall. John R. Clarke typifies the lecturers: "He touched upon everything which was elevated, pure, laughable, and homely. . . . His appeal for Christian charity, love in the home and to all, temperance, morality, good reading, carried conviction to everyone present."[3] The newspaper was so feeble that it steadily ran advertisements in its column of "personals." "A well-known Randolph woman remarked in C. D. Hills and Co's Store recently, 'I have always used two bars of rosin soap for a week's wash, but one bar of Russell's soap does the same work and the clothes look whiter than ever before.' "[4] Though Miss Wilkins' successes were noted from time to time, there was no effort to review her books or to raise the question, Do they have any conceivable meaning for Randolph? At least, the commemorative impulse was stirring: in 1891, the selectmen voted to prepare a celebration two years hence of the one hundredth anniversary of Randolph's incorporation. The committee was headed by J. White Belcher.[5]

Miss Wilkins touched only the edges of Randolph's industrial and cultural life; hers was of course the woman's world. If that world showed some of the effects of declining vitality in men's enterprises and was itself decadent to a degree, it was at least as much alive as corporate Randolph. Miss Wilkins could find little there which would direct her thought toward the life which still survived in New England.

In the spring of '92, she visited her cherished friend, Mrs. Severance, then living in Brattleboro, for her invalid husband had resigned his Shelburne Falls medical practice. Evie was still lovely, and she was proud of her brilliant son. But to Miss Wilkins it seemed outrageous that her social life was so limited by her husband's illness.

Driving the road to Putney, they met Brattleboro's celebrities, the Kiplings. They had known the wife, Caroline S. Balestier of a distinguished local family; and there was much to hear about her and Ruddy's life in the Bliss Farm cottage.[6] The Kiplings were also something to see as they sat in their basket phaeton—Caroline, slim, elegant, very pretty; Mr. Kipling, swarthy, black mustached, with brilliant dark eyes magnified by thick glasses; Matthew Howard, their coachman, in top boots, doe-skin breeches, blue coat, and top hat.[7] Mr. Kipling was bringing the trappings of the English manor to Vermont.

Chat was brisk and friendly. Miss Wilkins knew Kipling's stories and their enormous popularity; she was delighted to learn that he was keenly interested in Vermonters. She knew that his compliments for her work were sincere;[8] for he had said earlier that her stories would survive his own, that they touched him much too deeply.[9] Caroline Kipling suggested lunch at the Brooks House; Miss Wilkins declined. Her time in Brattleboro was limited, and she was promised to the family of the young man to whom her sister Nan had been engaged. She told Mrs. Severance later that they wanted her for herself, not as a writer.

Her stay in Brattleboro was limited because she was working on a novel for serial publication in *Harper's Monthly*.[10] The decision to attempt the larger form had been made in fear and trembling. A few years past, she had doubted her ability to write a short story, a "simple melody" as she called it. The art of the novel she considered a "very different affair" and much more exacting.[11] Here she agreed with her contemporary: Howells wrote *Suburban Sketches* and then gradually moved on to the solid novels of his mature period; Cable made his name with the stories of *Old Creole Days* and then attempted *The Grandissimes*. Mr. Alden of Harper's was not very encouraging.[12] But one suspects that the goad of ambition was in the flesh and knows that royalties for serial rights were a lure that caught most of the writers of the time.

Work on the novel was her intense activity of 1892, but lesser projects also claimed her time. She collected her recent juvenile stories in volumes named *The Pot of Gold* and *Young Lucretia*. In Boston and elsewhere, she negotiated for the production of her six act tragedy, *Giles Corey, Yeoman*. It was based upon an episode in the Salem witchcraft trials of 1692—the accusation, trial, and "pressing" of Giles Corey. In the spring of the next year, it would be presented in a garbled version by the Theatre of Arts and Letters in Boston and New York.[13]

It was about this time that Lieutenant Hanson Tyler married in California.[14] Miss Wilkins presumably learned of the event from her friend Mrs. Severance of Brattleboro.

At the Aldens' in Metuchen she met a young man of about the same sort. His head was finely moulded, his eyes clear and friendly; he moved with casual grace. Though he talked well of men and women and books, something of a boyish quality lingered in his manner. Kate Upson Clarke, who had arranged the introduction, said that Dr. Charles Manning Freeman refused to grow up: he drank too much, drove fast horses, courted all the girls, skillfully eluded marriage. Though a graduate of Columbia's College of Physicians and Surgeons, he did not practice medicine and was bored by the coal and wood business which he had managed since his father's death. He was said to be devoted to his mother and four sisters.

Miss Wilkins was interested in the legend and she liked the man. Herself a rebel, however timid and conventional in manner, she admired the rebellious streak in Charles Freeman. Several times each year she would visit the Aldens, and the Doctor was always one of the party. Inevitably, the Alden circle speculated about an engagement.[15]

She also met a Lion. The setting was the annual affair of Mrs. George Field's Literary Club in Brooklyn; the Lion was the beautiful F. Marion Crawford, then nearly at the peak of his great popularity. Miss Wilkins tells the story of the introduction.

"When I was introduced the hostess said, 'Mr. Crawford, I wish to introduce Miss Wilkins.'

"Mr. Crawford gave me a coldly polite bow, and I would have passed on perfectly satisfied, but not so my hostess. She felt that Mr. Crawford ought to have recognized in me a fellow-author, and she quickly followed the first introduction with an impressive:

" 'Mr. Crawford, this is Miss Mary E. Wilkins.'

"Again the delightful novelist gave me a polite bow of recognition. My friend was sorely distressed. Not even now did the lion of the evening deign to recognize this poor little body, but my friend would not be repulsed, so she returned afresh to the assault, and in a still more impressive manner, she said:

" 'But Mr. Crawford, this is Mary E. Wilkins, the author of those charming stories of New England life.'

"Mr. Crawford, I felt sure, had never heard of me. I did not wonder at it. Living so far away [in Rome], and naturally enough absorbed in his own work, he probably had never seen a line I had written, but he was equal to the occasion. . . . He bowed and smiled most graciously, and shaking me by the hand, he expressed great pleasure in meeting me. . . . His bewildered manner as he tried to make me believe he knew all about me, was most delicious comedy."[16]

In a few days, she was back in Randolph, working hard yet finding time for a letter to Mrs. Severance:

"I got home from Brooklyn Christmas night, and have been making a frantic attempt to finish my novel [the second novel, *Pembroke*] ever since. I am dodging everything that I can. I rather want to visit Mrs. Wynn in Chicago, in fact, I decidedly want to, and take in the Fair, if I can only get the novel finished. . . .

"I had a note from Mrs. Devens the other day, asking me to lunch and dine with her, but I could not possibly do so. If I had an astral body . . . , I should manage very well. But one cannot kill a boy with heart disease [Ephraim Thayer in *Pembroke*], and celebrate funerals and weddings, and at the same time lunch and dine with one's friends.

"I expect to go to the Vermont Dunns' Tuesday and hope I may see some old friends there. I wish you were to come. I go out to Wellesley this week for a day or two. I go there nearly every week and show my last chapters to my critical friends there. . . .

"The spell of Ruddy's [Kipling's] eyes have faded away, but my heart still clings to the coupé driver."[17]

Such was her bustling life. The first novel, *Jane Field,* was issued by Harpers in the same month, January of 1893.

The germ of *Jane Field* might have been some slight contact with one of the patients of the Vermont Insane Asylum who came to the door of the Wilkins house at 3 Chase Street in the late '60's. For at the close of the novel, Mrs. Field is obsessed in a way which will mark her as "queer" through all the rest of her life.

The setting permits the novelist to use more of her observation than had entered any earlier work. It is first Green River, almost any of the villages in the West River Valley near Brattleboro, then Elliott which strongly suggests Randolph. For purposes of humorous contrast, Miss Wilkins can play off the countrified awkwardness of her Green River ladies against the relative sophistication of Elliott manners. Customs and especially travel by railroad suggest a time in the '70's; the feeling is always retrospective. These are the quaint and twisted doings of ancient aunts and grandmothers. And here are poverty, pride, and the New England conscience doing their awesome work.

The elderly widow, Jane Field of Green River, was a good woman; like Sally in "A Humble Romance," "she could see the distinction between right and wrong with awful plainness."[18] Though apparently empty of feeling, she was in fact greatly devoted to her daughter Lois. When neighbors told her that the girl was showing symptoms of consumption, Jane Field cut them off with a show of cold impenetrability. Lois was perfectly well, she said, quite able to continue teaching. But when Lois collapsed, the neighbors learned what the reader has suspected. Mrs. Field has been worrying desperately and hopelessly, for she has no money for sending Lois away. It was pride that prompted her show of hardness.

Then came to her a letter from an Elliott attorney—addressed to her dead sister Esther Maxwell, saying that Esther is heir to the sizable property of her father-in-law. Jane knew that she closely resembled the sister. She remembered too that years ago she had entrusted her own little fortune of fifteen hundred dollars to Esther's husband, that he had lost the money in a speculation. Somehow she must get money so that Lois may have the rest and the change of scene which she needs.

Jane set off for Elliott, ready if necessary to impersonate her dead sister and claim the inheritance. She has a dimly formulated notion that she can obtain the portion of the estate which is more or less rightly hers and then turn over the remainder to the true heir, the widow of another son of old Thomas Maxwell.

Arriving in Elliott, Mrs. Field was welcomed as Mrs. Maxwell by the executor. She did not correct him. She moved into the huge empty Maxwell mansion, lived there for months almost at the point of starvation as she cannot bring herself to use the funds turned over to her from time to time. Lois came after a time; and Mrs. Field was forced to endure her condemnation because she could not tell the girl the reason for her strange behavior. After several months of this tortured existence, a visit by some old Green River neighbors, knowing her as Jane Field, hastened her decision to clear up the fraud. She confessed first to her Green River friends. Then she walked through the streets, announcing to the bewildered villagers, "I ain't Esther Maxwell."

"The stern will of the New England woman had warped her whole nature into a groove. Gradually she seemed more like herself, but never did she meet a stranger unless she said for greeting, 'I ain't Esther Maxwell.' . . . And she said it to her own daughter on her wedding-day, when she came in her white dress from the minister's with Francis. The new joy in Lois' face affected her like the face of a stranger, and she said, 'I ain't Esther Maxwell.' "[19]

Despite the amateurishness of the complications, the struggle at the center of *Jane Field* is meaningful and potentially dramatic. The deepest demands of a New England woman are pitted against each other: Mrs. Field must cherish her daughter; she must also maintain her selfhood by living within the village code, and especially the commandment, "Thou shalt not steal." Nor was Jane Field the only village mother who was caught within this dilemma; it must have occurred frequently in these unusually hard times. Equally significant is the denouement—the break, the confession, the mind which will never fully recover from a conflict too long sustained.

The most telling moments are those which take us into Mrs. Field's consciousness to suggest the terror of her lonely struggle. "Many a time through the night, voices which her straining fancy threw out . . . seemed actually to reverberate through the house. . . . Often the phantom voices would swell to a very pandemonium surging upon her ears; but she sat there rigid and resolute in the midst of it, her pale old face sharpening out into the darkness."[20] The New England conscience is taking its toll.

The effect of such probings of the spirit is heightened by the moral and religious norms implied steadily within the novel. Whatever Miss Wilkins' personal convictions may have been, she writes here in the spirit of a latter-day Calvinism. The majesty of God and the heroic temper of the "saints" are gone; but there is no questioning of His justice or of the finality of His commandments. It is precisely in her hours of guilty torment that Mrs. Field must cling most closely to the tenets of her faith. Here is the "touch of tragedy, still homespun but terrible," which was felt by *The Nation's* critic.[21]

One can notice these elements of power in *Jane Field* without being convinced that M. E. Wilkins could write a novel in 1892. The illusion is overwhelming when we are within the mind of her heroine; but the representation of the struggle in action and dramatic scene is commonplace, implausible, uneven in tone. Since the conception of the character precluded cleverness and quick thinking as attributes, Mrs. Field must move through endless scenes, in which Elliott people are always about to discover the deception, using no artifices beyond silence or mumbled words. Frequently the effect of her clumsiness is comic—moments of calculated humor for which the reader is grateful. More often one is simply impatient with the minor characters who are too easily deceived; they seem to be stooges cut carelessly out of the whole cloth.

Mrs. Field's neighbors—Miss Pratt, Mrs. Green, and Mrs. Babcock—serve well as supporting cast in the early, Vermont chapters; but when their interminable chatter about going to Elliott and the story of their journey and arrival are given three chapters at a time when Jane Field's Elliott doings are wearing thin, it becomes all too obvious that Miss Wilkins is struggling with little success to stretch a good short story into a novel.

One puts down this work with questions rarely raised by the short stories. Is *Jane Field* to be taken as a comic novel of village manners, touched with a little grimness? Is it "homespun tragedy"? Or was Miss Wilkins seeking again the note of tragicomedy maintained so firmly in some of the stories? The last is the most plausible answer. She seems to have attempted a maneuver which she had virtually mastered in the short form without fully understanding its difficulties in the novel.

The first months of '93 brought heavy snows, hard work on *Pembroke,* and a disturbing letter from Mrs. Severance. This is Miss Wilkins' reply:

"My dear Evie,

> 'If thou wert vanished far away,
> To regions hot and fiery,
> I'd be contented there to stay,
> If thou wert there, Elviry.'

"I am still in as right a mind as usual, the above comes simply from a frantic desire to amuse you, after your letter. . . My dear, I *wish* you could go to Chicago, I wish you could do something, and see some people who entertain you. You see you are fond of people and I never have been. I am bored by circumstances. I have a constant longing to go to a land where there are no circumstances. I have a fellow feeling, even for bores, as being also exposed to circumstances. If we could only swap susceptibilities, we could give each other a rest.

"Here is another verse:

'Have you a bananner?
No, I have no bananner.
But my sister Hannah,
She has a bananner—dam her.'

"I learned that at a very select luncheon in Boston.

"Do you know they are threatening to run electric cars through Boston Common? Well, I have seen Plymouth Rock, with a clam-bake in full swing on either side of it. . . .

"Don't you think we are having a tremendous amount of weather this winter? I am in the last agony of my new novel. Until I see how it develops I can't tell what it will be. I think now I may go down to Old Point Comfort, after that is finished, and then if my strength and purse are not exhausted, I *may* go to Chicago, but that is very doubtful.

"Evie, you really *have* a genius of a certain rather rare, and unfortunate kind, because it requires a very particular atmosphere for its development. . . . You are quite justified, in a way, in being bored by people because you require a *certain kind* of people for the needs of your own nature. They are your proper atmosphere. You ought to have flourished in a French salon, a century or so ago, and you might have been another Madam—who? De Stael, or—I can't think of the name of another who is in my mind.

"You might think this flattery, but it is simply what I have always thought. You have certainly uncommon powers which have never had full swing, their checking is bad for you, but they may have some day. I somehow believe in that sort of thing, that powers do get full swing, finally, in spite of everything. You've got your own individual *shine,* that you needn't lose, dear.

"I am going to Boston on the next train, and I must stop. I

don't know whether I cheered you up a bit, but I mean what I say, and I want to.

"With kind remembrances to the Doctor and love to Kenn. . . ."[22]

"Bored with circumstances," needing people with "an individual shine" and in Randolph, Dolly Wilkins turned to the Tolmans. She was sufficiently abetted by Miss Wales.

Isaac and Irving Tolman were cousins—most eligible bachelors just turned thirty. Isaac, the more dashing of the two, was a broker in Boston and would soon have his own firm—Rogers and Tolman. Irving was a buyer for the Boston Dry Goods Company, associated with Jordan Marsh, and made annual trips to Paris. They were really Miss Wilkins' neighbors: Irving's family lived in the Warren Wilkins house next to the Lothrops on South Main; Isaac's family, the Bert Tolmans, had a square and finely proportioned place just a few steps further south at Maple and South Main.

It began with an invitation to a Saturday evening of whist in Miss Wilkins' study, the cosy room behind the ornate parlor. Since it had once been the kitchen of the old house, the fireplace with its bake oven occupied all the right wall. That night the logs were burning, and a copper kettle hung from the crane. On the white mantel were books, a green bottle, a French peasant candlestick, a fine oil with the clear color and warm light of a Vermeer. Bright draperies all but covered the shuttered windows. On the table at the window were tea things and two chafing dishes. A desk, a divan, comfortable chairs—it was all inviting, and Mary John's humor and heartiness reassured the somewhat skeptical Tolmans.

Even light chat over whist was enough to mark off the types. Irving with his neat small face and kindly dark eyes was more manageable: he fell to Mary John. At a quick glance Isaac seemed the same sort, but Miss Wilkins noticed that he was playing hard to win even while he was pretending to despise a game without stakes. Names—the best of Randolph names and some better names of Boston—frequently entered his talk. Miss Wilkins could also play the game of names; in her own study, supported by Mary John, she could be pretty and impressive.

She liked chafing dish cookery and knew that her oysters and chicken in thick creamy sauce would be appreciated. They were. The talk turned to investments, and she learned that Isaac was very happy to advise and that his advice showed a keen knowledge of the market.

The Saturday evenings became part of the Randolph ritual. Dolly Wilkins usually devised the invitations, one of which reads:

"Crane!
Pot hooks!!
Kettle!!!
Stero!!!!
Come!!!!!"

Isaac and Irving were, one assumes, properly thrilled; they came, and they came again and again until Randolph tongues were wagging prodigiously. Was Mary John in love with Irving? Was Dolly Wilkins setting her cap for Isaac even while everyone knew he was virtually engaged to that nice Mabel Leach? And wasn't she much too old for him?[23]

On July 19, 1893, Randolph celebrated the centennial of its incorporation. The selectmen's committee had labored: from the first gun at dawn to the last moments of dancing, Randolph people and hundreds who came in from neighboring Brockton and the other towns were entertained, amused, possibly inspired. The centennial was a resounding success;[24] but for a thoughtful person like Mary Wilkins, it was presumably John V. Beal's address which would linger in mind.

This eminent lawyer, a descendant of one of the founding families, was in appearance completely representative of the old stock. A slim person of medium height, he had a high forehead, clear gray eyes, a mustache and neat Van Dyke beard.[25]

In his peroration, he extolled the private citizen—"humble, obedient, temperate, educated"—and these were, one suspects, his own best qualities.[26]

Since the occasion called for a linking of noble past, solid present, and glorious future, Mr. Beal did what he could in his quiet and sincere way. He alluded to the founding fathers and mentioned their descendants still in Randolph. "The following are the surnames of some of them: Adams, Alden, Baker, Beals, Belcher, Burrell, Chessman, Clark, Faxon, Hayward, Howard, Holbrook, Hubbard, Hunt, Hunting, Jones, Jordan, King, Mann, May, Newcomb, Paine, Porter, Sawin, Spear, Stetson, Strong, Sylvester, Taft, Thayer, Tower, Turner, Vinton, Wales, West, Whitcomb, White. These men with their families were not here as sojourners, they had come to stay. They with their sons built the walls in the forests about us; transformed the woodlands into pastures and fields; and year after year, generation after generation, sowed and planted and harvested the fruits of their toil. Their wives and daughters were no idlers. In every household were found the spinning wheel, the reel, the winder and the loom. These women, eager to perform their part, converted the flax, the wool, and later the cotton, into fabrics which clad the members of their respective families."[27]

In a more sombre tone, Mr. Beal touched the more recent history of the village. "One hundred years and more ago the principal employments of the people here were such as are common to a farming community. . . . At the middle of the past century [19th] it stood in the front ranks and was a centre of the boot and shoe industry. For miles around, the enterprise of Randolph then sought and fed the skilled mechanic. Men, women, and children then completed the boot and shoe on the homestead. . . . But alas! To the surprise of all, inventions for stitching and pegging and lasting came. [Mr. Beal apparently implied that Randolph was at its best during the period of balanced economy—farming and domestic industry.]

The little shop in the door yard consequently became vacated. Larger and larger grew the factory until its proportions became immense. Seven or three or even one year's apprenticeship became unnecessary. The machine, the great operator, 'knows it all.' . . . Of some he has required the sacrifice of a finger, a hand, an arm or a leg. Sometimes in case of gross inattention to his call the penalty has been death. He ignores the experience and knowledge of the gray-bearded workman, and seeks for his companions the active persons below fifty years of age. For the old he has no sympathy, but directs them to the alms house. Machinery and steam have said to our small manufacturers with limited capital, you can't compete with us, and they could not. They have therefore withdrawn from the contest and yielded to the two conquering giants. . . .

"Previous to 1845, about forty young men, who were either residents or identified with the interests of the town, had graduated from the colleges of New England. . . . Since 1845, the number of college graduates has been very limited.[28]

"Our farmer complains of the railroad because by it the market where once he found a ready sale is amply supplied. His wood no longer commands its former price because the railroad reaches the coal mines. His hay is no longer desired because of the room required to store it. His fruit and vegetables afford him no profit because the steam ship and freight train so frequently communicate with warmer climes, whose exports secure the early high prices. His fields which once waved with golden grain consequently now yield only pasturage, cedars, and birches. Beaten at every turn he makes, and with no abatement of taxation, he finally exclaims, indeed, indeed, what am I to do with my hills and valleys. [period sic]"[29]

With fine candor, Mr. Beal has said that the revolutions in industry and communication and the opening of the West were body blows to the Randolph economy. But what of the immediate present? He pointed with pride to streets and shade trees, the electric trolley, well kept cemeteries, train service, water works, fire department, and the electric street lights soon to come.

For the future of Randolph: "We now live in a day when it is considered an honor to be a private citizen,—an humble, obedient, temperate, educated private citizen. And whenever such an individual looks at himself, and shrinks to a realization of his own insignificance, let him remember that such no doubt was the experience of our ancestors when they adopted the motto of our country 'E Pluribus Unum.' "[30]

One assumes that old John Wales of the hundred acres understood Mr. Beal's remarks about the decline of agriculture; that the Tolman boys congratulated themselves that their futures were tied to Boston and not Randolph. And Miss Wilkins—perhaps for her the most disturbing words were those which touched the insignificance of the private citizen. If she did not know Emerson's phrase "the infinitude of the private citizen," she understood and believed its spirit. In her own curious way, in story after story, and even in her life, she had been contesting against the drift toward individual insignificance which Mr. Beal apparently considered unalterable.

For the immediate future at least, the orator's views proved prophetic. In Cambridge, Professor Barrett Wendell was saying of New England, "We are vanishing into provincial obscurity. America has swept from our grasp. The future is beyond us."[31] By September, Mr. Huxford of the *Randolph Register,* noting the effect of depression on a town built around a single declining industry, had only this to offer: "The country is for the business people and the working people, and they should see to it that politicians do not disturb their inalienable rights."[32] The decline of Randolph was not arrested.

Mr. Huxford also included a brief item about Miss Wilkins: "Miss Mary E. Wilkins of this town has been interviewed, and it is given out that she is about to write another story of New England life, entitled 'Pembroke,' treating upon the characteristics of a certain family in that town. Miss Wilkins considers it perfectly legitimate for the public to be curious about her literary work, but curiosity of another sort she does not look upon with favor."[33] Was the editor too much interested in the Saturday evenings for Isaac and Irving Tolman? Whatever the occasion, it seems that village Randolph was behaving like village Randolph, that proud and reticent Miss Wilkins was behaving like proud and reticent Miss Wilkins.

In January of '94, the boot factory of William Gibbons burned to the ground;[34] it was not rebuilt. Later in the month and early in February came heavy snow storms.[35] Coxey's Army marched on Washington late in March.

With *Pembroke* completed, Miss Wilkins went off to Metuchen, New Jersey, for another of the Alden house parties. She saw Charles Freeman again and also met Marian Boyd Allen, a portrait painter of Boston, who was to become a life-long friend. Soon Miss Allen would be inviting Miss Wilkins to luncheon at her Commonwealth Avenue house and presenting her to her mother Mrs. Stillman B. Allen and her brother Willis Boyd. Later there were innumerable meetings, for Mary Wilkins and the Allens discovered that they spoke the same language. Unsubdued by her impressive establishment, Mrs. Allen was a buoyant person, a great one for getting up parties and "roping in her friends for consequences or charades or capping verses." Marian and Willis were of the same sort: Marian painted portraits; Willis, though trained for the bar, was a writer and editor of juvenile stories. But they had not forgotten how to play. They liked Miss Wilkins for her simplicity, her readiness for all manner of fun, her dry humor.

She was often invited for the weekend and to stay on for Mrs. Allen's Monday reception. Interesting people came to these Mondays—Phillips Brooks, Nathan Haskell Dole, Julia Ward Howe, Louise Chandler Moulton, Mrs. Deland, Lucy Larcom, Henry M. Alden whenever he was in Boston. As the author of *A New England Nun* and *Jane Field,* Mary Wilkins was an honored guest; but she was rarely happy until, the "names" having departed, she and Mrs. Allen, Marian, and Willis could slip off to the "Owl's Nest," Marian's ivory-tinted room on the fourth floor. There almost lost in a huge wing chair beside the fire, Mary Wilkins was at her best. Though talk glanced toward many directions, the Allens chiefly prized her stories of Randolph and Brattleboro experiences, the incidents too slight or strange for writing. Later came a realization of the power and sweetness of her personality: Mr. Allen said, "She did not wear her heart on her sleeve, but she had real depth of feeling."[36]

Some of her depth of feeling worked its way into the novel *Pembroke* of 1894. For despite its nominally "happy" ending and its deference to a modish objectivity of treatment, this novel is a deeply felt plea for the natural expression of normal feeling. By the same token, it is also M. E. Wilkins' fullest exploration of the "diseased will" which blocks the expression of feeling, a theme touched frequently in earlier stories. By the nature of its subject, it is intensely dramatic, and the dramatic conflicts are boldly realized.

In *Pembroke,* Miss Wilkins wrote about her maternal grandmother's family, the Lothrops, about that incident in the life of Uncle Barnabas Lothrop recounted in the first chapter of this study. The setting is the locale which the writer knew best—the Lothrop house, the house next door in which she was born, and the immediate neighborhood. Barnabas Lothrop becomes Barnabas Thayer in the novel; his fiancée Mary Thayer is given the name Charlotte Barnard.[37] Though the chief incidents and the major traits of the leading characters were matters of family history, it would be unwise to assume that the entire novel has this factual basis.

On a Sunday evening in May, Barney's father Caleb Thayer was reading the Bible to his wife, his daughter, his younger son. Barney, bound for a call on his fiancée, stopped with the family for a moment, was told by his mother that he must return by nine. He said nothing but shut the door with a thud. " 'If he was a few years younger, I'd make him come back an' shut the door over again,' said his mother. Caleb read on; he was reading now one of the imprecatory psalms. Deborah's blue eyes gleamed with warlike energy as she listened: she confused King David's enemies with those people who crossed her own will."

On the way to his Charlotte's, Barney lingered for a moment in the house which he was building for her. Thinking of her and their life together as he imagined it, tears came into his eyes. "It was a fervent demonstration . . . to all life and love and nature, although he did not comprehend it." Then he went on to her father's house, and she came to the door to meet him. They kissed but only once because the sharp voice of the father drew them into the house. Barney took his place with the family in the kitchen. Fearing that the young man would hold his daughter's hand in the dusk, Cephas Barnard ordered that candles be lit. (Miss Wilkins could not have known the psychiatrist's terminology; but she was surely suggesting that the father, frustrated in one way or another, is attempting to hold his daughter within the pattern of a relationship going back to childhood.)

Cephas was small of head and body, but his eyes were sharp and bright. Barnabas, the son of proud Deborah, looked back at him without flinching, and "there was a curious likeness between the two pairs of black eyes. Indeed, there had been years ago a somewhat close relationship between the Thayers and Barnard. . . ." Though the women made talk, the men were grimly silent. Then Cephas was picking a quarrel, flinging out a topic on which he and Barney had previously disagreed. Insults flew fast. Cephas said, " 'Get out of this house, an' don't you ever darse darken these doors while the Lord Almighty reigns.' "[38] Barney went nor could Charlotte's pleas pull him back.

There is no need for recalling the incidents of the eight year estrangement which followed. Miss Wilkins was simply saying that Barney and Cephas were warped and twisted by what she terms a "will . . . in phases of disease";[39] that Charlotte, though slightly more pliable, was also one of the same breed. She said also, again and again, that the need for love continued and that neither Charlotte nor Barney could turn to other mates.

But it will be interesting to look closely at the reconciliation which she contrived. Charlotte learned that Barney was lying seriously ill and alone in the unfinished house in which they should have lived together. Ignoring inevitable censure and her father's terrible threat, she went to Barney's house and lived there nursing him. He was deeply grateful; but his "will" yielded only when he learned that a deputation from the church had condemned the girl and ordered her to return to her home. He asked her to go. Then he followed and stood at the door "with all that noble bearing which comes from humility itself when it has fairly triumphed. Charlotte came forward, and he put his arm around her. Then he looked over her head at her father. 'I've come back,' said he.

" 'Come in,' said Cephas.

"And Barney entered the house with his old sweetheart and his old self."[40]

Lest there be any doubt of the moral import of her novel, Miss Wilkins expressed it bluntly in her 1899 "Introductory Sketch" for the "Biographical Edition" of *Pembroke.* It was, she wrote, "originally intended as a study of the human will in different phases of disease and abnormal development, and . . . to prove the truth of a theory that its cure depended upon the capacity of the individual for a love which could rise above all consideration of self."[41]

Much needs to be said of Miss Wilkins' understanding of both *will* and *unselfish love,* but this interpretation must follow a glance at the interwoven subplots and characters. For the Barney-Charlotte story is merely the more lyrical of many contrapuntal variations on the theme of perverse wilfulness and its consequences. Charlotte's Aunt Sylvia Crane unwittingly offends her Richard Alger, who had been about to pop the question after a ten year courtship, is deserted by him, and restored to his good graces only when he sees her being carried off to the poor house. Deborah Thayer, Barney's mother, attempts to break the courtship of her daughter Rebecca and young William Berry because he was related to the Barnards who had insulted her son. Rebecca and William meet secretly. When Deborah discovers that the girl is pregnant, she orders her out of the house. There is a hasty marriage in a sordid setting; then Rebecca lives on in Pembroke as an outcast. Mrs. Thayer's iron rule also extends to her invalid son, the boy Ephraim. Disciplining him outrageously, she goads him into revolt, whips him against doctor's orders, and kills him. The steel rod of Deborah's spirit snaps, and she dies of a heart seizure.

Several lesser characters—Rose Berry, Tommy Ray, Thomas Payne—are introduced as foils. Rose and Tommy sacrifice pride to win love but are represented as rather inferior types. Wealthy, college-bred Thomas Payne manages to hold his form and also to remain a well-balanced person. But he is developed only slightly. Indeed, Miss Wilkins did little to modify our general impression that Pembroke was peopled chiefly by diseased wills. From this aspect of its design, from the conflicts rising from embattled wills, the novel derives its intense dramatic impact, an impact never equalled in her later works.

But to return to *will* and *unselfish love*. Here one may surmise that M. E. Wilkins, with her subtle penetration of New England character, came within a hair's breadth of very illuminating and quite modern insight.

Nothing is more obvious than the spiritual and material poverty of Pembroke and the other villages in which the stories are set. However noble the original Calvinism, its nineteenth century form no longer answered the needs of the spirit. It seemed to say chiefly, Thou shalt not . . . at a time when an invitation to life was needed. For land and local industry were also saying Thou shalt not. Careers for young men who stayed at home were increasingly difficult; and they hesitated to accept the responsibilities of marriage and family, thus closing to women the only career socially honored.

Yet these village Yankees were the descendants of a strong and self-respecting breed, the strongest who came to this land. Independence and self-respect—these qualities had been transmitted with little weakening; they were vital aspects of the code. To be sure, Mr. Beal had praised humility, obedience, temperance;[42] and there were always those, the weaker spirits, who would attain a limited happiness by adjustment to village ways in their most stultifying aspect. Theirs was the solution of what Erich Fromm names "automaton conformity,"[43] but Miss Wilkins rarely used such types as important characters. Her protagonists, including the chief figures of *Pembroke,* must live within the code, the cultural ideal, and especially within its glorification of independence and self-respect.

Yet the conditions of their lives, as has been shown, did not permit the development of healthy self-confidence. Both Barney Thayer and Charlotte Barnard were the children of weak fathers and strong mothers, of disordered homes. Bound by traditional marital patterns, these parents must play out the charade of an unreal relationship. All are twisted and thwarted.

Lacking natural independence and confidence, Charlotte and Barney, especially the latter, must form idealized images of themselves; their real selves fade away. They must struggle to build and defend these idealized images, using the dictates of the code and its emphasis upon independence in the process. They must become proud, neurotically proud.

Though we are likely to understand such a development by studying Karen Horney[44] and Erich Fromm, Miss Wilkins seems to have worked it out for herself. To follow her completely, it is necessary only to modify slightly her understanding of *will.* Her wilful characters are frequently called *proud or stiffnecked,* the latter an Old Testament term for the wilful, haughty, and arrogant. In context, *will* always means tenacity in clinging to a position involving false pride; it is always connected with some antecedent frustration or insecurity. We need only to see *will* (tenacity) as symptom and to stress the related pride to grasp her meaning. The sequence of development then becomes frustration and insecurity, the formation of an idealized image of the self, false or neurotic pride, wilfulness or tenacity.

Unselfish love, writes Miss Wilkins, is the "cure" for what has been called neurotic pride;[45] it is also related to Barney's "humility" and to his regaining of his "old self." Here the insight seems incomplete; the "recognition" is too simply pious, at least for those who wish to keep their religion and psychology in the same mental compartment. The attainment of a real or old self and with it humility and a rich capacity for love seems in modern thought to depend upon the discovery of self-love and healthy self-confidence. Miss Wilkins touched that insight in "A Tardy Thanksgiving," but she did not carry it over to *Pembroke*.

In one respect however the motivation of the conversions remains impressive. Barney Thayer and Richard Alger are subjected to eight years of loneliness and self-hatred and to intense emotional experiences—for Barney the realization that he has exposed his Charlotte to public condemnation, for Richard the sight of his Sylvia in a wagon bound for the poor house. To that extent, at least, they are prepared for new understanding.

Conan Doyle called *Pembroke* "the greatest piece of fiction since *The Scarlet Letter*."[46] Though his praise was excessive, the comparison with Hawthorne is interesting. Miss Wilkins at her best rivals her predecessor in understanding the dark side of human nature, nor is her method as far from his as might be supposed. She is of course more "realistic," yet the note of poetic suggestiveness is frequently heard. The unfinished house of *Pembroke* is a symbol of great power, a power fully and imaginatively developed. More strikingly reminiscent of the "A" which may or may not have disfigured Dimmesdale's breast is her physical embodiment of Barney's disease of the will. "Thomas stared at Barney; a horror as of something uncanny and abnormal stole over him. Was the man's back curved, or had he by some subtle vision a perception of some terrible spiritual deformity, only symbolized by a curved spine? In a minute he gave an impatient stamp, and tried to shake himself free from the vague pity and horror which the other had aroused."[47]

Pembroke, one concludes, was clearly Miss Wilkins' strongest work up to this point in her career. Could she grow further? She might one day contrive a more artistic novel—surer in the interweaving of plots, more skillful in the distribution of light and shade. Without digging deeper into the nature of neurotic pride, a perilous undertaking, she could hardly surpass the human insights of *Pembroke.* Nor was there any other twisting of the village personality which could offer a richer reward of understanding. This novel was at the center.

Miss Wilkins went to Chicago after the completion of *Pembroke* and also stopped off in Brattleboro to cheer Evie Severance. Together they traveled through the Berkshires in the spring of '94.[48] Of Deerfield, Miss Wilkins later wrote, "[It] is a gem among villages, with its wide street overarched as solemnly as a cathedral aisle by its wonderful old elms, its ancient dwellings whose first owners heard the war cries of savages, its strange terraces overlooking green valley-lands; and in Old Deerfield, too, survive, like the refrain of a song, the best blood of the land, in dignified gentlemen and gentlewomen who reflect in their past, not with ignoble pride, but with respect and appreciation of what it has done for them."[49]

Mrs. Allen spoke of these years, '91 to '94, as the happiest in Miss Wilkins' life. The driving, compulsive demand for prestige and financial security was satisfied—not completely of course but to a degree which the Miss Wilkins of Brattleboro would not have dared to imagine. She still enjoyed writing and properly respected her own talent. The serial rights for

Jane Field and *Pembroke* had brought handsome rewards; she had invested well, was nearing financial independence, and could securely indulge her taste for lovely clothes and frequent travel.[50] "Isn't it splendid," she said to a friend, "to think I can have all the money I need, and more too? I can go into a shop and order just the kind of hat I want without thinking anything about it."[51] And she enjoyed "doing things for people"—helping the Wales family in their financial difficulties; slipping a bill into the hand of Herbert Clark, the hired man: "Now I want you and Johnny [the Wales son] to run up to Boston to see a show."[52]

But the dark moods had not disappeared. At times she was completely unreconciled to the death of her mother, father, and sister; for *Harper's* in 1892 she wrote a bit of prose and verse on the tomb which closes:

"Only the living know [grief]?
Only the living.

Then, then the tombs be not for the dead, but for the living! I would, I would that I were dead, that I might be free from the tomb, and sorrow, and death."[53]

Usually she made the best of the pattern which had gradually taken shape. She had many interesting friends. In Mary Wales she had a mother and sister, who misunderstood her at times but always accepted her moods of petulance and rebellion. She had other sisters—the priceless Evelyn Severance and Marian Allen and probably Hattie Lothrop, when she could forget her village gentilities. Now that Uncle George was gone, she had no father though sometimes Mr. Alden almost acted this role. Of course she needed a husband, for she never dallied with the notion that a career could be substituted for a woman's "birthright." But for many reasons—some, one suspects, only slightly understood—that matter could not be hurried even though the years were flying.[54] On October 31, 1894, she and Mary John knew that her age was forty-two.

Meanwhile, old John Wales had made a discovery. Sent

across the road to reconnoiter the possessions of a new family moving in, he reported to Mrs. Wales and the two Marys, "They got a big piano. I guess they're some folks."

The W. F. Kingsburys were some folks though not in exactly the sense which Mr. Wales meant. Mother, father, and five young children —Alice, Molly, Persis, Harriet, and Emory, they were hearty, energetic, and friendly people. Mr. Kingsbury traveled New England, selling a freckle remover. Sometimes his wife accompanied him, and his demonstrator was a cousin of Mary John Wales. Miss Wilkins liked all of the Kingsburys and became especially fond of the children. From the mother, who was always telling anecdotes picked up in visiting other towns, she acquired characters and situations which could later be developed into stories.[55]

The year '95 was one of few events. Cousin Hattie's mother Mrs. Edward Lothrop died;[56] now, said Mrs. Wales, Hattie would surely marry.[57] For Miss Wilkins the pattern remained unchanged—visits to the Aldens in Metuchen; the Allens, Chamberlins, and others in Boston; and Mrs. Severance in Brattleboro. It was probably in this year that she first joined the Allens for a summer stay in the White Mountains of New Hampshire. Charles Freeman and Isaac Tolman were interesting though Tolman was still going everywhere with his Mabel Leach.[58]

As usual, she found many hours for reading in the comfortable study. She read much light fiction, also Emily Brontë, Dickens, Thackeray, Hardy, Howells, Jewett, Garland, Tolstoi, and Dostoevski. Knowing that her own vein was a little thin, fearing that she might be dominated by more powerful talents, she avoided close study of any of her major predecessors and contemporaries. To one note at least, life underground, she responded strongly. She said of *Crime and Punishment* to Mr. Chamberlin, "I am at odds with the whole thing, but it is a wonderful book. He writes with more concentrated force than Tolstoi. This book seems to me like one of my own nightmares, and told on my nerves."[59] It also worked its way into her novel *Madelon.*

Later she wrote of *Wuthering Heights,* "All that Emily Brontë is intent upon is the truth, the exactness of the equations of her characters, not the impression which they make upon her readers or herself. She handles brutality and coarseness as another woman would handle a painted fan. It is enough for her that the thing is so. . . . How she ever came to comprehend the primitive brutalities and passions, and the great truth of life which sanctifies them, is a mystery. . . . She had given to her a light for the hidden darkness of human nature, irrespective of her own emotions. . . . It [the love of Heathcliff and Catherine] is made evident as one of the great forces of life; . . . it does not deal with the social problem; it is beyond it. . . . *Wuthering Heights* from first to last is an unflinching masterpiece. There is evident no quiver of feminine nerves in the mind or hand."[60]

"The hidden darkness of human nature"—Miss Wilkins had herself put some of that darkness into *Jane Field, Pembroke,* and several of the strongest short stories. She would later attempt to represent more of it in her novels. Mainly, however, she was reading for pure enjoyment and getting what she wanted.[61]

In '95, she was working on stories, the novel *Madelon,* and, with Mr. Chamberlin, the crime story "The Long Arm." The crime and its solution are much less piquant than the characterization of iron-willed Phoebe Dole and Maria Woods, who had lived together for forty years. It is a typical Wilkins story plus a murder, a work of no great originality. But because it won the Bacheller Syndicate's prize of two thousand dollars and appeared in many newspapers, some of the very old people think of Miss Wilkins chiefly as the author of this story. Its success suggested to the writer that her fiction would be improved by the inclusion of more violence,[62] a notion which partly explains the novel *Madelon.*

For one of the Curtis publications, she was turning off sketches of local characters which would later appear as *The People of Our Neighborhood,* 1898. Though quietly pleasing, these pieces are mentioned only because they increased the tension between the writer and the Randolph majority. Folks said she was going too far in writing about her own neighbors, who were just as good as she was.[63]

Early in December, Miss Wilkins received an invitation to another meeting of Mrs. George Field's Literary Club. This lady was, it seems, disturbed because the papers had taken up that ludicrous meeting of 1892 and twisted it into the form, Lion F. Marion Crawford snubs Lioness Mary E. Wilkins. Mrs. Field proposed that the writers should meet again at her home on December 19, that in this way the rather embarrassing rumor could be killed. Miss Wilkins replied to the invitation:

" 'My Dear Mrs. Field:

My work is, at present, of such a very urgent nature that I am obliged to deny myself nearly every social recreation that comes in my way and keep closely at home. I am very sorry not to meet you and the members of your Club again. . . . I have always remembered with pleasure your delightful reception for Mr. Crawford. Lately, in reading over his "Witch of Prague," I came to the portion which I heard him read that evening, and it had a new interest for me.

Very sincerely yours,

MARY E. WILKINS

Randolph, Mass., December 8, 1895' "

Mr. Crawford's letter was written only a day later.

" 'My Dear Mrs. Field:-

It is very good of you to send me two invitations, and I wish I could accept either with any chance of being present. I am chiefly in Washington nowadays, and my movements are as uncertain as those of a mosquito! I have always remembered with pleasure my reading at your Club three years ago, as having been the first I gave in this country and one of the most pleasant. There was indeed that little story about Miss Wilkins! Do you remember? I shook hands with two or three hundred people whose names were murmured in the air quite outside my hearing; and for all I heard of an introduction, Miss Wilkins might have been the Queen of the Cannibal Islands. I have always regretted that I did not know who she was, as I have read some of her things with great pleasure, and we have never met again.

Sincerely yours,

F. MARION CRAWFORD

Washington, D. C., December 9, 1895' "

"Mrs. Field lost no time in communicating to Miss Wilkins the substance of Mr. Crawford's note. Her letter elicited this acknowledgement:-

" 'My Dear Mrs. Field:-

Thank you very much for all this interesting news about Mr. Crawford. Of course I saw the notices in the papers at the time, and people often spoke to me of the matter. I do wish Mr. Crawford knew how utterly irresponsible I held him for not knowing me; I live in too fragile a glass house myself, on such occasions. Then, too, I could never see why Mr. Crawford was in duty bound to know me; he had lived so much abroad, and I was, comparatively, a new writer. There were some funny features about the affair, which amused me, but in a most friendly fashion, to which Mr. Crawford would have taken no exception. I should like to tell him the story myself.

I admire Mr. Crawford so much, that I dislike to think he should consider me so very silly as to be hurt, because he did not, in such a crowded assembly, single me out from the others and begin to talk about my little stories. I was glad that he did not because I went to see him, and not for him to see me. . . . I wish you would please tell him this for me. I thought of writing to him, but I think perhaps it would be better for you to tell him, if you will.

MARY E. WILKINS

December 15, 1895' "

"By permission of the writers," continues *The Critic's* meticulous report, "these letters were read at the last month's meeting of the Literary Club at the home of Mr. and Mrs. Van Anden. Then Mrs. Field, at *The Critic's* request, wrote to Mr. Crawford and Miss Wilkins for permission to print them. Miss Wilkins' reply left the matter to Mr. Crawford; Mr. Crawford's, written at the same time, assented to Miss Wilkins' decision, whatever it should be."[64] For final comment, whatever it should be, on the entire incident, such as it was, or as it may have seemed to each of the protagonists, and to the literary world, the reader is referred to the spirit of Henry James.

Madelon of 1896 is Miss Wilkins' gesture toward violence and passion. Though the setting, Ware Center, Vermont, was familiar enough to her readers, the plot and its chief actors were cut from new cloth. Madelon Hautville is a half-breed, Indian and French Canadian; she is also wildly beautiful and intensely amorous. The tale is scarcely under way before she is stabbing Burr Mason because he prefers another girl. His cousin Lot Gordon takes the crime on his own head, substituting his weapon for hers, and goes to prison. As Madelon announces her guilt to everyone, she meets only blank incredulity, an irony reminiscent of Raskolnikov's confessions in *Crime and Punishment.* At length Burr Mason, who is still living, states that he committed the deed himself, an attempt at suicide. Then follows the whole second half of the novel—a confusion of cross purposes and twisted but uninteresting motives. Lot Gordon gradually emerges as an infinitely fine and poetic hero.

Clearly Miss Wilkins was attempting "strong" incidents and a frankly romantic tone even as she sought to preserve some of the sobriety in observation and character delineation of her earlier stories. Such a blending of styles is not impossible, but it is not achieved in *Madelon.* It is obviously and disturbingly uneven. Miss Wilkins' letter to Mr. Asa French—July 26, 1896—reveals her own doubts: "It is odd, but the very morning of the day I received your letter, I had been in a discouraged frame of mind. . . . I wished I could have some praise, quarts and gallons of it, to hearten me. Therefore you can readily understand that your letter was very acceptable. I am truly very glad that you liked Madelon, and I appreciate most gratefully your kindness in telling me so. I have felt especially sensitive about this book, it is such a deviation from my usual line of work."[65]

The December 12 issue of *The Randolph Register* brings us back to her personal life.

"Mr. and Mrs. Gilbert Tolman of Canton were the guests of Mr. and Mrs. George W. Wales last Saturday, at whose residence they dined. Mr. Isaac S. Tolman of the banking firm of Rogers and Tolman, Boston, was also a guest, and astonished those present by the statement that he was engaged to be married, and Miss Mabel W. Leach, recently of this town, now of Philadelphia, was the chosen one. Of course congratulations were at once offered by the several friends present, and other friends will offer equal as hearty congratulations when the opportunity arrives."

Miss Wilkins and Miss Wales did not abandon their Saturday evenings of whist, but there was no one who could replace Isaac Tolman.

CHAPTER
Seven

A FEW days after the new year of 1897 came a bracing letter from a dear friend, the actress Minnie Maddern Fiske: "A happy New Year and lots of love. Sometimes—I wonder—would you send me A New England Nun with a few words in the book written by yourself. I would so prize it among my most prized possessions."[1]

Such reassurances were needed, for life at the Wales place was becomingly increasingly difficult. Mr. Wales was feeble and failing rapidly. His son Johnny was worthless on the farm —lazy, sullen, dissolute: he would work only enough to get money for periodic sprees in Boston. His one mark of distinction, said a tolerant Randolph citizen, was a "good throat." Johnny could drink anything. It was the steady and devoted hired man, Herbert Clark, who kept the farm going in these days.[2]

Mr. Wales died of paralysis in April; the funeral was held on a Monday afternoon in the home. Of him Mr. Huxford wrote in *The Randolph Register,* "Mr. Wales united with the First Congregational Church in his youth, and his life was filled with the wonderful love that belongs with the Christ spirit. His influence was simply that of a bright, sunny, loving life, which was a blessing to all who knew him."[3] His life proved, the editor might have added, that it was no simple matter to support a family on a hundred Randolph acres from the '40's through the '90's.

A few days later Miss Wilkins was reading one of her stories to an audience in Harvard's Sanders Theatre. She was one of a group of authors—George Washington Cable, Thomas Bailey Aldrich, Louise Imogen Guiney, Edward Everett Hale, and others—who read for the benefit of the Radcliffe Scholarship Fund.[4] However such pleasing recognition could hardly provide more than momentary relief from the problem that was disturbing her.

She had been rebelling from time to time against what she called "circumstances," and now they were closing in upon her. With Mary John heading the Wales family, Mary Wilkins felt more than ever obligated to stand by. She was fond of her friend and grateful for this home which had been hers for thirteen years; she knew that the rental for her half of the house was even more necessary now than it had been before. All of the royalties on one of the novels were lent to Mary John; probably more would soon be necessary.[5] She was devoted to her friend, but was she quite ready to put aside all thought of marriage? That must have been the question she was asking, for by this time she was forty-five.

Feeling the need to think her own thoughts free from the pressure of Miss Wales' strong personality, she devised a scheme for having a few days alone. She proposed to Mary John and Hattie Lothrop that they all set off for Brattleboro: they would be packed and ready to leave next morning. When morning came, she was dressed for the house. "But, Dolly," said Mary John, "I thought we were going to Brattleboro."

"Well, I've changed my mind. I packed last night, and now I feel I've been there. But you and Hattie must go." Much against their will, they went.[6]

The death of John Wales brought another complication. For years Miss Wilkins had been having bad dreams; she would wake in terror and call across the hall to Mary John. When she came, they would talk until the terror had passed. Now Miss Wales must sleep on the first floor to be near her feeble mother. Left alone with her dreams, Mary Wilkins obtained a sedative, a rather powerful drug, from her physician and came to depend upon it rather alarmingly.[7]

Increasingly she was probing her own New England conscience. Years later she would start and leave unfinished a story which seems to reflect her darker moods of this period.

"I am a rebel and what is worse a rebel against the Over-government of all creation. . . . I even dare to think that, infinitesimal as I am, . . . I, through my rebellion, have power. All negation has power. I, Jane Lennox, spinster, as they would have designated me a century ago, living quietly, and apparently harmlessly in the old Lennox homestead in Baywater, am a power.

"I do not understand in what manner I am a power against the Whole, perhaps only through my antagonism toward the part. I do not imagine, I know, that my antagonism toward the little works definite harm. That I have proved.

"My life-long friend and next-door neighbor Julia Esterbrook . . . has just run across the lawn after borrowing vanilla to flavor the cake for the Friday bridge party which meets at her house this week. Julia has never returned the last vanilla which she borrowed, or the vanilla before that, and before that. Julia owes me an endless chain of vanilla, but what of it? It rather pleases me. I like to have a definite charge of either carelessness or dishonesty against her. It raises me in my own esteem. I have never seemed able to rise on stepping stones of my dead self to higher things for the excellent reason that my real self has as many lives as a cat.

"But I can rise on the faults of my friends if I do not call them to account. This morning I rather have a sensation of being seated on a little throne of vanilla bottles. . . . Another thing which pleases me, gratifies my pride in my astuteness is that Julia, without knowing it, never borrows very good vanilla. I keep my own vanilla in a separate bottle. Julia's is in a bottle by itself containing a cheaper vanilla, much diluted. . . .

"I often wonder if I might not have been very decent, very decent indeed, if I had laid hold on the life so many of my friends lead. If I had only had a real home of my own with a husband and children in it. That was my birthright, but I was deprived of it, with neither trade nor barter.

"And another thing which was my birthright: the character of the usual woman. I am a graft on the tree of human womanhood. I am a hybrid. Sometimes I think I am a monster, and the worst of it is, I certainly take pleasure in it.

"No mortal can exist without a certain satisfaction in herself. Satisfaction in myself I certainly have, or perhaps satisfaction may not be the right word. Perhaps pride is better, pride which intoxicates like forbidden stimulants. . . .

"I sometimes wonder what would have been the state of the world, had it not been for the Tables of Stone. Once made they could not be broken. They were broken. They are broken now. Could the Devil have existed, even in the imagination of men, had it not been for those terrible and sacred Tables of the Law? Did he exist in the fullest sense before?

"It is a pity that those tables could have been broken, that the will and strength of mortal man should have been sufficient to break them.

"Here am I, a woman, rather delicately built, of rather delicate tastes, perfectly able to break those commandments, to convert into dust every one of those Divine laws. I shudder before my own power, yet I glory because of it."[8]

Typically, Miss Wilkins phrased her tormented mood in terms partly of orthodoxy, partly of psychology. As a believer in God's power, she rebelled against the burden of freedom itself, using insights expressed by St. Paul in *Romans* 5. As the subtle analyst of her spirit, she described neurotic pride with extraordinary precision. And she knows there is no escape; for her "real self [Horney would substitute *idealized image of the self*][9] has as many lives as a cat."

Was Miss Wilkins indeed a "monster"? Of course not. She was simply a troubled woman, prone on occasion to looking hard at herself, much harder than is customary among most troubled women.

Mr. Huxford had a bit of news about her in his *Randolph*

Register for May 15: "Miss Mary E. Wilkins, Randolph's popular authoress and Miss Mary E. Wales, left for New York City Tuesday." There she met Charles Freeman and agreed to marry him; no date was set, nor was there any announcement.[10] In Randolph, folks were saying that having lost Isaac Tolman, she would now turn to Irving.[11]

Jerome, a Poor Man, the novel written through much of the preceding year, had now appeared. Warned presumably by the failure of *Madelon,* Miss Wilkins returned to the subject she knew—New England middle class character, represented with minimal sensationalism. She allowed herself room for turning around, for developing her protagonist from boyhood to a point of stability in his late twenties. Whereas *Jane Field* was little more than novella and *Pembroke* a short novel, *Jerome* contains nearly two hundred thousand words. Perhaps it should be viewed as her fairest and most generally acceptable treatment of a Yankee village; but frequently the reader is disturbed by new notes, new mannerisms which do not come off. Considering the long succession of weak novels which will follow, one concludes that *Jerome* is the watershed between Miss Wilkins' firm writing in the novel and her later unrewarded experimentation.

Despite its surface realism, *Jerome* is virtually an allegory of unhealthy pride expressed in compulsive rejection of gifts and in sacrificial generosity. This theme is lightly suggested in the first episode. Lucina Merritt, the pretty little daughter of the wealthy squire, held out her gingerbread to the boy. " 'I'd just as lives as not you had it,' said she timidly. . . .

"Jerome turned on her fiercely. 'Don't want your old gingerbread,' he cried. 'Ain't hungry—have all I want to home.' " Then he forced upon her a bit of sassafras root.[12] That was the attitude which this twelve year old boy had learned from his mother and father, Ann and Abel Edwards. Farming a poor piece of land in Upham, they were throttled by a mortgage and desperate poverty. But they were "beholden" to no one;

they were proudly sensitive in the presence of any act savoring of pity or charity. Shrewdly, Miss Wilkins touched the religious aspect of this trait, naming it a survival of the orthodox belief that "misfortune is the whiplash for sin."[13] The Edwards must be ashamed of poverty.

Soon Abel Edwards, another of Miss Wilkins' defeated husbands, disappeared under circumstances suggesting suicide. His wife maintained appearances by arranging a funeral though there was no body. Jerome was forced to recognize that it was his task, at twelve, to support his mother and sister. Amazing strength was in this boy; partly by his own industry, partly by the well-concealed generosity of Squire Merritt, he kept the family together. There was even, as in the tea with Lucina, the Squire, and Aunt Camilla, an occasional glimpse of a richer and gentler life. Mostly he worked in his fields, bound shoes, and found a little time for school. With the help of his Uncle Ozias, he also learned to hate the power of rich Dr. Prescott and Simon Bassett and to feel his oneness with all the poor of the village. At seventeen he quit school to have more time for work on shoes, but he continued studying at home.

Though the family was now beginning to prosper, Jerome felt that he must give up his hope for higher education and use his little knowledge of medicine by serving those who could not pay Dr. Prescott's high fees. He became a nurse and medical adviser, practicing without fees. His sister is in love with Dr. Prescott's fine son Lawrence, who cannot marry her because of his father's objection to an alliance with her lowly family. And Jerome, resisting at every point, must recognize that he loves and is loved by wealthy Squire Merritt's beautiful Lucina.

Since *Jerome,* despite its diatribes against the rich and avaricious, is in no sense a proletarian novel, the outcome is clearly in sight. These very nice young people must marry. But nearly half of Miss Wilkins' story is yet to be told. For the obstacles which separate boy and girl and the favorable turns which bring them together, it is only necessary to say that they are occasionally well-conceived but more frequently thin and awkward. One notes again that Miss Wilkins cannot maintain an even texture of incident through a sustained action.

But, as in *Jane Field* and in *Pembroke,* there is continued cogency in the psychological analysis. The essential obstacle is of course the warping and twisting of Jerome's spirit. He loves his Lucina in so far as such a nature is capable of love; he can get the respectable income without which he will not marry. He remains however the boy who refused the gingerbread and gave the sassafras root; he must give and give even though each sacrifice pushes back the wedding date and prolongs an intolerable situation. At length, like his cousin Barney of *Pembroke,* he is emotionally so exhausted that circumstances and the strong words of Lucina's mother can break the grip of pride. " 'You generous—you! Talk of Simon Bassett! You are the miser of a false trait in your own character. You are a worse miser than he unless you give it up. What are you that you should say, "I will go through life, and I will give and will not take?" What are you that should think yourself better than all around you? . . . If you love my daughter, prove it. Take what she has to give you, and give her . . . the pride of your heart.' "[14] Thus is another note added to the analysis of neurotic pride.

For significance of theme, *Jerome* must be ranked with the best short stories and with *Jane Field* and *Pembroke.* It resembles *Jane Field* in setting in that Miss Wilkins was drawing upon observation of both Randolph and Brattleboro. Jerome's "Upham" seems to be a rather successful fusing of the two towns. Steady references to shoe manufacturing in the domestic stage and a crucial episode concerning the building of a shoe factory suggest Randolph in the '40's and '50's. The landscape is hilly Brattleboro; important scenes mention the Hayes Tavern of West Brattleboro and the flooding of the "Graystone brook," rather obviously a reminiscence of the flooding of the Whetstone of Brattleboro, which was one of the town's memorable disasters. *Jerome* is like *Pembroke* in bringing to its readers a group of well-conceived minor characters—the broken father, the proud and domineering mother, the miser Simon Bassett, the spinster Camilla.

Yet it prefigures the later and inferior novels. Though closely kin in spirit to Barney of *Pembroke,* young Jerome differs from him significantly. He is a perfectionist, deadly set in his determination to grapple with his own spirit and a hostile world, and he is without humor. Granting that the type is worthy of study, one cannot escape an impression of sheer boredom. He will reappear in feminine guise as Ellen in *The Portion of Labor* and as Maria in *By the Light of the Soul.* Moreover this character will increasingly seem to be a projection—not of the whole Mary E. Wilkins, who is not dull but—of the writer in an attitude of tense spiritual striving.

Almost equally alarming are the village gentry who here appear for the first time in a Wilkins novel. The fact that they are, with the exception of avaricious Dr. Prescott, mannerly, charming, dignified, generous is not to be held against them as fictional creations. Such qualities were needed in Miss Wilkins' pages; such human beings certainly lived in the villages. It is rather that the writer, who is completely at ease with her middle class characters, seems uncomfortable when she introduces us to the Squire and his lady, a little too much on her own best behavior. There will be more of this uncertainty as later stories and novels bring more of the gentry to us.

One of the quiet sources of richness in the earlier stories and novels was the restrained employment of symbolism. Though treated only in connection with two or three stories and *Pembroke,* it is felt lightly in virtually all of Miss Wilkins' writing. The symbols work their way precisely because they seem to emerge from ordinary observation and casual reflection; they blend easily with surface realism because, for the most part, they do not suggest a conscious striving for symbolic effect. In *Jerome,* the symbolism is conscious, overt, sustained.

Into the mouth of the character Ozias Lamb, Miss Wilkins put words explaining its rationale, " 'Everything on this earth means somethin' more'n itself, if we could only see it. They're symbols, that's what they be, an' we've got to work up from a symbol that we see to the higher thing that we don't see.' "[15] From this point, it is only a short step to Jerome's moment of mystical insight.

Miss Wilkins created a scene of hushed loveliness—dusk, the fragrance of spring, the tolling of the meeting-house bell clear in the still air. Then—"The clearness of sight seemed to enhance hearing, and possibly that imagination which is beyond both senses. Jerome had a vague impression which he did not express to himself, that he had come to a door wide open into spaces beyond all needs and desires of the flesh and the earthly soul, and had a sense of breathing new air. Suddenly, now that he had gained this clear outlook of spirit, the world, and all the things thereof, seemed to be at his back, and grown dim, even to his retrospective thought."[16]

Such intuitions will come from time to time in later novels to the one who may be loosely called "the Wilkins character"; they will also be expressed in lyrics obviously speaking for the heart.

To set up a tight little standard for "realistic" fiction, to use it to condemn the spiritual validity of these intuitions would be absurd. But one may properly ask whether Jerome's momentary insights are fused with the general structure of his personality, whether they blend with the overall philosophical and religious tone of the novel. To both queries, the answer must be no. Essentially, Miss Wilkins remains the moralist and psychologist as she thinks through the nature of her hero. The effect of the mystical moments then appears to be decorative and sentimental rather than truly functional.

The social criticism of *Jerome,* expressed partly in the vaguely socialistic diatribes of the cobbler Ozias Lamb and in the previously unmentioned hocus-pocus about a will and gifts to the community, is also decorative and sentimental.

Miss Wilkins sympathized with the poor and was at least lightly aware of the 'nineties trend toward radical social and economic thought, but she was unready for close and honest fictional exploration of the issues.

Jerome is today a readable novel—less dramatic than *Pembroke,* equally mordant as an analysis of neurotic pride, better balanced as an interpretation of a New England village. But it raises the crucial question of Miss Wilkins' later career. Will she be able to extend her range and still retain the unity of effect of the early stories and novels? Will she be up to the fundamental brainwork which goes into the making of a profound and artistic extended work?

After strenuous work on *Madelon* and *Jerome,* she needed a rest; she did not attempt another lengthy novel until 1899. The situation of the Wales family was disturbing—so disturbing that sometime in 1898 or 1899, for this and probably other reasons, Miss Wilkins broke her engagement to Dr. Freeman.[17]

As usual she was getting away from Randolph occasionally—summers in New Hampshire with Marian and Willis Allen, frequent trips to Boston, less frequent to New York and Metuchen, an extended stay in Virginia in '99 in preparation for an historical novel set in the Tidewater.[18]

There were several new faces in Randolph. Mrs. Ellen Proctor had brought her sons and invalid husband to her family home, the Dubois place across from Hattie Lothrop's and the Tolmans'. Hers was a mind and an insight into New England character which easily matched Miss Wilkins' except in artistic capacity. For Mrs. Proctor, a partial cripple, had been reading well, observing keenly, airing her ideas in talk with men for many years.[19] Like Aunt Mary Emerson, she had no patience with women's talk, and she dominated every conversation. Miss Wilkins could have found her worth knowing; but she was afraid of the clear gray eyes which saw too sharply, of the tongue which spoke truth too accurately. "There are two kinds of intelligently helpless women," said Mrs. Proctor.

"For one, men do everything without even 'thank you'; for the second, they also do everything, and they receive a bit of gratitude. Miss Wilkins always said 'thank you.' "[20]

Avid of good talk, needing to escape from the house in which her husband was interminably dying, Mrs. Proctor would frequently look in on Irving Tolman and his sister after tea. From Irving, Miss Wilkins learned the story of the strange call at one in the morning. When Mrs. Proctor called in the evening, there was the customary question about her husband's health and the customary reply. He was just the same. Then the talk began, and Mrs. Proctor had her say—sharp, anecdotal, grimly humorous. She departed at ten. At a little after one, Irving was pulled out of bed by sharp rapping at the door. It was Mrs. Proctor and she spoke fast. "Behold the Widow Proctor. Now call the undertaker."

Irving Tolman, now nearing forty, was by this time Randolph's most eligible and elusive bachelor. Mrs. Wales considered him the property of her Mary and of Dolly Wilkins: he was still calling at the homestead. Mrs. Franklin Porter, who lived a few doors below the Tolman house, had other ideas for Irving. There was her niece Edith. She was a New England girl with southern manners, for her parents had moved from Randolph to Mobile, Alabama. There she had been educated. Twenty, flirtatious, very feminine, Edith played a guitar and sang ballads. When Mrs. Tolman died, Mrs. Porter gave Edith a note of sympathy to be handed to Irving. He seemed quietly pleased but a little uncertain of manner. Was Edith to be treated as a little girl or a young woman? But he called occasionally at the Porters'.

All this Miss Wilkins would learn from Hattie Lothrop who had it from Irving's sister. And Hattie had a beau. He was Edmund Belcher, a well-paid cutter in one of the shoe factories. Nearly fifty, a hard drinker, a famous man-about-village who had escaped a whole generation of mothers with willing daughters, Mr. Belcher was now showing signs of readiness to settle down in marriage. His blue eyes in their long thin face were still bright, and he had a fine collection of country jokes. Hattie liked Edmund Belcher, but wondered whether she could manage his drinking. She and Mary Wilkins discussed this question for many an hour with side glances toward Charles Freeman, who was also fond of his bottle.[21]

Now Cousin Hattie was even tinier than Mary Wilkins, a small-boned person under five feet; and Edmund was a big man who had been going his own way for a long time. Yet Hattie was a Lothrop, the daughter of a long line of domineering women. Miss Wilkins thought a Lothrop woman could manage a Belcher, and Hattie agreed.[22]

In 1898, Harpers issued *Silence and Other Stories.* Since so much of Miss Wilkins' time and best effort had gone into the writing of novels, the thinness of this collection is not surprising. Of the six stories, only one, "A New England Prophet," need be mentioned. Its germ was an incident in the Millerite Movement of 1843-44 which occurred in Randolph. We are given something of the wild prophecies and fierce eloquence of Solomon Lennox as he leads his followers to a high hill and watches there for the end of the world, but much more of his skeptical brother Simeon. Miss Wilkins never wrote a speech of more salty authenticity than his report to Solomon's protestation that his prophecies were inspired by Scripture: " 'Passages,' he says, 'that ye've had to twist hind-side foremost, an' bottom-side up, an' add, an' subtract, an' divide, an' multiply, an' hammer, an' saw, an' bile down, an' take to a grist mill afore you got to the meanin' you wanted. . . . What I want is a square up an' down passage that says without no chance of it's meanin' anything else, "The world is coming to an end next Thursday." I stump ye to show me sech a passage as that. Ye can't do it.' " Here is the flavor of man in a single speech and also a sufficient critique of such religious hysteria.

Through much of 1899 and 1900, Miss Wilkins was writing two novels simultaneously—the romantic *The Heart's Highway;* the more or less realistic, *The Portion of Labor.* On May

1 she sailed with Marion and Willis Allen for Paris and the Universal Exposition of 1900. There she seemed a little girl thrilled by everything and especially the streets of Paris. But she was timid about venturing far by herself; once she called a *fiacre* simply to cross a boulevard.

Liking the French, she felt a certain kinship with them and fancied that, without knowing their language, she understood the sense of what they were saying. At the Exposition she enjoyed watching the peasant types and especially one family—father, mother, grandmother, and two children—who were bending their necks to stare upward at the great arch topped with the "Frivolity of Paris." At noon she saw them calmly spreading their lunch of bread, salad, cheese, and red wine in a conspicuous corner of an arcade.[24] Later she put this family into a sketch for *McClure's*, "The Happy Day," which is as completely "Mary Wilkins" as anything she has written.[25]

On May 11, 1900, Hanson Tyler died in Vallejo, California.[26] The news may have been conveyed to Miss Wilkins by Mrs. Severance after the party returned from Paris.

Soon *The Heart's Highway* was out. It is an historical romance of seventeenth century Virginia, less robust than Mary Johnston's *To Have and to Hold*, a phenomenal best seller of the moment, but definitely superior in style and characterization. Presumably it was written partly to satisfy a craving for the frankly beautiful and romantic, partly to fall in with a literary fashion. It was praised by reviewers and widely read.

The Randolph Register for September 1 permitted itself a touch of coyness, an item headed "Those Literary Cats": "The St. Nicholas for August has a charming article on 'Some Literary Cats,' by Helen M. Winslow. Among the number she depicts two belonging to Miss Mary E. Wilkins, Randolph's noted authoress, 'Punch and Judy' by name. Judy was cruelly shot by a neighbor, but the right-hand cat (in the picture), with angelic expression still survives. 'Augustus,' too, moved from Brattleboro, Vt. to Randolph, after being the pet cat for many years, came to an untimely end. 'I hope,' says Miss Wilkins, 'that people's unintentional cruelty will not be remembered against them.' Speaking of Punch, Miss Wilkins says: 'I'm sure he loves me better than anybody else'; and yet it is hinted that by the time the chestnuts begin to fall, Miss Wilkins will have changed her name for a home with a man in it, and continued popularity and regard."

If Hattie thought she could manage Edmund Belcher, Mary Wilkins, though cautioned by friends, saw no need for fearing marriage with Charles Freeman. On October 27, *The Register* was more explicit: there would be a wedding sometime in November. "Dr. Charles Manning Freeman of Metuchen, N. J., is the fortunate man, and to his new home in that town the bride of forty-eight summers will go. It is said that he has seen about forty-two winters, and is still in his prime, being the proprietor of a large lumber business in his native town, having discarded the practice of medicine, it being distasteful to him. . . .

"The doctor has said that he thought her popularity would be improved by marrying. Miss Wilkins has written many years, and she is now reaping the fruit of her work. Her home on South Main Street is a bower of loveliness so the literary people say who visit here, and they are many. Although Miss Wilkins is a lady of quiet taste and of exclusiveness at her home town, she is an honored guest at society circles at the great centres, and is known by all the prominent people who worship at the shrine of the poets, the writers and the literate of the land."

November 17: "Miss Mary E. Wales entertained the Ladies Library Association at the Wales homestead on South Main Street, last Tuesday evening." Here, presumably, the engagement was announced to the literate of Randolph.

November 23: "Dr. Charles M. Freeman of Metuchen is expected to be the honored guest of Miss Mary E. Wilkins at the Wales homestead on South Main Street sometime during Thanksgiving week. Randolph's popular novelist will entertain graciously and hospitably." Miss Wilkins, one may be certain, did entertain the doctor "graciously and hospitably," but he did not take a bride back to Metuchen.

Meanwhile Miss Tolman told Hattie who told Dolly Wilkins that Irving Tolman had proposed to Edith Porter and that she had accepted. Mary John brought the news to Mrs. Wales in the kitchen. She said, "Can you imagine him marrying that child!"[27]

Two new works appeared in 1901—*The Love of Parson Lord and Other Stories* and a novel, *The Portion of Labor.* The first contains a single striking piece, "One Good Time." It is another story of revolt, the revolt of middle-aged Narcissa Stone against the long dullness of her life, and her decision to take her mother to New York to spend the entire fifteen hundred dollars of insurance left by her father before settling down with her faithful William Crane to a routine of wifely washing, scrubbing, and baking. Within a week Narcissa returned to the village and her fiancé to confess that she had spent all of the money in having "one good time." The recital of her adventures involves a contrasting of the complex sophistication of New York ways with the simplicity of the village ladies who had never seen a town of more than five thousand.[28] Had Miss Wilkins been seriously concerned with what we later learned to call the "revolt against the village," this situation would have led to something comparable to Carol Kennicott's stay in Washington and her return to "Main Street." The flatness of life in the little place would have been rendered in sharply satirical terms. But that was not her intention in this story. The contrasting of the different ways of life is imagined in a lightly humorous way, and Narcissa revolts against the dullness of her life rather than against the dullness of a generalized village life.

The Portion of Labor is Miss Wilkins' most ambitious and least successful novel. In some two hundred thousand words, the author attempted to build a companion piece for *Jerome,* to trace the development of a lower-middle class girl of a "shoe town" from childhood through adolescence and young womanhood into the safe port of a good marriage. The town is perhaps Brockton; the time, the troubled '80's and '90's; the chief incident, an unsuccessful strike of shoe workers.

Ellen Brewster, the heroine, is asking Jerome's question, "Where is my happiness?" The minor middle class characters are as usual limned with fine insight, but the mill owner and his family are seen through eyes too much dazzled by wealth and position. For close thinking and sound knowledge of the economic system of the '90's, Miss Wilkins substituted the moralism and sentiment which marred Elizabeth Stuart Phelps, *The Silent Partner*. After harrowing us with sharply observed details of worker degradation and poverty, she concluded that such was the will of God and a fine schooling in "character." Calvinistic determinism is linked with economic conservatism and decorated with a touch of self-righteousness. This, in general, is the "portion of labor"; but sentiment enters to arrange the marriage of the worker heroine with the owner's son.

Ellen is the "Wilkins character" mentioned in comment on *Jerome,* hardly as neurotic as the boy but sufficiently tedious in her ecstasies of self-sacrifice, her commitment to perfection, her tense demand for happiness. After this pattern is once grasped, it will bear repetition only if the writer is amplifying her analysis of its limitations. The amplification does not occur in *The Portion of Labor*.

Through a period of about thirteen months, Miss Wilkins postponed her wedding. "Six times it was announced that they were married, and as often it was denied."[29] On December 22, she wrote to Mrs. Severance: "At this extremely late hour of the day [age forty-nine], I am about to be married. Early in January, the day, I don't mention, even in my prayers, on account of the newspapers.

"I hope you haven't believed them. The unfortunate man is Dr. Chas. M. Freeman. I met him years ago at the Aldens' when I visited in Metuchen, N.J. We are very old friends, but have not been engaged as long as the newspapers state. They have married and postponed at their own discretion. I [shall] have a house in Metuchen with seventy-eight doors, and five pairs of stairs, otherwise it is quite pretty. I suppose I shall spend most of my time, being naturally of a somewhat indecided [sic] turn, trying to decide which door to go in or out of, and which stairs to descend. . . .

"Please give my love to your doctor. I don't forget you, old friend, if I don't ever see you. How I used to trot up to see you, and we used to pop corn and discuss life. How little we knew; even you knew none too much, and how much (or is it how little?) we have learned. Somehow just now, those old days seem very near, and I can see you, you tall, beautiful, golden-crowned thing, getting around and me tagging you."[30]

Though the day of Miss Wilkins' marriage could not be mentioned even to Mrs. Severance, there was no mystery whatever about the wedding of Hattie Lothrop and Edmund Belcher. It was announced simply in the *Randolph Register* for December 28, 1901:

"Married—

Belcher-Lothrop—In Saugus, Dec. 24, by Rev. John C. Labaree, D. D., at the Congregational parsonage, Mr. Edmund K. Belcher and Miss Hattie Lothrop, both of Randolph."

In the Wales homestead and by wires to Metuchen, dark plans were being formed. Miss Wilkins' wedding was to be in Metuchen because Dr. Freeman's mother was ill and could not come to Randolph. Such at least was the official explanation, but more feminine reasons may have entered. On the morning of the last day of December, Miss Wilkins and Miss Wales took a train south to Brockton: that would fool the curious ones of Randolph. From Brockton north to Boston, they rode a marketman's train, then on to New York on the New York, New Haven, and Hartford. Dr. Freeman met them in New York, and they went toward Metuchen. To elude New Jersey friends, they left the train a few miles above the town and drove to the homestead in Dr. Freeman's carriage.[31]

At eight in the evening of the next day, January 1, 1902, amid roses and smilax in the east parlor of the pretty house on Lake Avenue with seventy-eight doors, Miss Wilkins and Dr. Freeman were married by the Reverend J. G. Mason. The only witnesses were Miss Wales and the doctor's three sisters. *The New York Herald* later supplied the ages of the couple: Dr. Freeman was "forty-two"; his lady—"thirty-five."[32]

CHAPTER
Eight

BECAUSE of the illness of Dr. Freeman's mother, there was no honeymoon. On the morning of the second, he galloped through the streets of Metuchen, came to his coal and wood establishment, and returned to his work. Now the news was out, and there was great curiosity in Metuchen.[1] Mary John stayed on for several days before returning to Randolph.[2] Then Dolly was alone with her husband in a big house in a New Jersey town twenty-five miles southwest of New York and over two hundred from Randolph.

Charles Freeman quickly learned that being wedded to a temperament had its obligations: one had to know just how to treat this woman who could be merry, wise, tender—and difficult. There was the matter of sedatives. He was shocked when he learned that his wife had relied on them for many years; he encouraged her to try to sleep without them. She made a real effort. Perhaps she might have succeeded had not Letty, an old retainer of the Freeman family, threatened to quit if Mrs. Freeman did not stop walking the floor at all hours of the morning. She returned to her sedatives. During these early months, Dr. Freeman wrote frequently to Miss Wales in Randolph for advice.[3]

If his wife was still a creature of moods, the balance shifted toward the brighter side. On April 25, she wrote to Mrs. Severance: "I am very well and doing a great deal of work. I have written a great deal since I was married and besides have some care of my house. I have two maids and one of them is almost as good as a housekeeper. The other is not yet wholly materialized as 'help,' but I don't worry. I have made up my mind if my house is clean enough so there is no immediate danger of typhoid, and we have enough to eat, it is the principal thing.

"Still I must admit, that I wonder how I can really do as much as I ought to do. It is actually doing a man's work and a woman's at once, though my husband does everything he possibly can to spare me, and I did not know that mortal man could be so considerate. Moreover he eats everything and does not fuss about his food, and you know what a joy that is to a housekeeper. My cuisine makes me think of the Old Testament and the seven days of, or was it seven years, of plenty, and vice versa. I don't want to be extravagant, so I try to strike an average. One Sunday we had roast goose, and mushrooms, so the Saturday before, I made them eat salt cod fish, and Indian pudding and baked beans.

"My grounds are lovely. I have always wanted evergreen trees, and now I have them, such beauties, with the branches resting on the ground, and there are lots of flowering shrubs, which I am watching bud with a great deal of interest. And there is the loveliest birch tree that I ever saw right opposite my window. If our very souls were not harassed by drainage, the whole place would appear a sort of Eden. It is a very pretty place.

"I have four charming sisters-in-law, who are a great resource to me.

"I enjoyed your letter . . . , and I never forget the dear old Evie, and the dear old days. They are always deep down in my heart, and a part of me. . . ."[4]

After the recovery of Charles' mother, she and Mrs. Freeman drove out nearly every afternoon in the family Victoria.[5] If Metuchen lacked the simple dignity of her Randolph's elm-shaded street, its steepled meeting house, its trim cottages and mansions, it was still a pleasant town. Completely casual in planning, its streets wander over the gently undulating

New Jersey countryside. Overhanging the streets, shading the houses, everywhere, are old maples of luxuriant foliage. Though not as rich as neighboring Plainfield, Metuchen is comparatively a wealthy town. Its mansions in 1902 were too new to be good architecturally, but they did speak of comfort and quiet luxury.

If Mrs. Freeman seemed to be flourishing in her new life in a new setting, she did not forget her New England friends and relatives. She wrote steadily to Mary John and Hattie Belcher; she also maintained a room in the Wales place, partly as a graceful way of continuing her assistance to the family. In June she returned to Randolph for the wedding of Edith Porter and Irving Tolman. It was held in the Porter home just a few doors south of the Wilkins and Lothrop places.[6] Edith was pretty in her "white *crepe de chine* over taffeta silk, with trimmings of carrikin across the lace"[7] and excited too, for she and Irving were to have a stay in Paris.[8]

Though her dearest ones were in New England, Mrs. Freeman had friends of long standing in Metuchen. There were the couples—Henry M. Alden and his second wife Ada Murray Alden, the Schenks, the Carvahlos, Solomon S. and his wife Helen Cusack. Mr. Carvahlo had been Pulitzer's *alter ego* on *The World* and was at this time general manager of all of the Hearst papers. Metuchen also had its perennial bachelors—the Stevens boys who were illustrators for leading magazines. There were many quiet parties in the homes, sometimes for distinguished guests such as William Dean Howells, Thomas Bailey Aldrich, Mrs. Margaret Deland, F. Hopkinson Smith, and Lafcadio Hearn.

And, quite as in the Randolph pattern, there were the girls —Dr. Freeman's four sisters, two of them teachers in Brooklyn, all pleasant, fortyish, and unmarried; and the three daughters of Mr. Alden and his first wife—the kindergartner Carolyn, the teacher Harriet who "wanted to write," and lovely, sensitive Annie, who dabbled in oils and collected illustrators. Mrs. Freeman seemed to like this group, and she was closest to Annie and Harriet Alden.[9]

In the summers, the Freemans went to the Crawford House of Crawford Notch, New Hampshire, where they would see Marian Boyd and Willis Allen and other friends of earlier visits. Mrs. Allen remembered Charles' pride in his wife: he said she was not only a writer but a fine figure of a woman. She must even rise and turn around for the little group to prove his point.

The also traveled to Brattleboro in the summer of 1902 or 1903 to visit Mrs. Severance and other friends. There was even some talk at a Brooks House reception of their settling permanently in town.[10]

Though it is pleasing to record these lighter aspects of Mrs. Freeman's life, they create a somewhat false impression. By her choice and probably her husband's, she was still a hard working writer except during vacation periods. She was attempting that difficult maneuver—the combination of a full career and marriage though of course there were no children.

The day to day texture of her life was not unlike that of Randolph. She rose early and wrote steadily through the morning, then lunched with her husband. With him and Letty, she made the housekeeping decisions. In Randolph, she had relied on Mary John for much of the "managing" and for encouragement in moments of self-distrust; in Metuchen, Dr. Freeman quickly and shrewdly slipped into her role. He directed her reading: she should have only the frothiest books —adventure and crime stories, historical novels, and a nightly spree of giggling and emotion in the funnies and the murders of *The New York Evening Journal*. They agreed that more serious reading might draw her attention away from the plots which were always simmering in her mind. He limited her social engagements that she might conserve energy for writing.[11] Accepting some of the responsibilities of the household, he also discouraged Mrs. Freeman's occasional impulse to invade Letty's kitchen and try her hand at cooking. "What's all this?" he exclaimed, coming into the kitchen one day while his wife was stirring up a cake. "Making a cake when the same time would produce a story worth five hundred!" He criticized her stories in detail; and since his taste was tolerably good, his suggestions were useful.[12]

During the last Randolph years, the struggle between the tendencies roughly named *romantic* and *realistic* was clearly evident. *The Portion of Labor* had its element of accurate documentation of lower middle class worker life; *The Heart's Highway* was frankly romantic in subject and inner feeling; *Understudies* involved a symbolism original to a degree but related to Hawthorne's. Each of these works expressed real impulses though the deeper may well have been the romantic and symbolic. "The most of my work," Mrs. Freeman said, "is not the kind that I myself like. I want more symbolism, more mysticism. I left that out [presumably, of the earlier stories and novels] because it struck me people did not want it, and I was forced to consider selling qualities."[13] Now emboldened by affluence and the steady demand for her stories, Mrs. Freeman gave looser rein to these tendencies. Popular taste was still, as it is today, strongly romantic. Mr. Alden would use several stories each year in the *Monthly* at five or six hundred, and she could also sell at higher prices to *Everybody's* and *McClure's,* which were reaching a larger and less critical audience. Serial rights for a novel would earn seven thousand.[14] In short, Mrs. Freeman could afford to write as she pleased.

Twenty or thirty years ago, one would have phrased this situation by saying that the low and confused critical standards of the time and her commitment to financial success encouraged Mrs. Freeman to mistake her own finest talent and to betray the great cause of realistic fiction. Now that the greatness of the cause is somewhat suspect, it is no longer necessary to think in terms of betrayal and wasted talent. The question becomes more simply: was there in Mrs. Freeman a rich talent for the subjective and romantic and symbolic, or was this element of her sensibility more impressive when, as in her earlier stories, it was controlled by the conventions of a surface realism? Bluntly, did she continue to write good fiction?

The Wind in the Rose-Bush (1903) is a volume of ghost stories written for *Everybody's*. The settings are the New England villages used so often before; the characters are members of the gentry, studied with no more skill than appears in the treatment of similar figures in *Jerome* and *The Portion of Labor*. The ghosts do what they can to be ghostly, but Mrs. Freeman does nothing especially fresh or interesting with this sub-literary *genre*. This volume is simply mediocre fiction.

A better volume, *Six Trees,* appeared in the same year. In thought and feeling, the stories return to moments of nature mysticism which the writer may have experienced in Brattleboro and to the doctrine of symbols expressed by Ozias Lamb in *Jerome:* "Everything on earth means somethin' more'n itself if we could only see it." Seeking a literary source, if one is needed, one thinks of Emerson's *Nature* and especially of such words as these: "In the woods we return to reason and faith. . . . Standing on the bare ground,—my head bathed by the blithe air and uplifted into infinite space,—all mean egotism vanishes. I become a transparent eye-ball; I am nothing; I see all; the currents of the Universal Being circulate through me: I am part and parcel of God."[15]

Choosing six trees as symbols of the spirit of goodness and beauty at the center of all creation, Mrs. Freeman suggested their influence upon the sensitive men and women who could feel their power. The second story, "The Apple Tree," is the most successful as a fusion of nature mysticism with sharp comment upon New England character. It is built around a contrast between two ways of life: dedication to Work and Thrift against an easy reliance upon nature. We meet the typical New England housewife, Mrs. Blake, small, wiry, intense, working hard and fussing all the time, forever cleaning house, "merciless and miraculously untiring when it came to shaking a mat."[16] To her the shiftless Maddon family across the road is beyond comprehension. " 'What's the use of cleaning house?' Mrs. Maddon said. 'It gets dirty again.' " Knowing but not resenting the squalor of their house and garden, "they settled back on the soft side of their poverty." It seemed as if the rich beauty of their apple-tree had somehow passed into their lives, making them gentle, kindly, contented.

"There never was a more beautiful apple-tree; majestic with age, it yet had all the freshness of youth and its perfection. Not one dead branch was there on the tree, not one missing from its fair symmetry. The blooming spread of it was even to the four winds; it described a perfect circle of wonderful bloom. . . . The whole tree seemed to pant and sing, and shout with perfume. . . ."[17]

Looking at it lovingly, the pagan Maddon said, " 'It's a pretty handsome tree.' " Mrs. Blake made the inevitable retort of the codebound, " 'I don't care nothin' about the looks of a tree so long as it has good apples.' "[18] At the close of the sketch, Mrs. Freeman clearly notes her sympathy with the Maddons: "The splendid apple-tree bloomed and sweetened, and the man and woman, in a certain sense tasted and drank it until it became a part of themselves, and there was in the midst of the poverty and shiftlessness of the Maddon yard a great inflorescence of beauty for its redemption."[19]

"The Apple-Tree" and several others in this volume are lovely stories. Since incident and dramatic clash are unimportant, they have the freedom and the looseness of form of the sketch, a form relatively new to Mrs. Freeman. She was very fond of this volume, telling her cousin Mrs. Mann that these were her best stories. Perhaps she had discovered here a theme and a form which could be further developed. But could American readers aware of evolutionary thought and of the many current naturalisms be interested in pan-psychic optimism?

In the summer of 1903, Mrs. Freeman was asked by *The Ladies Home Journal* to write a few lines on what she would do with a million dollars; other distinguished women would supply their ideas. Her contribution to this feature stunt is unimportant except in so far as it reflects memories of struggling years in Brattleboro and the predicament of the proudly poor: "My sympathy goes out, as would some of my million to people who had had and lost and who undergo the keenest suffering. . . . Then I should set aside the income of perhaps a quarter of the million for other objects. I think I should like to pay off mortgages with some of it. I should like to assist young people to get educations and equip themselves for life. I should even like to buy some pretty things for young girls who have had to do without them and hunger for them. I should give to old people those pleasures of which they have dreamed all their lives, and of which they have been deprived because all their money had to go for the stern necessities. . . . I should not search the slums for deserving objects of charity, but I should give to the unacknowledged poor. . . . To such, of frugal habits, a very little a year would mean independence. . . ."[20]

Independence—Mrs. Freeman presumably wrote that word with feeling. And she was concerned that Mary John Wales, Mrs. Wales, and her spinster sister Aunt Lizzie should not lose theirs. Shiftless Johnny Wales was still shiftless; Miss Wales and the hired man, Herbert Clark, were still doing what they could to keep the place going. The Freemans always returned at Thanksgiving: the ritual dinner would help to draw the family together. It was always the same dinner—turkey, cranberry sauce, turnips, onions, potatoes, squash pie, nuts, raisins, figs, dates; always the same group—Mrs. Wales and her sister Aunt Lizzie, Mary John and her fiftyish bachelor Henry Whitcomb, Caleb Thompson and his Sarah, and the Freemans. Since the Freemans stayed with Hattie and Edmund Belcher in the old Lothrop house, there was also a Friday evening to which the Thompsons and Irving and Edith Tolman were invited. Most important in a practical way was Mrs. Freeman's talk at the Belchers with Herbert Clark. "I can trust you, Herbert," she would say. Then she would learn the real state of Wales' affairs and decide what she could do to help them. Regular checks to Mary John and Aunt Lizzie would follow.[21]

In 1904, some of Mrs. Freeman's stories for *Harper's Monthly, Harper's Weekly,* and the *Bazar* were collected in a volume called *The Givers and Other Stories.* Six of the eight pieces are Christmas stories—by no means the worst of this sentimental *genre* but sticky enough. In general, *The Givers* resembles in its relative realism *A Humble Romance* and *A New England Nun;* it is however distinctly inferior in incisiveness to the early collections.

It does contain one striking story, "The Butterfly," a triumph of delicate suggestiveness. In a series of homely scenes—B. F. Brown proudly inspecting the new sideboard bought in anticipation of his daughter's arrival; B. F. Brown awkwardly arranging on it "an old fashioned glass preserve dish . . . a little painted mug which had been his in babyhood, and a large cup and saucer with 'Gift of Friendship' in gold lettering"; B. F. Brown greeting the girl at the train with inarticulate emotion—Mrs. Freeman suggests the devotion of this man to a daughter who can be with him only half of each year. Another low-keyed scene, and we begin to suspect that the mother, from whom B. F. Brown has long been separated, is a despicable person. The concluding scene, the daughter's decision to live permanently with her father, comes with quiet inevitability.[22] The "broken home" was a new subject in these days, and it is interesting to see that Mrs. Freeman could treat it well.

Miss Wales' mother, Sarah Thompson Wales, died in her eighty-fourth year on March 13, 1905.[23] By this time Mrs. Freeman was avoiding funerals and probably did not go to Randolph. In the same year, Marian Boyd Allen, the painter, married William A. Allen—another late venture like Mrs.

Freeman's.[24] Willis Allen was still a bachelor and would never marry.

And Dolly and Charles Freeman—were they making the "best of a bad job" or was this for her a good marriage added to a good career? Dr. Freeman was certainly an ornamental husband: he was still handsome, was still idolized not only by the mother and sisters but by nearly all of his Metuchen friends. If he was not a "man's man" in reality, he acted like one. He had been gay during the "gay nineties": Metuchenites liked to remember that he had jilted many of the town's attractive girls, that he was a magnificent figure on a horse, that he was not above shooting dice with the boys—white or colored—in Lawless' Saloon. He was a local legend, living proof that something of the Bohemian and the Wild West could flourish in suburban New Jersey. And the coal and wood business did not greatly cramp his style.

Mrs. Freeman could, it seems, be proud of having brought this exotic male to heel. In these years he was drinking little and playing admirably his role as silent partner to a writing career. It seemed to be a good marriage. Even when her prevailing moods had been dark as in the later Randolph years, Dolly had always had her occasional moments of bright humor. Now they were frequent.[25] She told her Yankee anecdotes with assurance at parties; visiting the Harper's editors, she transformed business into a comic whirl; she played with nonsense verses:

"The ostrich is a silly bird,
With scarcely any mind.
He often runs so very fast,
He leaves himself behind.

"And when he gets there, has to stand
And hang about till night,
Without a single thing to do
Until he comes in sight."[26]

Colonel George Harvey, Harpers president, invited the Freemans to a banquet in Delmonico's great room to honor Mark Twain's seventieth birthday.[27] The date was December 5, 1905, five days later than the actual birthday, for the occasion must not conflict with Thanksgiving functions. There were nearly two hundred guests.[28] At Twain's table were Kate Douglas Riggs; his closest friend, the Reverend "Joe" Twitchell of Hartford; Ruth McEnery Stuart; Mr. Alden of *Harper's New Monthly;* Henry H. Rogers, Standard Oil millionaire; and Mrs. Freeman. She was at his right hand in a shimmering flowing gown of rose silk.[29] Was she honored as a writer or as a charming and amusing woman? Perhaps something of both.

Twain talked of many things; but by eight, he was beginning to feel fatigue. "O, this business of making speeches," he said, "I despise it. And they put me down for nine o'clock when everyone knows I always take a nap at eight. It's eight now."

Mrs. Freeman said, "Then why don't you take your nap?" Twain took his nap, so Mrs. Mann's story runs, and then returned for the speeches and his own with its fine closing moment: "I am seventy, seventy, and would nestle in the chimney-corner, and smoke my pipe, and read my book, and take my rest, wishing you well in all affection, and that when you in your turn shall arrive at Pier 70 you may step aboard your waiting ship with a reconciled spirit, and lay your course toward the sinking sun with a contented heart." The tears that had been waiting were not restrained.[30]

Mrs. Freeman would cherish the memory of this dinner for Mark Twain. He was a great writer and a lovable man; he played on the Harpers team, and that was her team too.[31]

All through this year she had been working on a serial for *Harper's Bazar;* it was issued in book form as *The Debtor* late in the year. A lengthy and weakly plotted novel of realistic and satiric tone, it added nothing to her reputation. Its interest now is biographical.

Work, Thrift, and the commandment, Thou shalt not steal—these were aspects of the Yankee code deeply ingrained in Mrs. Freeman's spirit. If on occasion, as in "The Apple Tree," she turned away from the worship of work, the revolt was only momentary and theoretical. The exaltation of industry, which is the theme of *The Portion of Labor* speaks her deeper conviction.

In Metuchen she formed the impression that New Jersey people lacked respect for work and business integrity. *The Debtor* is a Metuchen book and was immediately recognized as such by her neighbors though she called her setting "Banbridge." Captain Carroll, the debtor, a figure reminiscent of Twain's Colonel Sellers (*The Gilded Age*), runs up bills which he cannot pay, suffers disgrace in the community, and at length recovers his integrity by working in a job which only Mrs. Freeman at her worst could have devised for him. *The Debtor* is a preachy novel, interesting only because it supplies further evidence of the writer's ambivalent attitude toward the village code. Again and again she revolts against one or another of its commandments only to return in loyal support.

"Doc" Gordon, the New Jersey novel of 1906, may be ignored entirely.

Two slight events of this year are pleasant to record. Mr. Alden celebrated his seventieth birthday; Mrs. Freeman wrote for the occasion a tender and graceful bit of verse published in *Harper's Weekly* for December 15. And she was delighted when the Tolmans of Randolph named their second daughter —the first had died—after her. She sent a breast pin of coral and pearl.[32]

The serialized novel, *By the Light of the Soul* (1906), is Mrs. Freeman's boldest attempt to realize the possibilities of the subjective and religious elements of *Jerome, The Portion of Labor,* and "The Apple Tree." For precision and fullness of detail in the treatment of minor characters and of the New Jersey and New England setting, it is a realistic and regional novel—another *Pembroke;* in the development of the inner life of its heroine, Maria Edgham, it appears to be lightly disguised spiritual autobiography. The cousin, Mrs. Edmund K. Belcher, agrees with this opinion.

By the Light of the Soul is also a feebly plotted novel. The major complication, which shapes Maria's life more than any other external factor, is her unconsummated marriage at sixteen, under preposterous circumstances, to the boy Wollaston Lee. Contriving with little plausibility objections against annulment or divorce, Mrs. Freeman spun out the frustrations latent in this marriage through nearly three hundred pages; other complications are almost as thin. And one may also dismiss Maria Edgham, like Ellen Brewster of *The Portion of Labor,* as a tedious bore.

So much for *By the Light of the Soul* as another unsuccessful novel. It is rewarding however as a comment on Mrs. Freeman's emotional and spiritual growth, especially on her conception of the "old maid." For she would never forget that her own marriage had come very late.

The correspondences between her formative experiences and Maria's are striking. The Edghams, like the Wilkinses, are dominating mother and weak but lovable father; the daughter is bright, pretty, greatly conscious of her prettiness, emotionally insecure, and proud; there is a younger sister—sometimes loved; the father is the favorite parent; both mother and father die before Maria has outgrown her need for their protective love; she has a career which partly satisfied her demand for prestige; whatever the sentimental sound and fury of her involvement with men, she is too proud to be capable of love; the solution is "losing herself" in dependence upon a woman, a dominant figure "outside the pale."[33] At every point, Maria's beauty, pride, and strength of will are underlined.

Strongly religious, she moves through a development from rebellion against a persecuting Jehovah through nature mysticism into an ultimate dependence upon an incomplete and suffering God, known by mystical experience.[34] The final retreat from the conflict between drives toward mastery and toward love is the substitution of the love of God for the love of a man, and the renunciation of all ambition. " '[Maria] has been a little ill, but she is much better.' "[35]

Only at the close does the novel move away from the writer's emotional and spiritual development as it has been traced in these pages. And why this divagation at the close? Though another explanation is possible, the simplest is that Mrs. Freeman preferred to avoid marriage as a solution because it would lead her readers toward understanding of the novel's autobiographical elements.

On March 6, 1907, she answered a letter from a Miss Todd, a nurse, who had known her slightly at Mount Holyoke. After a few lines about autographing one of her books and the Mount Holyoke reminiscence already quoted, she wrote of her life in Metuchen: "I am living here in New Jersey, still pegging away at novels and stories, keeping house horribly, and not managing at all well my servants, angora cat and bull terrier. My husband I don't believe in managing, and he is so good he doesn't need it anyway.

"We are having a new house built, and expect to move on the first of May. The new house is on a hill with better drainage, so I hope not to need you in your professional capacity, but I hope that if you are in the vicinity you will come and see me some time. It is a grand thing to be a good nurse [;] I dare say you have done more good in the world than I. Of course I have much to be thankful for because I have been able to write and succeed (if you really do remember me, you must be astonished that I have succeeded) but after all there are other things, and good nurses among them. . . ."[36]

The house, a pleasant spready structure, vaguely colonial in design, was completed in the summer of 1907. The Freemans moved in; then, as Mrs. Freeman wrote to Marian Allen, the difficulties began: "It has in some respects been the hardest summer of my life. . . . I have had so much to do about this house. It is not really finished yet [September 23]. So much has come upon me. I have had to cajole electricians and hardware men and all sorts of men to do work which didn't belong to them to get anything whatever done. . . . I have been trying to get the sidewalk laid or rather Charlie has and doesn't seem to make out much, and I have serious thoughts of getting the Chinese laundryman or the barber to undertake it. . . .

"Sometimes I wish I could have a little toy house, in which I could do just as I pleased, cook a meal if I wanted to, and fuss around generally. Lettie and Leila are very good, but I have to do about as Lettie says, if we are to keep her, and we could not do without her. If I had my little toy house nobody could say anything, and if I get what I may for this serial I don't know but I shall have it. . . . Thank fortune I am allowed to run the upstairs. Of course it is no worse for me than for any woman who has an old family servant who thinks she owns the whole thing. It is unlucky that I have such a New England streak and do so want to amuse myself with housekeeping as a change from writing.

"I went to Randolph in June and stayed for two weeks and was ill nearly all the time when there. That is all the vacation I have had. . . . My in-laws have been away all summer at Lake George.

"Metuchen has every summer a new fad. This summer it was riding horseback. I went to a meet at Mrs. Carvahlo's. Her race track is the scene of the equestrian performances. I drove with some of my in-laws, and watched the show, and it was very funny. Harriet [Alden] rides her new horse, name John, but that day she was driving and looking on. Carolyn rode Merrylegs, or rather she sat on her. None of the women seemed to be riding much, but to simply sit on their horses, and mighty thankful for that!

"They have a riding mistress from Plainfield. She used to be in the Wild West Show and the Hippodrome, but I am assured that she is from one of the oldest families in Plainfield. Her stage age is nineteen and the Aldens have had her to luncheon. She told Carolyn she was so sorry that she didn't know that she wanted to go to Europe this summer, because the Hippodrome went over, and she could have gone with them as well as not.

"Miss Buffalo Bill (I can't remember her name) rode around the ring in a dashing manner. She is a rather pretty girl and has very gracious and condescending manners. . . . Then came the circus stunt. Everybody shivered when the whisper went around that Miss Buffalo Bill was about to ride Aristocrat. . . . She made an awful fuss about mounting, but appeared to do so at the peril of her life, but I am inwardly convinced that Aristocrat would have stood like a hitching post if she had wanted him to. Aristocrat is a big black horse and he wears bracelets on both front legs and his eyes stand out a good deal—makes you think of Pharaoh's horses. I didn't see any fire coming out of his nostrils, but I suppose she does that sometimes. Miss Buffalo Bill galloped about the track. I thought she favored Aristocrat's front legs a good deal, and depended more on the back ones. Maybe he stumbles. Then she galloped up before her admiring audience of women, and dismounted with grace.

"Then Mrs. Carvahlo insisted that I go out and speak to Aristocrat. So I did. You know I am cowardly in streaks and I am not afraid of speaking to horses. So I spoke to Aristocrat, and he was very amiable. Mrs. Carvahlo wanted me to take off my gloves and pat him, and I did. Then when I got back to the carriage in safety, she calmly informed me that Aristocrat liked me. If he hadn't, he would have struck out at me. I was also told that it took four men to put his bits in. All of which I don't believe a word of. . . . Mrs. Carvahlo kept leading more horses up to the carriage for me to speak to and I didn't mind as long as she kept the head end first, but I was awfully afraid she wouldn't. We had little cakes and punch, and the way the women ate and drank and still sat on their horses was really noble. The meet has been my one really large dissipation this summer.

". . . I undertook to write a serial in two months, and I have been ill and am now better, and writing three thousand words per day to get the serial done. Now Sallie [Freeman] has returned to her Brooklyn Polytechnic, and Gussie to her Pratt Institute, and Mother Freeman and Janie contemplate going abroad in two weeks. . . . I had thought that Charlie and I should have about two weeks vacation and go somewhere in October, but now Charlie has gone in for local politics . . . and I think I shall have to stay where I am. I can't leave him alone with so many of his family away. It seems mean. After I get my serial done I shall have plenty of amusement in fixing my upstairs rooms."[37]

Though much is to be said about the serial novel, it must be postponed for a word about *The Fair Lavinia and Other Stories,* published late in 1907. It contains stories originally used by *Harper's New Monthly* during 1907 and the preceding three or four years. "Gold" has the strength and intensity of Mrs. Freeman's early writing; the others, which pivot on the crotchets of the New England gentry, are thin and precious.

The serial turned off at three thousand words per day was *The Shoulders of Atlas,* written on commission for the *New York Herald's* "Anglo American Competition." A full page spread in the magazine section of the *Herald* for January 12, 1908 bore the first public announcement of this event. Mary E. Wilkins Freeman of the United States would engage Max Pemberton of England in a duel of narrative skill: on succeeding Sundays the *Herald* would print installments of Mrs. Freeman's *The Shoulders of Atlas,* a realistic novel of New England life, and Mr. Pemberton's *Sir Richard Escombe,* "a swashbuckling romance of old England." It was to be nation against nation and romance against realism, a titanic conflict. The public would "referee" the contest and register its preference by filling out ballots included with each installment. The winning author would receive a prize of five thousand dollars.

The inspired illustrator captured the spirit of the occasion by presenting on the left an heroic female figure, Columbia (Mrs. Freeman) mounted upon a curvetting white charger, the American Pegasus. On the right appeared a dour John Bull (Mr. Pemberton) balanced precariously on a testy black. In the background stands the great American public tensely awaiting the clarion which will speed the coursers into the international contest.

The element of the ludicrous is so obvious in this affair that it must be reported with an edge of satire. We of this advanced age are so clearly above such journalistic shenanigans that not even our crudest sheets would attempt an Anglo-American contest. But is there not something rather pleasing in this competition, based as it is on the conviction that newspaper readers would be sufficiently interested in a more or less literary issue to fill out ballots and mail them week by week? One suspects that no editor would have that conviction today.

Anyway America won! On May 24 the *Herald* announced: "Mrs. Freeman has won a great victory in the Anglo-American competition, defeating her rival by more than 14,000 votes. To her will therefore be awarded the $5,000 prize offered by the *Herald,* in addition to the original money paid for *The Shoulders of Atlas.*" Whatever her estimate of the glory, she could hardly question the monetary reward for those months of frenzied writing:

From the *Herald* for serial rights—$5,000
The prize in the competition—$5,000
Book rights to Harpers—about $10,000

Financially *The Shoulders of Atlas* was the consummate triumph of her career. It also came at the right moment, for that twenty thousand paid for the new house.[38]

Though writing under such conditions might well produce inferior stuff, *The Shoulders of Atlas* is certainly Mrs. Freeman's strongest novel of the Metuchen years as it is also superior to all but the two or three best pieces of the Randolph period. Wisely she returned to New England life: the setting is "East Westland," a small shoe town much like her own Randolph. The people of the novel might have walked directly out of "A New England Nun" or *Pembroke*. Structurally, the new novel also resembles *Pembroke,* for it is a series of variations on a single theme developed in the lives of closely connected characters.

It is the theme, principal or subordinate, of much realistic tragedy. "Everyone bore, seen or unseen, the burden of his or her world upon straining shoulders. The grand pathetic tragedy, inseparable from life, moved multiple at the marriage feast."

Mrs. Freeman wrote of the disparity between the strength of the shoulders of the shoe-worker, Henry Whitman and of his wife Sylvia, and the burden which they must bear. For bitter and rebellious Henry, life had always been a grim struggle against poverty. When he inherited a fine house and a competence from a distant relative, the burden seemed to fall away; but he soon discovered that he was unfitted for a life of ease, that his years of drudgery had dried up all the springs of sensitivity and enjoyment. Ultimately he slipped back to his old bench to recover a kind of negative satisfaction in his work.

The burden of his wife Sylvia was a tormented conscience, a New England conscience paid less than its due, a life of perfect integrity. Sylvia Whitman is another Jane Field. Knowing that the property which she and Henry had inherited actually belonged to Rose Fletcher under an earlier and supposedly effective will, she concealed this knowledge in order to retain the estate. There was no joy in her new comfort, for the mere presence of Rose was a steady reminder of her guilt. Only in the final chapter do we learn the nature of the sin. If the situation is hackneyed, one must still recognize that

Mrs. Freeman handled it well, that her probing of the tortured spirit of Sylvia Whitman is subtle and convincing.

Her "Miss" Farrell bears the burden of beauty and of a nature which demanded too much tribute to beauty. ". . . Possibly the knowledge of it made her demand too much, long for too much, so that people dimly realized it and were repelled instead of being attracted. I think she loved her husband for a long time after he left her. I think she loved women better than a woman usually does, and women could not abide her."[39] Lucinda Hart, the spinster tavern keeper, was groundlessly suspected of poisoning Miss Farrell and suffered the torment of social ostracism.

The burden of Lucy Ayres was an intensely erotic nature which drove her to pathetic devices of intrigue. Written with a full evocation of the rigid sexual code of the village and equal sympathy for one who could not live within it, this episode becomes intensely poignant.

The Shoulders of Atlas is a valuable complement to Mrs. Freeman's earlier comment on New England ways and character. Moving away from the theme of neurotic pride, it touches other abnormalities fostered by material poverty and an overly rigid cultural ideal. In thought and observation, it is a distinguished novel. The prose is always adequate and frequently pungent and suggestive in the manner of the early stories. Structurally, however, *The Shoulders of Atlas* is a poor thing; for Mrs. Freeman could not bring herself to attempt the hard thinking about incident and complication which her theme of "burdens" seems to require. She had undertaken a realistic subject, realistic in the sense that it seems to demand a matching of broadly typical traits with broadly typical incidents. Her plot draws much too heavily upon a hocus-pocus of concealed and altered wills and melodramatic poisoning. And the commonplace conclusion—a general pairing off of all unattached males and females—is merely a reiteration of the Victorian assurance that love is best.

Mrs. Freeman was ill in November or December of 1908, and she would never again attempt the feverish productivity of 1907. During the next two years she wrote only a chapter for Harper's collaborative novel, *The Whole Family,* and a dozen stories for various periodicals—*Harper's, Harper's Bazaar, Harper's Weekly, Collier's, The Ladies Home Journal.* If the peak of her critical reputation was reached by 1895, if the Twain dinner of 1905 was her richest honor as writer and woman, 1908 probably represents the highest point of her popular reputation. Absurd as the *Herald's* contest seems in retrospect, it was a great stunt in an age avid for stunts; and it carried the name of Mary Wilkins Freeman to thousands who had never heard it before. They could have read Dreiser, but they did not; they did read Mrs. Freeman, believing that she was one of the few advanced writers of the age.

Of course there were press interviews, one of which yields a useful note: "Mrs. Freeman meets the trite question, 'Do you like New Jersey as well as Massachusetts [she was never popularly associated with Vermont] and New York as well as Boston?' with a wavering and expressive, 'Well'—

"It is not necessary to say more.

" 'Oh, but I may in time,' she adds. 'The people here are very kind, indeed, and very likable.' "[40]

In March came a letter which offered a higher price than had ever before been bid for a Freeman story. "A young editor, knowing that I have the pleasure of your acquaintance has begged me to ask you for a story. He is the editor of the very popular Red Book . . . and has a number of very distinguished names among his contributors. He authorizes me to offer you one thousand dollars for a story of about five thousand words in length, preferably with a hint of Thanksgiving festivities.

"Faithfully yours,

JEANETTE GILDER"[41]

Max Pemberton testified in May to her solid English reputation: "Let me hasten to admit that there is no name more honored in England than that of Mary E. Wilkins. We have always been ready to place her among the first of American realists."[42]

The Nation's critic called *The Winning Lady and Others* (1909) "the best collection of short stories that Mrs. Freeman has published."[43] More accurately, it might be termed her most immediately pleasing collection. Lacking the pungency of the two first volumes, it offers greater variety of theme, some delightful touches of humor, an easy and flexible style, and an engaging mellowness of mood.

"A New Year's Resolution," a short incident centered in that stock character of homely fiction, the hen-pecked husband; "Flora and Hannah," a pallid improvisation on valentines and rival lovers; "The Winning Lady," a mild satire on cheating at bridge; "Her Christmas," the story of a little girl who stole her own Christmas stocking—these are inconsequential trifles. But the volume has better things to offer: two exquisite studies in child psychology, "Little-Girl-Afraid-of-a-Dog" and "The Joy of Youth"; "Billy and Susy," a droll anecdote about two old sisters who quarrelled over the identity of their pet kittens; a fine character study, "Eliza Sam"; above all, two of Mrs. Freeman's strongest stories, "The Selfishness of Amelia Lamkin" and "Old Woman Magoun."

CHAPTER Nine

In these years Mrs. Freeman enjoyed her house. The exterior would not be lovely until the awkward angles of gable and dormer were softened by a growth of ivy; the interior was superbly planned. The hall, entered directly from the porch, was a room of noble proportions. Since it had many windows, and walls timbered with yellow pine, it seemed bright even on dull days. The colors in paintings and oriental rugs were rich and warm; before the fire lay a tawny tiger skin. The library, which adjoined the far end of the hall, had its fireplace and bookshelves—a pleasant nook for reading. On the left, the dining room opened hospitably into the hall. It was an airy sunny house planned for ample ventilation, for Mrs. Freeman found the summer heat of New Jersey very trying.

She "had the say" about the rooms upstairs. For her own small bedroom, she had a four-poster, a handsome highboy, a drum table, a Chinese lacquer chair. Her study was a small adjoining room, just large enough to hold a typewriter on its table, another small table with a few books, and an old-fashioned chair between the tables. They were placed by a window overlooking a thicket of gum trees, white birches, and silver-stemmed beeches.[1]

Growing more interested in her house, Mrs. Freeman found less time for writing. Even more dangerous to her career was her gradual loss of hearing. Only a brazen person can easily cope with deafness: to say again and again, Sorry, but I didn't hear, was a humiliation which she would not accept. She would pretend to understand though her replies showed that she had heard almost nothing. Since she had always depended to a degree upon incidents from life for her stories, incidents reported by friends and relatives, her growing deafness would limit this source of materials.[2]

The ever-present sense of growing old was perhaps the wriest savor of these years. She had been a pretty woman; she was even then charming in her soft browns and grays. Her smoothly rounded arms and lovely neck and shoulders were still youthful. Her face—well, there were lines, and the mouth drooped pathetically at the corners. Yet she loved youth and refused to grow old.[3] She was, one feels, clearly expressing her own thoughts in the words given to Viola Longstreet in "The Amethyst Comb": " 'My dear, you [Jane Carew] insisted upon growing old—I insisted upon remaining young. You laid hold of age and held him although you had your complexion and your shape and your hair. I, my dear, have held youth so tight that he has almost choked to death, but held him I have.' "[4]

She was worried too by her husband's condition: he had returned to the heavy drinking of his bachelor days and was also using veronal. In 1909 he spent some time in a New York City sanitarium,[5] but the marriage survived this testing.

Mrs. Freeman still cherished her New England ties. She visited Hattie and Edmund Belcher and Mary Wales each year; she was "helping" not only Mary John but also the related Thompsons, Caleb and Sarah. She was fond of the Tolmans—Irving, Edith, her namesake Mary Eleanor, and the younger daughter Augusta. She decided that Augusta, a winning and imaginative girl with striking dark eyes, was really her favorite child. Mrs. Freeman said Augusta was "born with a lamp within."[6] She remembered Vermont and Brattleboro too but in a different way: "Often," she wrote to Miss Allie Morse, "my heart turns to Brattleboro, with an old homesick longing after all these years. I am not sure that even Massachusetts, the state of my birth, is as dear to me as Vermont. I know just how the Mountain looks with its winter colors of rose, and blue, and mauve, and I wish I could see it, and all the people who have not forgotten me. Oh well, some day I may look in on you and the mountain."[7]

Annie Alden, one of her closest friends in Metuchen, died in 1912.[8] Her own sixtieth birthday came in this year though her friends thought her to be much younger.[9] If her writing was by this time work and little else, she was still "pegging away" at a reduced pace. In the six years, 1909-1914, she wrote about three dozen short stories and several slight articles for *Harper's Monthly* and other periodicals.

There was also the short satirical novel, *The Butterfly House* of 1912. In it Mrs. Freeman paid her respects to women's clubs. Though the subject had its possibilities, they were not realized in this preposterous tale of "Fairbridge" or Metuchen.

Some of the *Harper's Monthly* short stories were collected in 1914 as *The Copy Cat and Other Stories*. Nearly all are set in New England villages; six are finely imagined studies of the character traits of youngsters of old stock, especially of their reversion to ancestral patterns. "The Cock of the Walk" is the lightest and most engaging.

Johnny Trumbull reverted to the traits of his grandfather. Though his own people were pious gentle folk "who wouldn't say boo to a goose," the boy was a fighter. He whopped the youngsters in his school; he even bowled over his spinster Aunt Janet when she attempted to whip him. After that atrocious lapse Johnny expected retribution. But Aunt Janet admired his pluck and was delighted to see that there was another fighter in the Trumbull family. She gave him his grandfather's fine old watch. Though slight enough, in all conscience, "The Cock of the Walk" is a delightful story—straight and simple in the telling, and moving because the writer so obviously likes her Johnny Trumbull.[10]

It was in this year that Austria declared war against Serbia, a distant affair which seemed for a time unimportant to the

Freemans in maple-shaded Metuchen. Later, world war would touch them too.

Mr. Thomas R. Wells of *Harpers* wrote encouraging news of Mrs. Freeman's English following: shilling editions of *Pembroke, Madelon, The Portion of Labor,* and *The Debtor* were to be issued.[11] This was also the time of the passing of two dear friends—Carolyn Alden[12] in Metuchen and Mary Wales in Randolph.

Mary John died on August 4,[13] and Mrs. Freeman did not go to Randolph. Soon, however, she was obliged to learn of the shabby aftermath. Dissolute Johnny Wales had married shortly before his sister's death, married a Boston woman who was interested in the property he would soon inherit. Johnny had talked grandly about its value. Knowing that her brother could not be trusted with the family place, Miss Wales, using the advice of Irving Tolman, had drawn a will which limited her brother to the income and vested title in other kin. When she died, Johnny and his wife took possession and employed a shrewd attorney to contest the will. Next year the will was proved: Johnny and his wife had lost their case. Soon she disappeared with everything she could carry away, leaving Johnny with the use of fifty acres which he refused to farm. When the attorney sued for fees, Johnny lost his fifty acres. Mrs. Freeman eventually took four thousand dollars in settlement of her claim for six thousand.[14]

Her December 29 letter to Edith Tolman reveals her sympathy with Irving, who had been drawn into the case because he had advised Miss Wales; her dismay as she thought of the jewelry which she had given her friend and "the old pieces of furniture which made my early broken-up home"—all at the disposal of John and his wife. "John is going a bee-line to his comeuppance."

The same long disjointed letter supplies flashes of her life in Metuchen: "We have a vocalion, but personally I don't care for it very much. . . . I did go to one very smart luncheon in New York. Had a pretty dress, too—green velvet trimmed with moleskin. . . . I am so glad Augusta [Mrs. Tolman's younger daughter] likes her pink corals, dear child.

"I have been in bed twelve days and now can sit up only a little while. . . . I have had a close call from bronchial pneumonia. . . . Then back of the whole nervous exhaustion which fondly lingers on. I have really not been well for a long time. . . . Now with the prospect of not being able to work for some time, I am worried about them [Aunt Lizzie and Uncle Caleb Thompson, to whom she had been sending money]. . . . I am writing things twice over.

"I look like a freak, have lost so much flesh. . . . I shall bob up all at once, must. Charlie is so worried about me I can't do anything else. . . . I hope I shall be able to go to New York New Year's, our fifteenth anniversary.

"Pollyanna is not in it with me. In bed Christmas day, so glad to have a bed. I must stop, am tuckered out. So glad to be able to write till I am tuckered out. . . . Taxes way up this year. So glad to have a house on which taxes can go up, might be a chicken coop. . . . Can't get any oysters here, had to live entirely on milk shakes today. So glad because oysters might give me ptomaine poisoning and then to think of saving so many innocent oysters' lives.

"I simply must stop. Best of love, and best wishes to you and Irving and the children for the New Year. God bless you all, for you are dear to

"CHERIE"[15]

Our entry into the war on April 6, 1917 appears to have been for a time a favorable turn for Mrs. Freeman. In the "Liberty Loan" drives, the speeches of the "Minute Men," the screaming posters of "Hun atrocities," the exciting stories of "big pushes" which she read every night in the *New York Evening Journal,* she found an interest which took her mind away from the annoyances of daily life. She became an ardent patriot; she hated the Huns with satisfying bitterness.[16] When asked to contribute to Louis Raemaker's *America in War* (1918),[17] an anthology of lurid cartoons of "atrocities" with accompanying texts by seventy Americans, she responded with a bit of spirited verse:

"Wake Up, America!"

"America wakes! The White Christ has called her;
She has seen the devils abroad in the world;
Evil flaunting himself has appalled her;
To the War-wind of Heaven her flag is unfurled!

"America wakes—with his murder and lust
Let the Hun take the path he has carved into hell.
No longer blaspheming the Cross with his trust.
America wakes, the sick world shall be well. . . ."

Later she would come to feel the war as "a general upheaval of all familiar things,"[18] but in 1918 it was exciting.[19]

In the autumn of 1918, Harpers issued *Edgewater People,* stories written in the preceding four years for *Harper's Monthly* and other periodicals. As Mrs. Freeman's last volume, it is, as it should be, a collection of Yankee village stories. The villages are called "Barr Center," "South Barr," "Barr-by-the-Sea," and "Leicester," all of which were settled, the writer tells us, from an original "Barr."[20] She was apparently thinking of the settling of Randolph and adjacent towns from early Braintree.

If some of the stories are thin and sentimental, several reach her best level. "Value Received" looks back to the theme of *Jerome*—the pride which results in compulsive generosity—but manages this subject in humorous style. Ann and Dora Matthews are elderly spinsters, genteel, finely bred, deeply conscious of their good old name, and proudly independent of spirit. They are also exceedingly poor, and their dependence upon the generosity of wealthy Sarah Edgewater is a galling humiliation. Outwardly appreciative, they hate their benefactor. But eventually comes an opportunity for repayment:

Sarah complains that she cannot find a hat suitable to wear at her niece's wedding. Dora seizes this opportunity to make a hat as a gift. " 'And for once, just once, Sarah Edgewater will have to take, and we can give. . . . ' "[21]

"Ann looked at her sister, and her wan face gathered intensity. Her cheeks bloomed; her eyes brightened. 'And,' said she, very slowly, with almost terrible emphasis, 'if Sarah Edgewater does not take that bonnet and wear it to the wedding—' "[22]

The hat is a bonnet, an "affair of flowery black and shimmering silver and long floating black ribbons,"[23] suitable for a little old lady, ridiculous for buxom middle-aged Miss Edgewater. There is also the problem of wedding gift for Margy Ellerton, which Ann solves by untombing a glass shade containing a stiff group of wax tuberoses and lilies of the valley. These too, Ann vows, must be accepted.

Mrs. Freeman was in a genial mood when she wrote "Value Received"; the gifts were accepted and admired, for Sarah and Margy were shrewd enough to penetrate to the inner motive for giving. And the old ladies departed stronger in spirit, able at last to feel a little of their old independence.

Sarah Edgewater appears in several of the tales and is the central figure of the collection. She has the sturdiest elements of New England character. A spinster whose life would ordinarily be called unhappy, she has attained stability only after a prolonged struggle. More wordly, less neurotic than Maria Edgham (*By the Light of the Soul*), she seems typical of many of the finer women one meets in New England villages. Poverty is not one of Sarah's problems; she is in comfortable circumstances. Mrs. Freeman maneuvers her through a number of quietly dramatic episodes involving family snarls and emotional upheavals. Though the situations are not worth recording, it is interesting to notice that Miss Edgewater is up to all of them. For she is a warm and sturdy woman, unflawed by sentimentality or perfectionistic demands. At long, long last, we are given a heroine without heroics.

By 1919 the war had been won, and Americans were moving toward "normalcy" and the Jazz Age. For Mrs. Freeman, now nearing seventy, grim experience was drawing close. It was hard to lose Mr. Alden, that best of friends at *Harper's* for over thirty years.[24] It was harder, one assumes, for her to arrange the commitment of her husband to the New Jersey State Hospital for the Insane at Trenton. But by this time the Doctor was far gone in alcoholism.

Early in 1921, he escaped and returned to his home; no doubt there had been some improvement in his condition. He made out a will in August, naming his wife and sisters as principal beneficiaries. Soon he was again drinking heavily, drinking necessarily the dubious stuff supplied by bootleggers. Mrs. Freeman and her advisers arranged for his return to the Trenton Institution in October.[25] He was released in November and lived for a short time in his home. Then he moved to the house of his chauffeur, Mohring; Mrs. Freeman obtained a legal separation. Next summer he made another will, leaving most of his estate to Mr. and Mrs. Mohring.[26]

Life for Mrs. Freeman seemed stale and bitter: she returned to her questioning moods and to morbid preoccupation with the problem of evil. She had her small compensations, for she could always call Ashby, her colored chauffeur, and set out for a drive through the pleasant North Jersey countryside. Her flowers—a superb circular clump of rose bushes—offered their moments of grace.[27] She attempted to put this feeling into verse.

> "Save for the roses I am blest to hold
> Sweeter than love and lovely as the day,
> If I were made of precious beaten gold
> I'd count myself as dross to fling away."[28]

On the night of March 7, 1923, Dr. Freeman died suddenly at Mohring's home.[29] At his wife's order, the body was brought home for the funeral ceremony.[30]

Death did not close this episode. The second will included

bequests of only two hundred dollars for each of the four sisters, of one dollar for his wife; the total remainder of the estate, later valued at $225,000, was bequeathed to the Mohrings.[31] Mrs. Freeman and the Doctor's sisters contested this will and broke it after a tedious litigation. To avoid further legal bother, Mrs. Freeman sold her rights in the estate to the sisters.[32]

Soon she would be writing her sympathy to Edith Tolman after the death of Irving and alluding to her own husband: "It is a wonderful thing to be able to feel that your husband was your unshattered ideal. I cannot feel badly because I can hardly say that of my husband, for I doubt very much if I ever had an ideal to shatter anyway, and I reckon Charles may have thought I smashed his to smithereens. After all my husband had splendid traits. . . . Sometimes I think the Volstead Act was what really finished him. If he could have had good whiskey he might have weathered the gale. But that is over, and if I can hold to my religion, he may have better now. And if you dare laugh at that! !"[33]

Though the last years of her life were lonely, they had many moments of brightness. For a time she had only her servants with her in the big house; then in the winter of 1925 Hattie and Edmund Belcher came to stay for a time. She could slip back into old customs—checkers with Edmund, and rubbers of three-handed bridge every evening. She was now very deaf but could occasionally see that even deafness has its comic aspect. She put it into a tiny dialogue:

> "Come."
> "Did anybody speak?"
> "Come to supper, you must be hungry."
> "Yes, I am tired."
> "Come to supper."
> "Yes, I see the blue-bird."[34]

When the Belchers returned to Randolph, Mrs. Freeman's cousin on the Wilkins side, Mrs. Arthur B. Mann, lived with her. In January, 1926, Mrs. Freeman wrote to Mrs. Severance: "I am living along here with a cousin . . . Carrie Mann. Her husband is a cotton broker in New York, and a very nice sort. He comes out twice a week. . . . I am trying to write if I can ever get over an exclusive form of grip. . . . I am just home from New Brunswick, New Jersey—a business errand and marketing. Life is a hustle, at least for me, but perhaps it is better so. . . . I must have a very tough streak in me. I did not look so but time has proved it. . . . I am not strong but I live along and fear I shall continue to until I look like John D. Rockefeller, in spite of cold cream. I really wonder if he ever had his barber put cold cream on him. . . . "[35] She wrote later in the year to Mrs. Allen that she felt "like a small and ineffectual push."

On April 23, the members of the American Academy of Letters—George Pierce Baker, Childe Hassam, William Lyons Phelps, Stuart Sherman, Grant Mitchell, Dr. Paul Shorey, Lorado Taft, Dean Wilbur L. Cross, Percy Mackaye, and others—gathered to witness the presentation of the Academy medal to Miss Cecila Beaux for distinction in painting and the Howells medal for Mrs. Freeman for distinction in fiction.[36] It was Hamlin Garland who presented the Howells medal, saying, "Book after book flowed from her pen each containing unfaltering portraits of lorn widowhood, crabbed age, wistful youth, cheerful drudgery, patient poverty, defiant spinsterhood, and many other related and individual types of character, each with proper background of hill, town, or village street; all making an unparalleled record of New England life. . . ."[37]

"Unfaltering portraits . . . crabbed age . . . unparalleled record—" such were the phrases of an old friend who surely wished to say the right thing briefly and kindly. None is flatly wrong, none says what the modern reader is likely to feel as he remembers Mrs. Freeman's writings. For Mr. Garland was bracketing her among realists and local colorists without capturing her special quality.

It is first sheer readability. She pleased Howells and James, and she was read avidly by thousands who could be interested in just any good story. It is hard to resist the tale which is clear, direct, poignant in detail, grounded in basic motives, and simple and warm in feeling, and these were qualities which could be expected in the Freeman story whether the subject was "wistful youth" or "cheerful drudgery."

And it is pleasant to return to her stories because they distill the flavor of life in a New England village. Writing of an old house, she expressed the feeling perfectly: "The rank and bitter emanations of life, as well as spices and sweet herbs and delicate perfumes, went to make up the breath which smote one in the face upon opening the door. Still it was not disagreeable, but rather a suggestive and poetical odor, which should affect one like a reminiscent dream." If this is only one side of the total effect of the stories, it is none the less a very real one; and it suggests her kinship with the poet Frost.

And the truth which seemed to her so sacred? It is not the truth of sociological surveys, for it would not and should not have occurred to her that she could use sampling techniques. In selecting characters and situations and traits, she was guided naturally by her own sensibility. She exaggerated the numerical importance of the women and of the elderly people; she made little attempt to represent fairly the variety of "adjustments" to village life which must have existed. It is hard to believe that no New England villagers of the last half century were able to come to fruitful terms with themselves and their culture, but no fully rounded figure appears in a Freeman story or novel. Though the great majority must have lived as easy, if mediocre, conformists, such people appear only rarely in the writings and then in minor roles. The reader gains no sense of their numerical weight in the towns.

Her truth is of a narrower and more precious kind—a superb understanding of the undefeated neurotics, occasionally men, more often women. Always they are dowered with the primary virtues of a traditional society—courage and loyalty and a strong sense of duty. If they are intensely individualistic, they must also bear the individual's burden of alienation from family and group and ultimately from self. Neither code nor church can bring them peace, yet their gestures of revolt are never quite conclusive, never fully satisfying. Necessarily, they are frustrated and neurotic to a degree. Yet the thrust toward love and achievement and a sense of belonging cannot be killed. They are all—these striving neurotics—seeking a wholeness of spirit and a fullness of life almost impossible of attainment in the village as Mrs. Freeman knew it.

That much is the fruit of sympathetic understanding, but there is something more. For in the loose and popular sense of the term, Mrs. Freeman was a philosophic writer; for herself and her major characters, she sought meaning in life and believed that fulfillment and happiness were not unattainable. And it is interesting to look back at several of the clues woven into her stories of strivers.

One has been called the mood of tragicomedy. In many of the stories, it is nothing more than a literary trick, an easy device for untieing the knots of a plot prevailingly tragic in cast; in others, however, it seems to have been felt with some honesty. It also appears in the letters. And at its best, the mood of tragicomedy rises to the level of a homespun, regional wisdom. It becomes an acceptance of life as it is and a canny reliance on humor for breaking tension and avoiding meaningless conflict and rebellion.

Another clue emerges as one thinks back to the stories and novels which probe neurotic pride. It was the recognition of the need for self-esteem, for confidence as a phase of growth in capacity to love. The analysis is most seaching in *Pembroke* and *Jerome;* the positive suggestion, now familiar to the Freudian revisionists, is in the stories "A Tardy Thanksgiving" and "A Solitary."

But the most resonant note is one that sounds in nearly all of Mrs. Freeman's writing and finds pithy expression in "The

Revolt of Mother": "Nobility of character manifests itself at loop-holes when it is not provided with large doors." In a New England village of the second half of the last century, in such a village today, wherever the middle class is hanging on within an order in which the best of middle class virtues are threatened, this tactic of seeing and using loop-holes makes sense. It is the tactic of all those in industry, education, and government service who must "get things done" without overturning the system and without heroics or the invocation of high, literary ideals. Conceivably, it might have thematic value for the "sensitive" young men and women who write the novels of this era.

"Unfaltering portraits of lorn widowhood, crabbed age, and wistful youth"—yes, Mrs. Freeman wrote them all. But Mr. Garland should have remembered the Mary E. Wilkins whom he knew at Edgar Chamberlain's in the early 'Nineties. He should have remembered, and he should have accented her thrust toward all that is not lorn and crabbed and wistful. There was life in this woman and in nearly everything she wrote.

Anyway, her own response to the ritual of the medal brings us back to solid feminine realities. She wrote to Mrs. Allen: "I made only a bit of a speech—had to cut it. . . . I think they were relieved to have so little said by me. . . . My dress was all right, I think. At the last minute I had to get a rose-colored slip to wear under it as there is a tinge of rose in the gray. . . . I had a rose-colored embroidered scarf and my gray hat lined with rose.

"I am getting the usual aftermath of honor, catty letters and more honors. . . . My gold medal weighs a ton and I don't know what to do with it. Hamlin Garland told me I could hock it. . . . I am going to display it to a few friends, shall take it to New Brunswick to P. J. Young's store where the girls all know me and will be interested, and to my lawyer in Perth Amboy. Finally I shall put it in my safe deposit box in Boston although I doubt if a burglar would consider it. I simply don't know what to do with it!"[38]

More honors. On November 10, the National Institute of Arts and Letters elected Mrs. Freeman, along with Mrs. Wharton, Mrs. Deland, and Miss Repplier, to its membership. Here was distinction, indeed, for these were the first women writers to be honored by the Institute.[39] Membership did not involve custodianship of a gold medal.

Mrs. Freeman was now a very old lady and in precarious health, yet in letters, at least, she could give illness a twist of humor. "I have to diet," she wrote in September 1927 from the Crawford House, "which is difficult in a hotel. I am threatened with something which I don't think will get me. . . . No meat, eggs, corn, beans. I don't mind it, but it means living like I wasn't weaned."[40] The human body, she decided in 1929, "is not such a very good job. They simply do not match souls—out of alignment." Aged? "O deaf, I suppose I am! but I don't live up to it a bit."[41]

She did not live up to it. When she had dinner at Mrs. Carvahlo's, she broke into chortles when she saw the coffee bubbling and chuckling in a new percolator.[42] She became indignant at the Braintree home of a niece when thick slices of bread and butter were forced on the little girls of the family. "Bread and butter. Why, you'll make them heavy and pudgy. Little girls should be fed cowslips and butterfly wings."

If she had recently published only several stories and poems, she refused to think of her writing career as a finished thing. She was planning a sequel to *Pembroke*.[43]

Occasionally she drove down to Princeton to visit Mrs. Alpheus Hyatt, a blind old lady of ninety who still retained remarkable mental clarity. They spoke of death.[44] After one of their talks, Mrs. Freeman wrote to Mrs. Allen: "Annihilation to me is unimaginable. Change is not, but nothing really ceases to exist. . . . Such tremendous vitality as is in Mrs. Hyatt cannot cease to exist in some form. I think her soul deserves a splendid new house of flesh, and I know it will have it. . . . She will not descend from her heights. Of course you will understand that I believe in transmigration—almost."[45]

When Mrs. P. K. White of Brattleboro visited Mrs. Freeman, she noticed that her dressing gown was brave with the buttons of the naval uniform.[46] She talked frequently with Mrs. Mann of Hanson Tyler. By this time, the story had been reshaped in her memory: loving him, she had put him aside because he had no money. "But," she said, "if there is an afterlife, he is the one person I should like to see."[47]

In the autumn of the Wall Street crash, Mrs. Freeman visited Randolph and Brattleboro. It was good to be in these old towns again, to talk with Hattie and Edmund Belcher in the small south parlor of the house which had once been Grandfather Lothrop's. She insisted on going to a nearby lake which she had always loved. In the glow of the afternoon sun, she stood on the bank gazing at the reflection of gold and copper leaves in the water. "You don't know what this means to me," she said softly. She stayed for two weeks. Noticing her feebleness, Hattie and Edmund decided that she would not come to Randolph again.[48]

In Brattleboro, she saw Evelyn Severance, her friend of nearly sixty years. Though her hair was white, her blue eyes were clear and lovely, her figure straight and slim. They drove to a spot whence they could look over the roofs of the town and the trees bright with color to the dull green of the Connecticut and the curve of Mount Wantastiquet. Deep lights came into Mrs. Freeman's eyes as she stood looking—looking.[49]

During the winter of 1929-1930, she was very weak; yet she could write in February to Marion Boyd Allen of Boston: "I am stronger but do not yet count too much on my strength. My heart may suddenly rebel, and I feel out of the scheme. . . . As near as I can make out I have been tearing around for years when I was unable. Then the crash came and now I shall be better."[50] There was no withstanding the next crash, a heart attack early in March. The end came in the evening of March 15, 1930.[51]

Notes

CHAPTER ONE

[1] Mr. Herman W. French, Mr. Joseph Belcher, and Mr. William J. Good, of Randolph.

[2] Town Records of Randolph, Massachusetts. In nearly all treatments of Miss Wilkins' life preceding the *DAB* article, 1862 appeared as the date of birth.

[3] Mrs. E. K. Belcher, née Harriet Lothrop.

[4] J. A. Vinton, *The Vinton Memorial . . . A Genealogy of the Descendants of John Vinton . . . Also Several Allied Families,* Boston, 1858, pp. 340 et passim.

[5] Mr. Joseph E. Belcher.

[6] Mr. J. Edgar Chamberlin.

[7] Mrs. E. K. Belcher.

[8] E. B. Huntington, *A Genealogical Memoir of the Lo-Lathrop Family,* Ridgefield, Conn., 1884, pp. 319-320.

[9] Mrs. E. K. Belcher.

[10] Mrs. E. K. Belcher.

[11] Mr. J. E. Chamberlin.

[12] Mrs. E. K. Belcher.

[13] Mr. J. E. Chamberlin.

[14] W. R. Cutter, *Genealogical and Personal Memoirs of the Families of Boston and Eastern Massachusetts,* New York, 1908, vol. III, p. 1536.

[15] *Vital Records of Salem, Massachusetts, to the End of the Year 1849,* Salem, 1916-1925, vol. VI, p. 333.

[16] *Vital Records,* vol. IV, p. 470. "Amos S. Wilkins of Cambridge m. Mary W. Moulton [Salem], Sept. 2, 1827."

[17] Town Records of Randolph, Mass.

[18] *Randolph Register,* June 14, 1890, p. 2.

[19] *Vital Records,* vol. VI, p. 333.

[20] *Vital Records,* vol. IV, p. 470.

[21] H. W. Moulton, *The Moulton Annals,* Chicago, 1906, pp. 89 et passim.

[22] Moulton, p. 407.

[23] Mrs. E. K. Belcher.

[24] Mrs. E. K. Belcher.

[25] Mrs. E. K. Belcher.

[26] Mrs. E. K. Belcher.

[27] Mrs. E. K. Belcher, supplemented by a description in Mary E. Wilkins, *Pembroke,* New York, 1894, p. 235.

[28] Mrs. E. K. Belcher.

[29] Mrs. E. K. Belcher.

[30] John C. Labaree, *Proceedings of the One Hundred and Fiftieth Anniversary of the First Congregational Church, Randolph, Mass.*, Boston, 1881, p. 8.

[31] Mr. E. K. Belcher and Mr. J. E. Belcher.

[32] Mrs. E. K. Belcher.

[33] Mr. J. E. Belcher.

[34] Salem Town, *Salem Town's Second Reader, or the Speller's Companion,* Cooperstown, New York, 1844, p. 11.

[35] Mr. J. E. Belcher.

[36] Mrs. E. K. Belcher.

[37] Mrs. E. K. Belcher.

[38] Mary E. Belcher, "The Atherton Wales Homestead," Randolph, c. 1905, an unpublished paper in the collection of Mrs. E. K. Belcher.

[39] Mrs. E. K. Belcher.

[40] Mrs. E. K. Belcher, supplemented by *Pembroke,* p. 302.

[41] Mrs. E. K. Belcher.

[42] Mrs. E. K. Belcher.

[43] Mrs. Arthur B. Mann, née Caroline Wilkins.

[44] Harry R. Butman, *The History of Randolph, Massachusetts,* c. 1950, unpublished.

[45] Blanche E. Hazard, *The Boot and Shoe Industry in Massachusetts,* Cambridge, Mass., 1921, pp. 99 et passim.

[46] Mrs. E. K. Belcher.

[47] Labaree, pp. 136-137.

[48] Labaree, p. 48.

[49] Mr. J. E. Belcher.

[50] Mrs. E. K. Belcher.

[51] In the collection of Mrs. E. K. Belcher.

[52] Mrs. E. K. Belcher.

[53] Fred Lewis Pattee, "On the Terminal Moraine of New England Puritanism," *Sidelights on American Literature,* New York, 1922, p. 178.

[54] "The Prism," *Century,* LXII, July, 1901, p. 474.

[55] Mrs. C. E. Severance, née Evelyn Sawyer.

[56] Town Records, Randolph, Mass.

[57] Town Records, Brattleboro, Vermont. Deed of Wells Goodhue and wife to Eleanor L. Wilkins, July 21, 1866.

[58] United States Census.

[59] Mr. H. W. French.

[60] Quoted by Mary R. Cabot, *Annals of Brattleboro,* Brattleboro, 1921, vol. I, p. 556.

[61] Cabot, vol. II, pp. 572-573.

[62] Quoted by Cabot, vol. II, p. 719.

[63] Charles E. Crane, *Winter in Vermont,* New York, 1947, pp. 56 ff.

[64] Labaree, p. 48.

[65] Mr. J. E. Belcher.

[66] "The Burial Hill Declaration Adopted in 1865," C. G. Atkins and F. L. Fagley, *History of American Congregationalism,* Boston, 1942, p. 400.

[67] Joseph Haroutunian, *Piety versus Moralism: The Passing of New England Theology,* New York, 1932, p. 144.

[68] Mr. J. E. Belcher.

[69] Mrs. E. K. Belcher and Mr. J. E. Belcher.

[70] Mr. J. E. Belcher.

[71] Mrs. E. K. Belcher.

[72] Edwin S. Sanborn, *Social Changes in New England of the Past Fifty Years,* Boston, 1901, p. 13.

[73] Mrs. E. K. Belcher.

[74] Mrs. E. K. Belcher.

CHAPTER TWO

[1] Mr. George H. Clapp, of Brattleboro, who had a shop near Warren Wilkins'.

[2] Mrs. Robert Dunklee, who lives at 3 Chase Street and knows the traditions of the house and neighborhood.

[3] Mr. G. H. Clapp.

[4] Mrs. P. K. White, née Virginia Sargent, a classmate and lifelong friend.

[5] Mrs. C. E. Severance, née Evelyn Sawyer.

[6] Mrs. Robert Dunklee.

[7] Reverend Edward Dahl, Center Congregational Church, Brattleboro.

[8] M. H. P. Tyler, *Grandmother Tyler's Book,* ed. Frederick Tupper and Helen Tyler Brown, New York, 1925, p. 349, and Mrs. George W. Tyler.

[9] Henry Burnham, *Brattleboro . . . Early History,* Brattleboro, 1880, pp. 101-102.

[10] Mrs. Edward Twitchell, née Elizabeth Shuster, a friend.

[11] Mrs. C. E. Severance.

[12] Cabot, vol. II, p. 830.
[13] G. L. Walker, quoted by Cabot, vol. I, p. 552.
[14] Town Records of Brattleboro.
[15] Cabot, vol. I, p. 416.
[16] Mr. G. H. Clapp.
[17] Cabot, vol. II, pp. 844-846.
[18] *Reformer,* March 1, 1938, Section A. p. 1.
[19] Town Records of Brattleboro.
[20] Mrs. G. W. Tyler.
[21] S. D. Stow, *History of Mount Holyoke Seminary, 1837-1877,* Springfield, Mass., 1887, p. 161.
[22] Stow, p. 36.
[23] Dr. Cornelia Clapp, a Mount Holyoke student in the early '70's, later a faculty member.
[24] *Thirty-fourth Annual Catalogue of Mount Holyoke Seminary, 1870-1871,* Northampton, Mass., 1871, p. 20.
[25] M. D. E. Morse, "Reminiscences of the Early 'Seventies," *Mount Holyoke Alumnae Quarterly,* May, 1931, pp. 25-26.
[26] Stow, p. 231.
[27] Letter to Miss Helena L. Todd, March 6, 1907, from the collection of Miss Todd.
[28] Mr. Frederick Adams, Vermont Savings Bank, Brattleboro.
[29] Cabot, vol. II, p. 939.
[30] Mrs. C. E. Severance.
[31] Mrs. C. E. Severance and Pattee, *Sidelights,* pp. 177-178.
[32] Mrs. C. E. Severance.
[33] From a photograph in the collection of Dr. Allan D. Sutherland, "a Tyler," and the memories of Mrs. G. W. Tyler.
[34] Mrs. G. W. Tyler and Miss Helen Tyler Brown.
[35] Mrs. C. E. Severance; Mrs. E. B. Barrows of Brattleboro for courting customs.
[36] Dr. Allan D. Sutherland and Pension File, Naval Archives.
[37] Letter given to the writer by Mrs. John Steele Tyler, widow of Hanson Tyler's son, Emmaus, Pennsylvania.
[38] Mrs. C. E. Severance.
[39] Allan Nevins, *The Emergence of Modern America, 1865-1878,* New York, 1927, pp. 295 ff.
[40] Mrs. C. E. Severance.
[41] Cabot, vol. II, p. 855.
[42] Mr. Frederick Adams.
[43] Mrs. Nellie Root.
[44] Cabot, vol. II, p. 938.
[45] Mrs. C. E. Severance.

[46] Letter given to the writer by Mrs. John Steele Tyler.

[47] Mrs. C. E. Severance.

[48] H. W. Lanier, ed., "Introduction," *The Best Stories of Mary E. Wilkins,* New York, 1927, p. viii.

[49] *Dictionary of American Biography.*

[50] Lanier, pp. viii-x.

[51] Mrs. E. K. Belcher.

[52] Lanier, p. ix.

[53] *The Vermont Phoenix,* June 2, 1876, p. 2.

[54] Mrs. P. K. White.

CHAPTER THREE

[1] Mrs. P. K. White.

[2] Cabot, vol. II, p. 830.

[3] Cabot, vol. II, pp. 201-204.

[4] Mrs. Patrick Fenton, one of the neighbors during the Grove Street years.

[5] Mrs. C. E. Severance.

[6] Miss Florence Pratt, librarian of the Brooks Library, Brattleboro.

[7] Mrs. C. E. Severance.

[8] Mrs. G. W. Tyler.

[9] Mrs. G. W. Tyler and Tyler, p. 353.

[10] Commander Pierce Brown.

[11] Pension File, Naval Archives.

[12] Letter given to the writer by Mrs. John Steele Tyler.

[13] Commander Pierce Brown.

[14] Tyler, p. 187.

[15] Tyler, pp. 279 ff.

[16] Mrs. G. W. Tyler.

[17] Pattee, *Sidelights,* p. 177.

[18] U. S. Census.

[19] T. M. Adams, *Windham County, Basic Facts and Figures,* Burlington, Vermont, 1949, p. 3.

[20] *U. S. Census.*

[21] Adams, p. 3.

[22] *U. S. Census.*

[23] Adams, p. 3.

[24] *U. S. Census.*

[25] Adams, p. 3.

[26] Harold F. Wilson, *The Hill Country of Northern New England,* New York, 1936, p. 13.

[27] Wilson, p. 27.

[28] Wilson, p. 95.

[29] C. C. Nott, *Nation,* XLIX, November 21, 1889, p. 407 quoted by Wilson, p. 95.

[30] J. H. Walbridge, *Picturesque Putney, Newfane, Townshend, and Jamaica,* Brattleboro, 1901, p. 9.

[31] Stewart H. Holbrook, *The Yankee Exodus,* New York, 1950, pp. 264 *et passim.*

[32] Mrs. G. W. Tyler.

[33] *Brattleboro Daily Reformer,* July 30, 1913, p. 1.

[34] "Bank Smash," *Brattleboro Weekly Reformer,* June 16, 1880, p. 1.

[35] Cabot, vol. II, p. 939.

[36] Mrs. C. E. Severance.

[37] Mrs. G. W. Tyler.

[38] Mrs. Edward Twitchell.

[39] Lanier, p. ix.

[40] "The Beggar King," *Once upon a Time,* Boston, 1897, pp. 147 ff.

[41] *Vermont Phoenix,* April 1, 1881, p. 2.

[42] Lanier, p. ix.

[43] Cabot, vol. II, p. 840.

[44] "The Girl Who Wants to Write: Things to Do and Avoid," *Harper's Bazar,* XLVII, June, 1913, pp. 272 *et passim.*

[45] Mrs. P. K. White.

[46] Miss Allie Morse, a Brattleboro friend.

[47] Mrs. P. K. White.

[48] "Good Wits, Pen and Paper," G. H. Dodge et al., eds., *What Women Can Earn,* New York, 1899, pp. 28-29.

[49] "Two Old Lovers," *A Humble Romance and Other Stories,* New York, 1887, pp. 25-36.

[50] *The Boston Evening Transcript,* March 14, 1930, p. 13.

[51] *New York Times,* April 24, 1926, p. 7.

[52] Mrs. C. E. Severance and Miss Allie Morse.

[53] *The Vermont Phoenix,* April 20, 1883.

[54] Mrs. E. K. Belcher.

[55] *By the Light of the Soul,* New York, 1906, p. 211.

[56] Mrs. C. E. Severance.

[57] Mrs. C. E. Severance.

[58] Mr. Henry W. Lanier in conversation.

[59] *DAB*

[60] *A Humble Romance,* pp. 1-24.

[61] Perhaps an overly severe judgment. Charles Norman includes this

story in *A Golden Book of Love Stories,* New York, 1947, along with tales by Pushkin, Galsworthy, Maugham, Chekhov, de Maupassant.

[62] Town Records, Brattleboro.

[63] Mrs. E. K. Belcher.

[64] From a photograph in the collection of Mrs. E. K. Belcher.

[65] Mrs. Ellen T. Proctor.

[66] Mrs. E. K. Belcher.

[67] "The Girl Who Wants to Write," p. 272.

[68] Mrs. Ellen T. Proctor.

[69] Mr. William J. Good.

[70] Mrs. E. T. Proctor.

[71] Mrs. C. E. Severance.

[72] Mrs. E. K. Belcher.

[73] Mrs. E. K. Belcher.

CHAPTER FOUR

[1] XI, July 16, 1887, p. 30.

[2] XVII, June 25, 1887, p. 203.

[3] LXXV, September, 1887, p. 203.

[4] Mrs. E. K. Belcher.

[5] Alexander Cowie, *The Rise of the American Novel,* New York, 1948, pp. 536-537.

[6] "Editor's Study," *Harper's New Monthly,* LXXIV, February, 1887, pp. 482-486.

[7] See p. 33.

[8] See pp. 51, 52.

[9] See p. 33.

[10] See p. 88.

[11] *A Humble Romance and Other Stories,* New York, 1887, pp. 37-48.

[12] *Humble Romance,* pp. 250-265.

[13] *Humble Romance,* pp. 148-163.

[14] *Humble Romance,* p. 150.

[15] *Humble Romance,* pp. 156-157.

[16] *Humble Romance,* pp. 382-398.

[17] *Humble Romance,* pp. 388-390.

[18] *Humble Romance,* pp. 49-59.

[19] *Humble Romance,* p. 57.

[20] *Humble Romance,* p. 59.

CHAPTER FIVE

[1] Randolph Register, June 28, 1890, p. 2.

[2] Mrs. E. T. Proctor.

[3] Mrs. E. K. Belcher.

[4] Mr. J. E. Chamberlin.

[5] Hamlin Garland, *Roadside Meetings,* New York, 1952, p. 33.

[6] Herbert Clark, the Wales' hired man.

[7] Mary E. Belcher, "The Atherton Wales Homestead."

[8] Mrs. E. K. Belcher.

[9] Mrs. E. T. Proctor.

[10] Register, May 24, 1890, p. 2.

[11] Mrs. E. K. Belcher.

[12] *Register,* May 24, 1890, p. 2.

[13] Mrs. E. K. Belcher.

[14] *Register,* June 14, 1890, p. 2.

[15] *Register,* June 7, 1890, p. 2.

[16] Mrs. Ada Murray Alden, the second wife.

[17] *DAB*

[18] Mrs. A. M. Alden.

[19] "Fifty Years of Harper's Magazine," *Harper's,* C, May, 1900, p. 956.

[20] Mrs. S. S. Carvalho, of Metuchen, N. J.

[21] Mrs. E. K. Belcher and a photograph in her collection.

[22] "The Girl Who Wants to Write," p. 272.

[23] Mrs. E. K. Belcher.

[24] Letter quoted by F. O. Matthiessen, *Sarah Orne Jewett,* Boston, 1929, p. 84.

[25] "Miss Wilkins' Prize Story," *Boston Evening Transcript,* June 29, 1895, p. 15.

[26] Quoted by Pattee, *Sidelights,* p. 186.

[27] Letter from the collection of Judge Thomas Brown, Perth Amboy, N. J.

[28] The American editions of *A Humble Romance* and *New England Nun* contained no prefaces. In the Edinburgh edition of stories from *A Humble Romance* (1890), Miss Wilkins wrote, "These little stories are written about the village people of New England. They were studies of the descendants of Massachusetts Bay colonists, in whom can still be seen traces of the features of will and conscience, so strong as to be almost exaggerations and deformities, which characterized their ancestors. These traces are, however, more evident among the older people; among the younger they are dimmer and more modified. It therefore seems better worth while to preserve in literature this old and probably disappearing type of New England character. . . ." The term *realism*

is not used, but it is implied by the employment of *studies* and the whole tone of the statement.

[29] " 'Adverse criticism does not help me very much, I think,' she said; 'I don't always know what people mean. But then I don't seem to know very much anyway. I didn't even know I'm a realist until they wrote and told me.' " (M. C. Smith, "Mary E. Wilkins at Home," *Author,* II, July 15, 1890, p. 100.)

[30] "Miss Wilkins—An Idealist in Masquerade," *Atlantic Monthly,* LXXXIII, May, 1899, p. 665.

[31] *A New England Nun and Other Stories,* New York, 1891, pp. 448-468.

[32] *Saturday Evening Post,* December 8, 1917, p. 25.

[33] *New England Nun,* pp. 37-53.

[34] *New England Nun,* p. 51.

[35] *New England Nun,* p. 53.

[36] Hans Kurath, *A Word Geography of the Eastern United States,* Ann Arbor, 1949, p. 90.

[37] *New England Nun,* p. 53.

[38] *New England Nun,* p. 37 et passim.

[39] *New England Nun,* p. 46.

[40] *New England Nun,* p. 41.

[41] *Young Lucretia and Other Stories,* New York, 1892, p. 10.

[42] *New England Nun,* p. 244.

[43] *New England Nun,* p. 112.

[44] *New England Nun,* p. 245.

[45] Mrs. S. S. Carvahlo.

[46] *New England Nun,* p. 39.

[47] *New England Nun,* p. 44.

[48] *New England Nun,* pp. 39-40.

[49] *New England Nun,* p. 40.

[50] *New England Nun,* pp. 37-38.

[51] *New England Nun,* pp. 38-39.

[52] *New England Nun,* p. 52.

[53] *New England Nun,* pp. 268-287.

[54] *New England Nun,* pp. 268-270.

[55] *New England Nun,* p. 270.

[56] *New England Nun,* p. 272.

[57] *New England Nun,* pp. 215-233.

[58] *New England Nun,* p. 219.

[59] *New England Nun,* pp. 231-232.

[60] *New England Nun,* p. 232.

[61] *Hyroglyphics,* London, 1923, pp. 160-161.

[62] *New England Nun,* pp. 1-17.

[63] *New England Nun,* p. 5.
[64] *New England Nun,* p. 17.
[65] *New England Nun,* p. 7.
[66] For the Garland "inference," see p. 84. The title of *The Boston Evening Transcript* obituary of Mrs. Freeman (March 14, 1930, p. 1) was "A New England Nun"; it was signed by Willis Boyd Allen.

CHAPTER SIX

[1] *Tenth Census, Twelfth Census, Seventh Census.*
[2] *Register,* April 16, 1887, p. 2.
[3] *Register,* January 18, 1890, p. 2.
[4] *Register,* June 14, 1890, p. 2.
[5] *Register,* December 5, 1891, p. 2.
[6] Mrs. C. E. Severance.
[7] Frederic F. Van de Water, *Rudyard Kipling's Vermont Feud,* New York, [c. 1937], pp. 35-46.
[8] Mrs. C. E. Severance.
[9] Harkness and Johnston, p. 154.
[10] Mrs. C. E. Severance.
[11] Fred Lewis Pattee, *The Development of the American Short Story,* New York, 1923, p. 317.
[12] Mr. J. E. Chamberlin.
[13] *Critic,* XII, April 29, 1893, p. 27.
[14] Mrs. John Steele Tyler.
[15] Mrs. A. M. Alden and Mrs. Samuel Schenck.
[16] Harkins, E. F. and Johnston, C. H. L., *Little Pilgrimages among the Women Who Have Written Our Books,* Boston, 1902, pp. 141-143.
[17] Letter from the collection of Mrs. C. E. Severance.
[18] *A Humble Romance,* p. 6.
[19] *Jane Field,* New York, 1893, pp. 266-267.
[20] *Jane Field,* p. 92.
[21] LVI, February 23, 1893, p. 146.
[22] Letter from the collection of Mrs. C. E. Severance.
[23] Mrs. Nathan Irving Tolman and Mrs. E. K. Belcher.
[24] Mr. J. E. Belcher.
[25] John V. Beal, *An Address in Commemoration of the One Hundredth Anniversary of the Incorporation of Randolph, Mass.,* Randolph, 1897, the photograph.
[26] Beal, p. 42.
[27] Beal, pp. 22-23.

[28] Beal, pp. 33-36.
[29] Beal, pp. 36-37.
[30] Beal, p. 42.
[31] Quoted by Van Wyck Brooks, *New England Indian Summer,* New York, 1940, p. 409.
[32] September 9, 1893, p. 2.
[33] September 16, 1893, p. 2.
[34] *Register,* January 20, 1894, p. 2.
[35] *Register,* February 17, 1894, p. 2.
[36] Mrs. Marian Boyd Allen and Mr. Willis Allen.
[37] Mrs. E. K. Belcher.
[38] *Pembroke: Biographical Edition,* New York, 1894, 1899, pp. 1-14.
[39] "Introductory Sketch," *Pembroke,* p. iii.
[40] *Pembroke,* pp. 329-330.
[41] p. iii.
[42] Compare p. 122.
[43] Erich Fromm, *Escape from Freedom,* New York, 1941, pp. 185-186.
[44] Especially Karen Horney, *Neurosis and Human Growth: The Struggle toward Self-Realization,* New York, 1950, which is essentially a study of the nature of neurotic pride.
[45] *Pembroke,* p. iii.
[46] *Harper's Weekly,* XXXXVII, November 21, 1904, p. 1880.
[47] *Pembroke,* p. 298.
[48] Mrs. C. E. Severance.
[49] "New England, Mother of America," *Country Life,* XXII, July, 1912, p. 32.
[50] Mrs. E. K. Belcher.
[51] F. W. Halsey, ed., *Women Authors of Our Day,* New York, 1905, pp. 211-212.
[52] Herbert Clark.
[53] *Harper's,* December, 1892, p. 148.
[54] Mrs. E. K. Belcher.
[55] Mrs. Harold Howard, née Molly Kingsbury.
[56] Mrs. E. K. Belcher.
[57] Mrs. E. T. Proctor.
[58] Mrs. E. K. Belcher.
[59] Mr. J. E. Chamberlin.
[60] "Emily Bronte and Wuthering Heights, *The Book Lover's Reading Club Hand-Book . . . The World's Great Woman Novelists,* Philadelphia, 1901, pp. 88-89.
[61] Mr. J. E. Chamberlin.
[62] Mr. J. E. Chamberlin.
[63] Mrs. N. I. Tolman.

[64] "Mr. Crawford and Miss Wilkins," *The Critic,* XXVIII, January 18, 1896, pp. 48-49.

[65] Letter from the collection of Mrs. E. K. Belcher.

CHAPTER SEVEN

[1] Letter from the collection of Mrs. E. K. Belcher.

[2] Mr. W. J. Good.

[3] April 10, 1897, p. 2.

[4] *Critic,* XXX, May 1, 1897, p. 311.

[5] Mrs. M. B. Allen.

[6] Mrs. C. E. Severance.

[7] Mrs. E. T. Proctor.

[8] Manuscript given to the writer by Mrs. A. B. Mann.

[9] Horney, pp. 22 et passim.

[10] Mrs. E. K. Belcher.

[11] Mrs. E. T. Proctor.

[12] *Jerome,* New York, 1896, pp. 4-6.

[13] *Jerome,* p. 454.

[14] *Jerome,* p. 502.

[15] *Jerome,* p. 194.

[16] *Jerome,* pp. 281-282.

[17] Mrs. E. T. Proctor.

[18] Mrs. E. K. Belcher.

[19] Mrs. N. I. Tolman.

[20] To the writer in conversation.

[21] Mrs. N. I. Tolman.

[22] Mrs. E. K. Belcher, "Hattie."

[23] *Silence and Other Stories,* New York, 1898, pp. 201-202.

[24] Mrs. M. B. and Mr. W. B. Allen.

[25] XXI, May, 1903, p. 89.

[26] Pension File, Naval Archives.

[27] Mrs. N. I. Tolman.

[28] "One Good Time," *The Love of Parson Lord and Other Stories,* New York, 1901, pp. 225-232.

[29] *Boston Evening Transcript,* March 14, 1930, p. 13.

[30] Letter from the collection of Mrs. C. E. Severance.

[31] *New York Times,* January 3, 1902, p. 7.

[32] *New York Herald,* January 3, 1902, p. 6.

CHAPTER EIGHT

[1] *New York Herald,* January 3, 1902, p. 6.
[2] *Register,* January 11, 1902, p. 2.
[3] Mrs. E. T. Proctor.
[4] From the collection of Mrs. C. E. Severance.
[5] Mrs. S. S. Carvahlo.
[6] Mrs. N. I. Tolman.
[7] *Register,* June 7, 1902, p. 2.
[8] Mrs. N. I. Tolman.
[9] Mrs. S. S. Carvahlo.
[10] Mrs. C. E. Severance.
[11] Mrs. S. S. Carvahlo.
[12] Mrs. A. M. Alden.
[13] Pattee, *American Short Story,* p. 322.
[14] Mrs. E. K. Belcher.
[15] *Nature,* Boston, 1836, in *The Complete Essays . . . ,* ed. Brooks Atkinson, New York, 1940, p. 6.
[16] "The Apple Tree," *Six Trees,* New York, 1903, p. 181.
[17] "The Apple Tree," pp. 173-174.
[18] "The Apple Tree," p. 198.
[19] "The Apple Tree," p. 207.
[20] "If They Had a Million Dollars," *Ladies' Home Journal,* September, 1903, p. 10.
[21] Herbert Clark.
[22] "The Butterfly," *The Givers,* New York, 1904, pp. 229-265.
[23] Town Records, Randolph, Mass.
[24] Mrs. M. B. Allen.
[25] Mrs. S. S. Carvahlo and Mrs. Samuel Schenck.
[26] "Nonsense Verses," *Harper's,* CXI, August, 1905, p. 483.
[27] Mrs. A. B. Mann.
[28] Albert Bigelow Paine, *Mark Twain: A Biography,* New York, 1912, vol. III, p. 1250.
[29] *Life,* XVI, May 8, 1944, p. 96.
[30] Paine, vol. III, p. 1252.
[31] Mrs. A. B. Mann.
[32] Mrs. N. I. Tolman.
[33] *By the Light of the Soul,* New York, 1906, p. 482.
[34] *By the Light,* p. 437.
[35] *By the Light,* p. 494.
[36] From the collection of Miss Helena L. Todd.
[37] From the collection of Mrs. M. B. Allen.
[38] Mrs. E. K. Belcher.

[39] *The Shoulders of Atlas,* New York, 1908, p. 78.
[40] *New York Herald,* January 5, 1908, p. 3.
[41] From the collection of Judge Thomas Brown, Perth Amboy, N. J., date March 14, 1908.
[42] *New York Herald,* May 31, 1908, Magazine Section, p. 5.
[43] XC, January 13, 1910, p. 36.

CHAPTER NINE

[1] Mrs. S. S. Carvahlo.
[2] Mrs. Samuel Schenck.
[3] Mrs. M. B. Allen.
[4] "The Amethyst Comb," *The Copy-cat,* New York, 1914, pp. 217-218.
[5] *New York Times,* November 22, 1923, p. 19.
[6] Mrs. N. I. Tolman.
[7] Letter of December 18, 1911 from the collection of Miss Allie Morse.
[8] Borough Records of Metuchen, N. J.
[9] Mrs. S. S. Carvahlo.
[10] "The Cock of the Walk," *The Copy-cat,* pp. 35-54.
[11] Letter of July 7, 1916 from the collection of Judge Thomas Brown.
[12] Borough Records of Metuchen, N. J.
[13] Town Records of Randolph, Mass.
[14] Mrs. N. I. Tolman and Mr. W. J. Good.
[15] Copy from the collection of Mrs. N. I. Tolman.
[16] Mrs. S. S. Carvahlo.
[17] New York, 1918, p. 54.
[18] "The Bright Side," *Harper's,* CXLVI, April, 1923, p. 637.
[19] Mrs. A. B. Mann.
[20] *Edgewater People,* New York, 1918, p. 128.
[21] *Edgewater People,* p. 87.
[22] *Edgewater People,* p. 88.
[23] *Edgewater People,* p. 97.
[24] *DAB*
[25] *New York Times,* November 22, 1923, p. 19.
[26] *Times,* April 7, 1923, p. 13.
[27] Mrs. A. B. Mann.
[28] "The Vase," *The Literary Digest,* August 19, 1922, p. 38.
[29] *Times,* March 9, 1923, p. 15.
[30] *Times,* March 17, 1923, p. 1.
[31] *Times,* April 7, 1923, p. 13.

[32] Letter of January 15, 1926 from the collection of Mrs. C. E. Severance.

[33] Letter from the collection of Mrs. N. I. Tolman.

[34] Mrs. A. B. Mann.

[35] Letter from the collection of Mrs. C. E. Severance.

[36] *New York Herald-Tribune,* April 24, 1926, p. 13.

[37] *Times,* April 24, 1926, p. 7.

[38] Letter from the collection of Mrs. M. B. Allen.

[39] *Times,* November 12, 1926, p. 10.

[40] Letter of September 13, 1927 from the collection of Mrs. M. B. Allen.

[41] Letter of December 13, 1929 from the collection of Miss Allie Morse.

[42] Mrs. S. S. Carvahlo.

[43] Mrs. A. B. Mann.

[44] Mrs. M. B. Allen.

[45] Letter of April 3, 1928 from the collection of Mrs. M. B. Allen.

[46] Mrs. P. K. White.

[47] Mrs. A. B. Mann.

[48] Mrs. E. K. Belcher.

[49] Mrs. C. E. Severance.

[50] Letter of February 2, 1930 from the collection of Mrs. M. B. Allen.

[51] *Times,* March 15, 1930, p. 19.

Bibliography

I. THE WRITINGS OF MARY E. WILKINS FREEMAN

A. Short Stories Collected or Reprinted in Book Form

A Humble Romance and Other Stories, New York and London, 1887.
A Humble Romance—Two Old Lovers—A Symphony in Lavender—A Tardy Thanksgiving—A Modern Dragon—An Honest Soul—A Taste of Honey—Brakes and White Vi'lets—Robins and Hammers—On the Walpole Road—Old Lady Pingree—Cinnamon Roses—The Bar Light-house—A Far-away Melody—A Moral Exigency—A Mistaken Charity—Gentian—An Object of Love—A Gatherer of Simples—An Independent Thinker—In Butterfly Time—An Unwilling Guest—A Souvenir—An Old Arithmetician—A Conflict Ended—A Patient Waiter—A Conquest of Humility.

A Humble Romance and Other Stories, Edinburgh, 1890. The first fourteen stories of the original edition.

A Far-away Melody and Other Stories, Edinburgh, 1890. The second fourteen stories of the original edition of *A Humble Romance.*

A Far-away Melody and Other Stories, Leipzig, 1891. The contents are identical with the preceding entry.

A New England Nun and Other Stories, New York and London, 1891.
A New England Nun—A Village Singer—A Gala Dress—The Twelfth Guest—Sister Liddy—Callah Lillies and Hannah—A Wayfaring Couple—A Poetess—Christmas Jenny—A Pot of Gold—The Scent of Roses—A Solitary—A Gentle Ghost—A Discovered Pearl—A Village Lear—Amanda and Love—Up Primrose Hill—A Stolen Christmas—Life Everlastin'—An Innocent Gamester—Louisa—A Church Mouse—A Kitchen Colonel—The Revolt of "Mother."

A New England Nun and Other Stories, Leipzig, 1892, two volumes.

The Long Arm by Mary E. Wilkins [and J. Edgar Chamberlin] and Other Detective Stories by George Ira Brett, Professor Brander Matthews, and Roy Tellet, London, 1895.

A Humble Romance and Other Stories, New York, 1897.

The People of Our Neighborhood, Philadelphia, [cop. 1895-1898].
Timothy Sampson; the Wise Man—Little Margaret Snell; the Village Runaway—Cyrus Emmett; the Unlucky Man—Phebe Ann Little; the Neat Woman—Amanda Todd; the Friend of Cats—Lydia

Wheelock; the Good Woman—A Quilting Bee in Our Village—The Stockwell's Apple-paring Bee—The Christmas Sing in Our Village.

Silence and Other Stories, New York and London, 1898.

Silence—The Buckley Lady—Evelina's Garden—A New England Prophet—The Little Maid at the Door—Lydia Hersey of East Bridgewater.

A Humble Romance and Other Stories, New York and London, 1899.

Evelina's Garden, New York and London, 1899. [This story previously appeared in Silence and Other Stories.]

The Love of Parson Lord and Other Stories, New York and London, 1900.

The Love of Parson Lord—The Tree of Knowledge—Catherine Carr—Three Old Sisters and the Old Beau—One Good Time.

The Love of Parson Lord and Other Stories, Leipzig, 1900.

Understudies, New York and London, 1901.

The Cat—The Monkey—The Squirrel—The Lost Dog—The Parrot—The Doctor's Horse—Bouncing Bet—Prince's Feather—Arethusa—Mountain-laurel—Peony—Morning-glory.

The Homecoming of Jessica . . . [by Mary E. Wilkins]. An Idyl of Central Park . . . [by Brander Matthews]. The Romance of a Soul . . . [by Robert Grant], Springfield, Ohio, and New York, 1901.

Six Trees, New York and London, 1903.

The Elm Tree—The White Birch—The Great Pine—The Balsam Fir—The Lombardy Poplar—The Apple Tree.

The Wind in the Rose-bush and Other Stories of the Supernatural, New York, 1903.

The Wind in the Rose-bush—The Shadows on the Wall—Luella Miller—The Southwest Chamber—The Vacant Lot—The Lost Ghost.

A New England Nun and Other Stories, New York and London, 1903.

The Givers, New York and London, 1904.

The Givers—Lucy—Eglantina—Joy—The Reign of the Doll—The Chance of Araminta—The Butterfly—The Last Gift.

The Fair Lavinia and Others, New York and London, 1907.

The Fair Lavinia—Amarina's Roses—Eglantina—The Pink Shawls—The Willow-ware—The Secret—The Gold—The Underling.

The Winning Lady and Others, New York and London, 1909.

The Winning Lady—Little-girl-afraid-of-a-dog—The Joy of Youth—Billy and Susy—The Selfishness of Amelia Lamkin—The Travelling Sister—Her Christmas—Old Woman Magoun—Eliza Sam—Flora and Hannah—A New Year's Resolution.

The Yates Pride: A Romance, New York and London, 1912.

The Copy-cat and Other Stories, New York and London, 1914.

The Copy-cat—The Cock of the Walk—Johnny-in-the-woods—Daniel and Little Dan'l—Big Sister Solly—Little Lucy Rose—Noblesse—Coronation—The Amethyst Comb—The Umbrella Man—The Balking of Christopher—Dear Annie.

Edgewater People, New York and London, 1918.

Sarah Edgewater—The Old Man of the Field—The Voice of the Clock—Value Received—The Flowering Bush—The Outside of the House—The Liar—Sour Sweetings—Both Cheeks—The Soldier Man—Ring with the Green Stone—"A Retreat to the Goal."

A New England Nun and Other Stories . . . with an introduction by Professor Fred Lewis Pattee, New York and London, [cop. 1920].

The Best Stories of Mary E. Wilkins selected and with an introduction by Henry Wysham Lanier, New York and London, 1927.

A Humble Romance—The Revolt of "Mother"—Little-girl-afraid-of-a-dog—A New England Nun—One Good Time—The Last Gift—A New England Prophet—A Village Singer—Old Woman Magoun—The Joy of Youth—Billy and Susy—The Butterfly—Both Cheeks—A Solitary—Two Old Lovers—Gentian—The Wind-in-the-Rose-bush—A Conflict Ended—A Conquest of Humility—The Apple Tree—Noblesse—The Outside of the House—Coronation—The Gold—The Gospel According to Joan.

B. Uncollected Short Stories

The Shadow Family, *The Boston Budget,* January 1, 1882.

The Story of Little Mary Witlow, *Lippincott's,* XXI, May, 1883, p. 500.

The Wandering Samaritan, *Cosmopolitan,* II, September, 1886, p. 28.

Serena Ann's First Valentine, *The English Illustrated,* XVII, June, 1897, p. 235.

Susan Jane's Valentine, *Harper's Bazar,* XXXIII, February 17, 1900, p. 132.

Pumpkin, *Harper's Bazar,* XXXIII, November 24, 1900, p. 1863.

The Christmas Ghost, *Everybody's,* III, December, 1900, p. 512.

About Hannah Stone, *Everybody's,* IV, January, 1901, p. 25.

A Tragedy from the Trivial, *Cornhill,* LXXXIII, January, 1901, p. 63.

An Easter Card, *Everybody's,* IV, April, 1901, p. 372.

Two for Peace, *Lippincott's,* LXVIII, July, 1901, p. 51.

Prism, *The Century,* LXII, July, 1901, p. 469.

The Happy Day, *McClure's,* XXI, May, 1903, p. 89.

The Revolt of Sophia Lane, *Harper's,* CVIII, December, 1903, p. 20.

She Who Adorns Her Sister Adorns Herself, *Harper's Bazar,* XXXVIII, May, 1904, p. 456.

Hyacinthus, *Harper's,* CIX, August, 1904, p. 447.
Humble Pie, *Independent,* LVII, September 1, 1904, p. 477.
The Slip of the Leash, *Harper's,* CIX, October, 1904, p. 669.
For the Love of Oneself, *Harper's,* CX, January, 1905, p. 303.
Other People's Cake, *Collier's,* XLII, November 21, 1908, p. 14.
The Cautious King and the All-round Wise Woman, *Harper's Weekly,* LIII, June 26, 1909, p. 22.
Julia–Her Thanksgiving, *Harper's Bazar,* XLIII, November, 1909, p. 1079.
The Christmas Lady, *Ladies' Home Journal,* XXVII, December, 1909, p. 17.
Josiah's First Christmas, *Collier's,* XLIV, December 11, 1909, p. 9.
The Fighting McCleans, *The Delineator,* LXXV, February, 1910, p. 113.
The Slayer of Serpents, *Collier's,* XLIV, March 19, 1910, p. 16.
The Steeple, *Hampton-Columbian,* XXVII, October, 1911, p. 412.
The Horn of Plenty, *Collier's,* XLVIII, November 18, 1911, p. 22.
A Guest in Sodom, *Century,* LXXXIII, January, 1912, p. 343.
Doll Lady, *Harper's,* CXXIV, January, 1912, p. 279.
The Blue Butterfly, *Woman's Home Companion,* XL, January, 1913, p. 3.
Something on Her Mind, *Harper's Bazar,* XLVI, December, 1912, p. 607.
Friend of my Heart, *Good Housekeeping,* LVII, December, 1913, p. 733.
Criss-cross, *Harper's,* CXXIX, August, 1914, p. 360.
The Saving of Hiram Sessions, *Pictorial Review,* XVI, May, 1915, p. 20.
Sweet-flowering Perennial, *Harper's,* CXXXI, July, 1915, p. 287.
Emancipation, *Harper's,* CXXXII, December, 1915, p. 27.
Honorable Tommy, *Woman's Home Companion,* XLIII, December, 1916, p. 15.
Boomerang, *Pictorial Review,* XVIII, March, 1917, p. 22.
Cloak Also, *Harper's,* CXXXIV, March, 1917, p. 545.
Thanksgiving Crossroads, *Woman's Home Companion,* XLIV, November, 1917, p. 13.
Prop, *Saturday Evening Post,* CXC, January 5, 1918, p. 12.
Jade Bracelet, *Forum,* LIX, April, 1918, p. 429.
The Return, *Woman's Home Companion,* XLVII, August, 1921, p. 21.
Mother-Wings, *Harper's,* CXLIV, December, 1921, p. 90.
The Bright Side, *Harper's,* CXLVI, April, 1923, p. 630.
The Jester, *The Golden Book,* VII, June, 1928, p. 821.
The Brother. [in manuscript, c. 1927.]
One. [in manuscript, c. 1928.]

C. Novels

Jane Field, New York, 1893.
Pembroke, New York, [cop. 1894].
Madelon, New York, 1896.
Madelon, New York and London, [cop. 1896].
Jerome, A Poor Man, New York and London, 1897.
Jerome, A Poor Man, New York and London, 1898.
The Jamesons, New York and Philadelphia, 1899.
Pembroke, Biographical Edition, New York and London, 1899.
The Heart's Highway, A Romance of Virginia in the Seventeenth Century, New York, 1900.
The Heart's Highway, A Romance of Virginia in the Seventeenth Century, New York, [cop. 1900].
Pembroke, Powiesc z Amerykananskiego, Przelad z Angielskiego, Warzawa, 1900.
The Portion of Labor, New York and London, 1901.
The Portion of Labor, New York, 1905.
The Debtor, New York and London, 1905.
By the Light of the Soul, New York and London, 1906.
"Doc." Gordon, Toronto, New York, and London, [cop. 1906].
Doctor Gordon, London, 1907.
The Shoulders of Atlas, New York and London, 1908.
The Whole Family, A Novel by Twelve Authors: William Dean Howells, Mary E. Wilkins Freeman . . . New York and London, 1908.
The Butterfly House, New York, 1912.
An Alabaster Box, by Mary E. Wilkins Freeman and Florence Morse Kingsley, New York, 1917.

D. Poems

Sweet Phyllis, A Pastoral, *Century,* XXIV, September, 1882, p. 799.
Decorative Plaques: Designs by George F. Barnes. Poems by Mary E. Wilkins, Boston, [cop. 1883].
Boy's Love, *Century,* XXVI, October, 1883, p. 959.
It Was a Lass, *Century,* XXVII, April, 1884, p. 959.
A Maiden Lady, *Century,* XXX, August, 1885, p. 654.
Once Upon a Time and Other Child Verses, Boston, [cop. 1897].
Cyrano de Bergerac, *Harper's,* IXC, June, 1899, p. 37.
The Lode Star, *Scribner's,* XXVII, May, 1900, p. 572.
Nonsense Verses, *Harper's,* CXI, August, 1905, p. 483.
Wake Up, America! [in] Louis Raemakers, *America in the War,* New York, 1918, p. 34.
Morning Light, *Harper's,* CXLII, December, 1920, p. 17.

The Prisoner, *Literary Digest,* LXXIV, August 19, 1922, p. 38.
The Vase, *Literary Digest,* LXXIV, August 19, 1922, p. 38.
A sheaf of unpublished verse, written in the main after 1910, in the possession of Mrs. Freeman's executor, Judge Thomas Brown, Perth Amboy, New Jersey.

E. Stories for Children and Miscellaneous Prose

The Cow with the Golden Horns and Other Stories, Boston, [cop. 1884].
The Adventures of Ann: Stories of Colonial Times, Boston, [cop. 1886].
The Pot of Gold and Other Stories, Boston, [cop. 1892].
Young Lucretia and Other Stories, New York, 1892.
"Pastels in Prose: In the Marsh Land, Camilla's Snuff Box, Shadows, Death," *Harper's,* LXXXVI, December, 1892, p. 147.
Giles Corey, Yeoman: A Play, New York, 1893.
Comfort Pease and Her Gold Ring, New York and Chicago, 1895.
In Colonial Times: The Adventures of Ann . . . Boston, [cop. 1899].
"Good Wits, Pen and Paper," [in] G. H. Dodge et al., *What Women Can Earn,* New York, 1899.
"Emily Bronte and Wuthering Heights," [in] *The World's Great Women Novelists,* Philadelphia, [cop. 1901].
Little Lassies, by Mary E. Wilkins et al., Akron, Ohio, New York, 1904.
The Green Door, New York, 1910.
"New England, Mother of America," *Country Life in America,* XXII, July, 1912, p. 27.
"The Girl Who Wants to Write: Things to Do and Avoid," *Harper's Bazar,* XLVII, June, 1913, p. 272.
The Pilgrim's Progress: Adapted to a Motion Picture Play, by Mary E. Wilkins and William Dinwiddie, New York, 1915.

BOOKS AND ARTICLES CONSULTED

An Account of the Proceedings of the Centennial Celebration of the Town of Randolph, Randolph, Mass., 1897.
Adams, James Truslow, *The Founding of New England,* Boston, 1921.
——— *Revolutionary New England,* Boston, 1923.
——— *New England in the Republic,* Boston, 1926.
——— *New England Prospect,* Boston, 1933.
Adams, T. M., *Windham County: Basic Facts and Figures,* Burlington, Vt., 1949.

Alden, Henry Mills, "Editor's Study," *Harper's,* LXXIV, February, 1887, pp. 482-486.

——— "Editor's Study," *Harper's,* LXXV, September, 1887, p. 640.

——— *God in His World: An Interpretation,* New York, 1890.

——— *Magazine Writing and the New Literature,* New York, 1908.

Allen, Willis Boyd, "A New England Nun," *Boston Evening Transcript,* March 20, 1930, part 2, p. 3.

Beal, John V., *An Address in Commemoration of the One Hundredth Anniversary of the Incorporation of Randolph, Mass.,* Randolph, 1897.

Beard, Charles A. and Mary R., *The Rise of American Civilization,* New York, 1930.

Beach, Joseph Warren, *The Twentieth Century Novel: A Study in Technique,* New York, 1932.

Beer, Thomas, *The Mauve Decade: American Life at the End of the Nineteenth Century,* New York, 1926.

Belcher, Mary E., "The Atherton Wales Homestead," [Randolph, c. 1905, an unpublished paper in the collection of Mrs. E. K. Belcher.]

Bentzon, Theophile, "Un Romancier de la Nouvelle-Angleterre," *Revue des Deux Mondes,* CCCXLVIII, August 1, 1896, pp. 544 ff.

Bishop, W. H., "Hunting an Abandoned Farm in Upper New England," *Century,* XXVI, May, 1894, pp. 30-43.

Blankenship, Russell, *American Literature as an Expression of the National Mind,* London, 1931.

Boutwell, G. S., "The Decadence of New England," *Forum,* X, October, 1890, pp. 142-151.

Bradford, Gamaliel, *Portraits of American Women,* Boston, 1917.

Bridenbaugh, Carl, *The New England Town: A Way of Life,* Worcester, Mass., 1947.

Brooks, Cleanth and Warren, R. P., *Understanding Fiction,* New York, 1943.

Brooks, Van Wyck, *New England Indian Summer,* New York, 1940.

Burnham, Henry, *Brattleboro, Windham County, Vermont; Early History with Biographical Sketches of Some of Its Citizens,* Brattleboro, 1880.

Bureau of Census, *A Century of Population Growth: 1790-1900,* Washington, 1909.

Butman, Harry R., *History of Randolph, Mass.* [Randolph, c. 1950, unpublished].

Cabot, Mary Rogers, *Annals of Brattleboro,* two volumes, Brattleboro, 1921-1922.

Canby, Henry S., *A Study of the Short Story,* New York, 1913.

Carter, Robert M., *Studies in Vermont History, Geography, and Government,* St. Johnsbury, Vt., 1937.

Chamberlin, J. Edgar, "Miss Mary E. Wilkins at Randolph, Massachusetts," *Critic,* XXXII, March 5, 1898, p. 155.

Chapman, Edward M., *New England Village Life,* Cambridge, 1937.

Chase, Mary Ellen, *A Goodly Heritage,* New York, 1932.

Commager, Henry Steele, *The American Mind: An Interpretation of American Thought and Character since the 1880's,* New Haven, 1950.

Courtney, W. L., *The Feminine Note in Fiction,* London, 1904.

Crane, Charles E., *Winter in Vermont,* New York, 1947.

Crawford, M. C., *Social Life in Old New England,* Boston, 1914.

Crockett, W. H., *History of Vermont,* five volumes, New York, 1921.

Cutter, W. R., *Genealogical and Personal Memoirs of the Families of Boston and Eastern Massachusetts,* New York, 1908.

Dame, Lawrence, *New England Comes Back,* New York, 1940.

Davidson, Donald, "Regionalism and Nationalism in American Literature," *American Review,* V, April, 1935, pp. 48-61.

Dean, William H., "Decay of New England," *Nation,* VIII, May 27, 1869, pp. 410-411.

Deegan, D. Y., *The Stereotype of the Single Woman in American Novels,* New York, 1951.

DeVoto, Bernard A., "New England, There She Stands," *Harper's,* CLXIV, March, 1932, pp. 405-415.

——— *The World of Fiction,* Boston, 1950.

Dictionary of American Biography, eds. Allen Johnson and Dumas Malone, New York, 1928-1936.

Earle, A. M., *Customs and Fashions in Old New England,* New York, 1893.

Emerson, Ralph Waldo, *Complete Essays . . .,* ed. Brooks Atkinson, New York, 1940.

Federal Writers Project, *Massachusetts: A Guide to Its Places and People,* Boston, 1937.

——— *Vermont: The Green Mountain State,* Boston, 1937.

Firkins, I. T. E., *Index to Short Stories: Second and Enlarged Edition,* New York, 1923.

——— *Index to Short Stories: Supplement,* New York, 1929.

Fiske, Howard S., *Provincial Types in American Fiction,* New York, 1903.

Forster, E. M., *Aspects of the Novel,* New York, 1927.

Foerster, Norman, ed. et al., *The Reinterpretation of American Literature,* New York, 1928.

Foster, F. H., *A Genetic History of New England Theology,* Chicago, 1907.
Fromm, Erich, *Escape from Freedom,* New York, 1941.
——— *Psychoanalysis and Religion,* New Haven, 1950.
Garland, Hamlin, *Crumbling Idols,* Chicago, 1894.
——— *Roadside Meetings,* New York, 1932.
Gilchrist, Beth B., *The Life of Mary Lyon,* Boston, 1910.
Gould, John, *New England Town Meeting,* Brattleboro, 1940.
Halsey, F. W., ed., *Women Authors of Our Day in Their Homes,* New York, 1903.
Hanscomb, Elizabeth Deering, *The Heart of the Puritan,* New York, 1917.
——— "Mary E. Wilkins Freeman," *Dictionary of American Biography.*
Hard, Walter, *Salt of Vermont,* Brattleboro, 1931.
——— *This Is Vermont,* Brattleboro, 1936.
Harkins, E. F. and Johnston, C. H. L., *Little Pilgrimages among the Women Who Have Written Famous Books,* Boston, 1902.
Haroutunian, Joseph, *Piety versus Moralism: The Passing of New England Theology,* New York, 1932.
Harper, J. Henry, *The House of Harper,* New York, 1912.
Hart, Albert Bushnell, ed., *The Commonwealth History of Massachusetts,* five volumes, New York, 1930.
Hazard, Blanche E., *Organization of the Boot and Shoe Industry in Massachusetts before 1875,* Cambridge, Mass., 1921.
"The Herald's Anglo-American Competition," *New York Herald,* January 5, 1908, Magazine Section, p. 3.
Herron, Ima Honaker, *The Small Town in American Literature,* Durham, N. C., 1939.
Hicks, Granville, *The Great Tradition: An Interpretation of American Literature since the Civil War,* New York, 1933.
Holbrook, Stewart H., *Yankee Exodus,* New York, 1950.
Horney, Karen, *The Neurotic Personality of Our Time,* New York, 1937.
——— *Neurosis and Human Growth,* New York, 1950.
Howe, M. A. DeWolfe, *Boston: The Place and Its People,* New York, 1924.
Howells, William Dean, *Criticism and Fiction,* New York, 1892.
——— *Literary Friends and Acquaintances,* New York, 1901.
Huntington, E. B., *A Genealogical Memoir of the Lo-Lathrop Family,* Ridgefield, Conn., 1884.
James, Henry, *The Art of Fiction: Critical Prefaces,* New York, 1937.
Jones, Howard Mumford, "New England's Dilemma," *Atlantic,* CLXV, April, 1940, pp. 458-467.
Kempton, K. P., *The Short Story,* Cambridge, Mass., 1948.

Kipling, Rudyard, *Something about Myself,* New York, 1937.
Knight, Grant C., *The Critical Period in American Literature,* Chapel Hill, N. C., 1951.
Kurath, Hans, *A Word Geography of the Eastern United States,* Ann Arbor, 1949.
Labaree, John Codman, *The Plymouth Pilgrims;* A Sermon, Randolph, Mass., 1871.
——— *Proceedings of the One Hundredth and Fiftieth Anniversary of the Organization of the First Congregational Church, Randolph, Mass., June 8, 1881,* Boston, 1881.
Lanier, Henry Wysham, "Introduction," *The Best Stories of Mary E. Wilkins,* New York, 1927.
Levy, Babette, "Mutations in New England Local Color," *New England Quarterly,* XIX, September, 1946, pp. 338-358.
Lewisohn, Ludwig, *Expression in America,* New York, 1932.
Lieberman, E., *The American Short Story: A Study of the Influence of Locality in Its Development,* Ridgewood, N. J., 1912.
Lunt, George, *Old New England Traits,* New York, 1873.
Machen, Arthur, *Hyroglyphics,* London, 1903.
Mann, Henry, *Features of Society in Old and New England,* Providence, R. I., 1885.
"Mary E. Wilkins," *Bookman* [London], 1, December, 1891, pp. 102-103.
"Mary E. Wilkins," *Critic,* XX, January 2, 1892, p. 13.
"Mary E. Wilkins as Prize Winner," *Critic,* XXVI, June 29, 1895, p. 484.
Matthews, Brander, *The Philosophy of the Short Story,* New York, 1912.
Matthiessen, F. O., *Sarah Orne Jewett,* Boston, 1929.
——— "New England Stories," in Macy, John, ed., *American Writers on American Literature,* New York, 1931.
——— *The American Renaissance,* London, 1941.
Mathews, Lois K., *The Expansion of New England: 1820-1865,* Boston, 1909.
McKenney, L. T., *The New England People: Builders of America,* Boston, 1942.
McWilliams, C., *The New Regionalism in American Literature,* Seattle, 1930.
Miller, Perry, *The New England Mind,* New York, 1939.
Millett, Fred B., *Reading Fiction,* New York, 1950.
"Miss Mary E. Wilkins," *The Book Buyer,* VIII, March, 1891, pp. 53-54.
Mitchell, E. V., *It's an Old New England Custom,* New York, 1946.
——— *Yankee Folk,* New York, 1948.
More, Paul Elmer, "Hawthorne: Looking Before and After," *Independent,* LVI, June 30, 1904, pp. 1489-1494.

——— "The Spirit and Poetry of Early New England," *Shelburne Essays,* Vol. XI, Boston, 1921.

Morison, Samuel Eliot, *Builders of the Bay Colony,* Boston, 1930.

Morse, M. D. E., "Reminiscences of the Early Seventies," *Mount Holyoke Alumnae Quarterly,* May, 1931, pp. 23-26.

Moss, Mary, "Representative American Story Tellers," *Bookman,* XXIV, September, 1906, pp. 21-29.

Mott, Frank Luther, *A History of American Magazines,* three volumes, New York, 1930-1938.

Moulton, Henry W., *Moulton Annals,* Chicago, 1906.

Mumford, Lewis, *The Brown Decades, 1865-1895,* New York, 1931.

Murdock, Kenneth Ballard, *Literature and Theology in Colonial New England,* Cambridge, Mass., 1949.

Nevins, Allan, *The Emergence of Modern America, 1865-1878,* New York, 1927.

"New England in the Short Story," *Atlantic Monthly,* LXVII, June, 1891, pp. 845-850.

Odum, Howard and Moore, Harry E., *American Regionalism: A Cultural Historical Approach to National Integration,* New York, 1938.

Orvis, Mary B., *The Art of Writing Fiction,* New York, 1948.

Paine, Albert Bigelow, *Mark Twain, A Biography,* three volumes, London, 1912.

Parrington, Vernon L., *Main Currents in American Thought,* three volumes, New York, 1927-1930.

Patterson, Emma V., "Mary E. Wilkins," *The Book News Monthly,* XXXVI, November, 1917, p. 75.

Perry, Bliss, *The American Mind,* Boston, 1912.

Pattee, Fred Lewis, *A History of American Literature since 1870,* New York, 1915.

——— "On the Terminal Moraine of New England Puritanism," *Sidelights on American Literature,* New York, 1922.

——— *The Development of the American Short Story,* New York, 1923.

——— *The New American Literature,* New York, 1930.

Pomeroy, Frank T., *Picturesque Brattleboro,* Northampton, Mass., 1894.

Quinn, Arthur Hobson, *American Fiction: An Historical and Critical Survey,* New York, 1936.

——— ed. et al., *The Literature of the American People,* New York, 1951.

Sanborn, Edwin S., *Social Changes in New England in the Past Fifty Years,* Boston, 1901.

Schneider, H. W., *The Puritan Mind,* New York, 1930.

Schorer, Mark, ed., *Criticism: The Foundations of Modern Literary Judgment,* New York, 1948.

——— *The Story: A Critical Anthology,* New York, 1950.

Smith, M. C., "Mary E. Wilkins at Home," *Author,* II, July 15, 1890, p. 99.

Spiller, Robert E. et al., *Literary History of the United States,* three volumes, New York, 1948.

Stallman, Robert Wooster, ed., *Critiques and Essays in Criticism, 1920-1948,* New York, 1949.

Stow, S. D. L., *History of Mount Holyoke Seminary, 1837-1887,* Springfield, Mass., 1887.

Taylor, W. F., *The Economic Novel in America,* Chapel Hill, N. C., 1942.

Thirty-fourth Annual Catalogue of Mount Holyoke Seminary, Northampton, Mass., 1871.

Thompson, Charles Miner, "Miss Wilkins—An Idealist in Masquerade," *Atlantic Monthly,* LXXXIII, May, 1899, pp. 665-675.

Thompson, Elroy S., *History of Plymouth, Norfolk, and Barnstable Counties,* three volumes, New York, 1928.

Town, Salem, *Salem Town's Second Reader,* Cooperstown, N. Y., 1844.

Turner, Frederick Jackson, *The United States, 1830-1850: The Nation and Its Sections,* New York, 1935.

Tutwiler, Julia R., "Two New England Writers," *Gunton's Magazine,* XXV, November, 1903, p. 419.

Tyler, Mary Hunt Palmer, *Grandmother Tyler's Book,* ed. Frederick Tupper and Helen Tyler Brown, New York, 1925.

Van de Water, Frederic F., *Rudyard Kipling's Vermont Feud,* New York, [c. 1937].

Van Doren, Carl C., *The American Novel, 1789-1939,* New York, 1940.

Vinton, John Adams, *The Vinton Memorial . . . A Genealogy of the Descendants of John Vinton . . . Also Several Allied Families,* Boston, 1858.

Virkus, F. A., ed., *The Abridged Compendium of American Genealogy,* four volumes, Chicago, 1925-1930.

The Vital Records of Salem, Massachusetts, to the End of the Year 1849, Salem, 1916-1925.

The Vital Records of Wenham, Massachusetts, to the End of the Year 1849, Salem, 1904.

Walbridge, J. H., *Picturesque Putney, Newfane, Townshend, and Jamaica,* Brattleboro, 1901.

Walker, George Leon, *Some Aspects of the Religious Life of New England,* New York, 1897.

Walker, Williston, *History of the Congregational Churches in the United States,* New York, 1894.
Wardwell, Mary E., "About Miss Wilkins," *Citizen,* IV, April, 1898, pp. 27 ff.
Warfel, Harry R. and Orians, G. H., *American Local-Color Stories,* New York, 1941.
Warner, W. L. and Lunt, P. S., *The Status System of a Modern Community,* New Haven, 1942.
——— *The Social Life of a Modern Community,* New Haven, 1948.
Washburn, O. R., *John Calvin in New England, 1620-1947,* Montpelier, Vermont, 1948.
Webster, C. M., *Town Meeting Country,* New York, 1945.
Welch, M. H., "Mary E. Wilkins," *Harper's Bazaar,* XXXIII, January 27, 1900, pp. 68-69.
Wellek, René and Warren, Austin, *The Theory of Literature,* New York, 1949.
Wendell, Barrett, *History of Literary America,* New York, 1909.
Westbrook, P. D., *Acres of Flint,* Washington, 1951.
Wharton, Edith, *The Writing of Fiction,* New York, 1925.
Whicher, G. W., *This Was a Poet,* New York, 1938.
Whiting, Edward E., *Changing New England,* New York, 1929.
Williams, Blanche Colton, *Our Short Story Writers,* New York, 1920.
Wilson, Edmund, *Axel's Castle,* New York, 1931.
Wilson, Harold F., *The Hill Country of Northern New England: Its Social and Economic History, 1790-1930,* New York, 1936.
"The Works of Mary E. Wilkins," *Harper's Weekly,* XLVII, November 21, 1903, pp. 1879-1880.
Wrifford, Anson, *Traits of Character . . . the Inhabitants of the Northeastern States . . .,* Portland, Me., 1837.

Index

WRITINGS